The Stackpole Social Science Series
LAURENCE FOSTER, General Editor

An Introduction
to
Social Research

Edited by
JOHN T. DOBY
Wofford College

With the assistance of
EDWARD A. SUCHMAN
Cornell University

JOHN C. MCKINNEY
Michigan State College

ROY G. FRANCIS
University of Minnesota

JOHN P. DEAN
Cornell University

THE STACKPOLE COMPANY
Harrisburg, Pennsylvania

Authors of Chapters

JOHN P. DEAN
Co-author of 8; 9
Cornell University

JOHN T. DOBY 2, 3
Wofford College

ROBERT L. EICHORN
Co-author of 8
Cornell University

ROY G. FRANCIS
1, 4, 5, Co-author of 6
University of Minnesota

JOHN C. MCKINNEY 7
Michigan State College

EDWARD A. SUCHMAN
Co-author of 6; 10
Cornell University

PREFACE

THIS INTRODUCTORY TEXTBOOK in research methods has been written to meet the methodological needs of undergraduate college students who are concentrating in the social and/or psychological sciences.

No one needs to be reminded today of the tremendous importance of the findings of science to modern man. This is evidenced by the great changes which science has made possible in our way of life, and the many courses in high school and college curricula concerned with the dissemination of the findings of science. It is one of the most talked-about subjects of modern times, and perhaps one of the least understood. It is this latter aspect which we are primarily concerned with in this text; *i.e.,* the understanding of science. What is the nature of science? What is the goal of science? How does science go about achieving its goal?

One does not answer the above questions by ascertaining what science is about. Rather one has to determine what science does, and how it does it. While our curriculum has no doubt put a premium on the *findings* of science, it has overlooked or under-emphasized the more important function of how these findings were made. If the methods of inquiry as used by science have been so effective in producing the great ideas, and the findings of science, then it is obvious that considerable attention should be given to the important task of learning the logic and procedures for deriving "truth." This does not imply, however, that scientific logic and procedure have reached perfection, but it does intend to imply that more attention should be devoted to the study of them in order to continue to improve upon them.

Our aim is to introduce the student to the task of how to do research in the social and psychological sciences. To accomplish this end we have presented the scientific endeavor as a special type of problem-solving activity. The first part of the book is designed to present the logic and the procedural rules for scientific problem-solving, while the second half is devoted to the methods and techniques for carrying out these rules in actual research.

This book is designed as a basic introductory text for courses in the logic and methods of research, and as such, it does not pretend to be exhaustive of the field. It is planned so as to provide the *core* material for a one semester course. The instructor will note that there is not sufficient material here for an entire semester course without some supplementing. This arrangement is intended. Since the needs of different instructors in the area of methodology in the social sciences are varied, (*i. e.,* some undergraduate students have some formal training in logic, and sufficient training in mathematics, while others do not) this opportunity to supplement should facilitate the meeting of the needs of their own situation.

The logic for the particular ordering of the content of Part II, follows two major considerations: *First,* that the methods and techniques to be considered first be those which will provide an overall picture of the logical and temporal steps in scientific research. Such ordering eliminates needless repetition in subsequent chapters. For example, if an adequate treatment of sampling is made in the discussion of statistical methods, then it is necessary only to refer to such when discussing survey research. *Second,* since the control of variables in social and psychological research is almost all by indirect means of randomization and statistical measurement, then it seems advisable to present statistical methods first. This becomes more apparent when we observe that most research designs (especially experimental, survey, and field observation research) in the behavioral sciences assume some knowledge of statistics.

In connection with the carrying out of the above task a few words should be said concerning the division of labor. The conception and overall outline of the basic content and organization of the book are the responsibility of the senior author and editor. While specific acknowledgment of the individual authors of particular chapters has been made in place, it is also desired to give summary acknowledgment here.

Chapters 1, 4, and 5 were written by Roy G. Francis of the University of Minnesota. Chapters 2 and 3 were written by John T. Doby of Wofford College. Chapter 6 was jointly written by Edward A. Suchman of Cornell University and Roy G. Francis. Chapter 7 was written by John C. McKinney of Michigan State College. Chapter 8 was jointly written by John P. Dean and Robert L. Eichhorn of Cornell University. Chapter 9 was written by John P. Dean. Chapter 10 was written by Edward A. Suchman of Cornell.

Thanks are due to Edward A. Suchman, Roy G. Francis and John C. McKinney who kindly read Chapter 2 and made helpful suggestions. Also, to Mr. Francis thanks are due for his reading and helpful criticism of Chapter 3.

Finally, I am indebted to Professor Sir Ronald A. Fisher, Cambridge, to Dr. Frank Yates, Rothamsted, and to Messrs. Oliver and Boyd Ltd., Edinburgh, for permission to reprint Table No. 3 from their book "Statistical Tables for Biological, Agricultural and Medical Research" and Table No. 5 from "Statistical Methods for Research Workers." Other acknowledgments are made in place.

JOHN T. DOBY

Spartanburg, South Carolina
August, 1954

TABLE OF CONTENTS

Part I: Introduction: The Logic of Science

Part II: Scientific Methods

Part I

Introduction: The Logic of Science

Chapter 1

THE NATURE OF SCIENTIFIC RESEARCH*

1. Introduction

THE student of research methods is faced with a two-fold task. He must first learn to "unlearn" some commonplace ideas about science and at the same time he must learn contemporary ideas about scientific activity. The student is probably already aware of the extensive writings about "science" in sociology. Indeed, the extent of such writings is so great as to suggest to some that we "declare a moratorium on the use of the word 'science' "[1] in order to avoid arguments as to whether a given piece of research is or is not "scientific."

Such a moratorium might be well for the peace of mind of the research practitioner. However, since the student does in fact pick up ideas, erroneous as well as correct ones, about science, such a moratorium would seem to work at the expense of the beginning student.

Our culture has put a premium upon science. It is true that some scientists themselves have begun to mistrust the "Sacred Cow" of science. Nonetheless, the fact that advertising agencies utilize pictures of doctors, graphs and terminology about "scientific proof" that this or that product is superior to all competitors, forces one to conclude the importance of scientific procedure as a value in our culture. Nor does this limit the access to ideas about science from nonscientific sources. Popular literature, the comics, movies, radio and television shows, often involve the scientist in the key role of the story being told.

The consequence is often a dramatized and erroneous account of the behavior of scientists, at least as scientists. The medical practitioner is often regarded by the lay public as the epitome of the scientist in action. Cigarette advertisements proclaiming the medical superiority of a given brand through the publication of "scientific tests" never reveal the research design which would enable one to assess more accurately the value of the test. The result is that the lay public is more likely to develop an attitude about, rather than knowledge of, scientific activity.

In addition to misleading conceptions of science gleaned from his everyday world, the student often brings with him preconceived ideas about his subject matter. When a sociological proposition about the behavior of man contradicts folk-belief, the student needs some way of deciding between the two propositions. To convince the student that the sociological one is to be preferred simply on the authority of the professor

---

* Written by Roy G. Francis.
[1] Samuel A. Stouffer, "Sociology and Sampling" in L. L. Bernard (ed.) *The Fields and Methods of Sociology* (NY: Long & Smith, 1934), pp. 486-487.

or that it is "scientific" may be temporarily expedient. In terms of the development of a field of inquiry such expediency has nothing in its favor; the future generation of sociologists are now students. Properly to take the role of scientists, they must, obviously, learn correctly how the scientist goes about his business.

We may draw an analogy between the student learning to be a scientist and an immigrant becoming a naturalized citizen of his adopted country. Certain similarities of belief and behavior exist between the "mother country" and the adopted one; at the same time, the immigrant must "unlearn" those values of his former country which conflict with a happy adjustment to his new one. Similarly, the student must prepare himself to unlearn some notions about science and to learn the contemporary "customs, traditions and mores of science." Of course, the analogy is limited: no one is "born into" a scientific culture.

There is probably one more major reason why sociologists, and, indeed, social scientists in general, are acutely methodology conscious. Science is a form of human behavior. A theory which is sufficiently general to explain the behavior of the "man in the street" must also be able to explain the behavior of the scientist himself. The behavior of the scientist which his theory must explain is not only his non-scientific behavior but his behavior as a scientist as well. No other scientific theory is called upon to perform this task. A theory of nuclear fission, for example, could not be properly used to explain the behavior of the physicist. In the so-called physical sciences, then, the relation between the scientist and his theory is not problematic.

In the social sciences, however, it is highly problematic. It would seem gratuitous, if not egotistical, to assume intellectual processes on the part of the scientist and deny them to the object the sociologist studies. In other words, to say that the scientist thinks and that his thinking is related to his behavior but that the "man in the street" either doesn't think or that his thinking is unrelated to his behavior involves a basic inconsistency.

In short, the social scientist is highly concerned with methodology for two basic reasons. He is a member of a culture which he seeks to study, and to arrive at a general theory, he must develop methods which permit generality by avoiding personal and cultural biases. Further, his behavior as a scientist is a form of human behavior and is properly an area of scientific inquiry.

We earlier commented to the effect that the medical practitioner is to the layman (who would not use terminology) an "ideal type" as a scientist. Such a conception of the scientist ignores the distinction between pure and applied science. The medical doctor, in his role of administering to the sick, is applying (more or less) scientific knowledge. He may or may not be engaged in discovering new knowledge which is the activity of the "pure" scientist. While there is, presumably, a relation between pure and applied science, the two are not the same and we will restrict our considerations only to "pure science."

Pure science, as the attempt to discover and systematize new knowledge, is intimately related to philosophy in at least three ways.

A. It is related to metaphysics; which, briefly, is concerned with basic ideas about "reality." Three assumptions are often made. The first is, that we live in a knowable real world. The second is, that that real world is not changed by our knowledge of it. The third is that our relation to the world may be changed by that knowledge. An example, however trivial: if we observe a "stove," it may be hot or cold. Knowing that it is, say, hot, does not change the stove, although our behavior towards it would be different than if it were cold.

Not all sociologists are willing to make these assumptions. Although none will disagree with the assumption of a knowable real world, the others are not as easily granted. It is a common argument that sociological knowledge itself modifies the world we seek to explain. If one develops a theory of cultural determinism, this theory becomes a part of the culture and hence differs from the culture out of which the theory grew. If we have a theory about voting behavior the politician eagerly uses this theory, modifying the voting behavior of the next series of observations. If a scientist develops a test to "measure" intelligence, and if this test becomes part of a system by which career judgments are made, those subjected to the test often try to improve their score (though their intelligence remains unchanged, presumably).

The ramifications of the assumptions we are willing to make are sometimes more extensive than we realize. The effect seems to be greater to the degree that our metaphysical assumptions remain implicit. An unawareness of basic assumptions can lead to contradictions if, basically, the assumptions were contradictory. Regarding the place of man in the universe, should a social scientist conceive of his object of inquiry as a thing, like other things in the universe, or should he ascribe to man a "human coefficient" that makes him different from other things in the universe? Does one subscribe to a dualistic philosophy of "mind and matter," or is "kind" in some sense epiphenomenal? It should be clear that one's research methods will be partly contingent upon the answers given to these questions.

B. Science is related to epistemology, which concerns theories about how "we know what we know." Conceptions of how we know is, obviously, related to research methods. For the most part, the issue will be treated subsequently (in Chapter two). However, we will draw a distinction between "belief" and "knowledge." The former is a matter of conviction, and the latter is a matter of "proof." "Proof" exists only within a complete theoretical system, its assumptions, definitions, admissable data and rules of inference. Thus, we may "believe" what we "know" but, in this terminology, we may not "know" what we "believe."

C. Science is related to ethics, which is concerned with beliefs about what is good and bad, particularly, what behavior ought or ought not to be engaged in. We will here assume that knowledge about science is itself "good," *i.e.,* that the student of human behavior "ought" to know how science proceeds. Further considerations will be discussed in Section 6 of this chapter.

It is quite clear that the philosophic basis of science is itself a justifiable area of inquiry. Our topic is not that of philosophy, however, so we will have to be content with this restricted treatment.

2. Characteristics of Science

Science includes both a goal and the means for obtaining that goal. Briefly, the goal of science is a theory. By "theory" we mean a "verifiable generalization of a high order which in some sense explains observed phenomena." The student is warned not to think of a theory as being "less good" than a "scientific law." Indeed, according to our usage of the term a theory systematizes "laws," "hypotheses," and other generalizations of a science. Thus, science is held to include the means for obtaining a theory and, as a matter of fact, we may well consider those means as an aspect of theory. Certainly, one's methodology contains theoretical implications and the student ought to be aware of that fact.

Some of the more important characteristics of science, both as substantive theory and methodology, follow:

(1). Science is "empirical." At some point science rests upon sense data. This characteristic of science excludes neither abstract concepts nor inferential knowledge. It merely means that science is concerned with a knowable real world.

(2). Science is propositional. It deals with propositions, *i.e.,* statements which have a truth-value, *about* things rather than with things. That is, sociology for example deals with propositions about human behavior; whatever is empirical about sociology must be reducible to propositional form.

Moreover, there are several distinct levels of logical abstraction of the propositions dealt with. A statement of the order "John Jones said he would vote Democratic" is less abstract than a statement of the order "The lower-class, Catholic, urban factory worker tends to prefer Democratic candidates." Both propositions may be admissable to a science; the latter may, and in fact does, rest upon the correctness of propositions of the former type. Clearly, the way one argues about a proposition will depend largely upon its level of abstraction.

In some respects, the propositional character of a science is basic to an understanding of scientific activity. Kaufmann[2] holds that the fundamental scientific act is that of deciding whether or not a given proposition ought to be incorporated into the theory of that science. In general, we concur in this position; however, the specific situation faced by the scientist often involves not merely one proposition but a set of alterna-

---

[2] Felix Kaufmann, *Methodology of the Social Sciences* (NY: Oxford Press, 1944).

tives. In this case, he must have some rules which will permit him to decide upon the choices open to him.

It should not be imagined, however, that once a proposition has been admitted to a science it is never again questioned. In Kaufmann's terms, science has "complete control" over its propositions. This means, simply, that a statement which is acceptable to science at a given time may be rejected or modified in the future. This propositional control exists at all levels of abstraction; the assumptions, definitions and procedural rules are all subject to re-examination. This control, however, should not suggest to the student that there is no stability to the structure of scientific theory.

Indeed, the changes in science seem to follow the same general patternings of any observable type of change. It would be easy to show, for example, how the three processes discerned by Teggart in social history are present in the history of science.[3] These processes are: (1) The persistence of certain elements. (2) The relatively slow change of certain elements. (3) The eventful changes of certain elements. The analysis of these changes belong properly in the field of the history of social thought and will not be further treated here. The main purpose of indicating their existence is to aid the student in realizing the significance of propositional control in science.

(3) Science is logical. Logic is defined as the discourse of argument. Analytically, logic is separable from any science; it constitutes a field of inquiry itself. However, science is not independent of the logic supporting it: at some point in his inquiry, the scientist reaches a conclusion regarding the acceptability of some proposition (or set of propositions). Some justification for the conclusion must be made. Logic is simply the rules by which inferences are made and hence is the structure of scientific argument.[4]

(4). Science is operational. Logic is completely formal; the formal correctness of an argument does not depend upon the empirical content of the argument. One may logically argue about mice with superior intelligence since, formally, logic does not guarantee the empirical existence of the classes used in the argument. How one is able to get empirical members into a logical class depends upon the operations which one is willing to perform.

As an example, consider the class of things "neurotic personalities." Logically, we may create a definition of the class in question and proceed to engage in argument about the "neurotic personality" without any reference to the real world. But science deals with a real knowable world. In order to become accepted into science, the logical class "neurotic personalities" must be accompanied by an operational procedure by which one can say "X has a neurotic personality." The operations by

---

[3] Frederick J. Teggart, *Theory and Processes of History* (Berkeley: University of California Press, 1941).

[4] We will discuss this further in Section 3 of this chapter.

which class members are identified allow us to give empirical content to formal classes.

(5). Science is public. In saying that science is propositional, we lay the groundwork for also asserting that science can be communicated from one scientist to another. Whatever is private to the individual researcher, his motivations, his value judgments, etc., do not properly belong to science (although such private convictions often do creep into scientific publications).

In its propositional form, science is symbolic.[5] Through consensus on the symbols utilized in a science, the objects studied by the scientist may be so well represented as to allow another scientist who does not observe the objects himself to judge the correctness of the inferences drawn. This, in turn, allows for replication of any scientific study. That is, a given piece of research can be duplicated by others and the same results may be obtained. If replication is not possible, then elements unique to the study are present and the acceptability of the study is commensurably reduced.

(6). Science is problem-solving. Ordinarily, we mean by "problem" some observations which need explanation. The lack of an acceptable explanation may be due to the presence of incorrect propositions in the theory, or it may be due simply to the inadequacy of the theory.

A problem is general, and does not adhere to a unique set of observations. When unique elements are present—as, for example, when the time and space setting of the observations are intrinsically important—we speak of a "difficulty".[6] In sociology, we draw the distinction between "sociological problems" and "social problems." Generally speaking, the "problem" belongs to "pure science" and the "difficulty" belongs to "applied science."

In the solution of a problem, the scientist formulates a *hypothesis* (or set of hypotheses). The hypothesis is a proposed solution to the problem. It is sometimes difficult to trace the source of hypotheses. Sometimes they are, originally, the result of the unique background of the scientist. When subjected to the formal test in a science, the source of a hypothesis is not particularly relevant as long as the criteria of scientific procedure are met. For the sake of semantic purity, we will say that the source of hypotheses is "inquiry" while the test of hypotheses is "research".

The correctness of the statement of the problem is paramount to subsequent scientific activity. One's conception of the problem at hand gives rise to the hypotheses to be tested, and the hypotheses, in turn, indicate which data are needed to satisfy the test. Although one may begin with only a vague feeling of the problem, eventually, it must be reduced to

---

[5] Susanne K. Langer, *Philosophy in a New Key* (NY: Penguin Books, Inc., 1948).

[6] This follows the formulation made by Professor John M. Foskett of the University of Oregon.

propositional form in order that its solution may be incorporated into science.

(7). Science tends to be abstract. Recall that we assumed a knowable real world. The propositions about the real world often are lacking in abstraction. All empirical observations, if part of science, are stated in this form. Though such propositions may depend upon rather abstract definitions and operations, such "atomic" propositions and abstract definitions are not the same thing.

As these propositions are formulated into a problem and hypotheses offered to solve the problem, the subsequent propositions become more and more abstract. At times, historically at least, scientific propositions may tend to be largely empirical; in part, science always contains at least some empirical statements. However, with the development of a theory, scientific propositions move away from the specific time-and-space statements to more general ones. Although some empirical reference is always necessary, a general scientific theory is highly abstract. As an example, the equation for "the law of gravity" is simply a set of abstract symbols.

(8). Science tends towards a system. As scientific knowledge gets more and more abstract, as the hypotheses and laws increase both in number and generalization, scientific theory tends to incorporate uniformities among the generalizations themselves.

Since science rests so heavily on logic, there is always the danger that the system tends towards "logical closure"—*i.e.,* is unable to accept certain empirical observations or generalizations. But science has complete control over its propositions. While certain propositions may be rejected because they contradict other known propositions, it is sometimes true that a new discovery may force a modification along the whole system of scientific theory.[7]

One of the major problems of "theory," as a major component of science, is the development of a system which is able to render empirical findings consistent with each other. At the same time, the attempt to systematize empirical research gives rise to new problems, and reformulation of old ones. Indeed, we must admit that some sort of dialectic relation obtains between the concepts, definitions and permissible operations.

(9). Science is on-going. We may re-state the theoretical problem of systematization of scientific knowledge to indicate the vast intellectual heritage upon which any piece of scientific research rests. No one piece of research stands alone, nor does it stand and fall by itself. Of course, the source of the problem may result from this intellectual heritage. We may inherit "bad" ideas as well as "good" ones.

---

[7] Such a proposition would result in "eventful change," while those which are consistent but empirically new would be an example of relatively slow change, and the basic theory against which consistency is measured would be "persisting elements" referred to earlier.

3. The Role of Logic in Research

Earlier, we held that at some point the scientist reaches a conclusion and is forced to justify the correctness of his inference. We should also recall that science deals with propositions about things. Scientific propositions may or may not be mathematical in form. But there is always a formal structure to the propositions of science. We recall, also, that science is public: it is to be shared by others, and others must agree upon the correctness of the argument. Moreover, science is operational in that the content of logical classes is made possible through the operation performed.

By *definition* logic is the rules by which we proceed from premises to conclusions. Scientific argument, then, involves relations between propositions. Thus, if one were given the premises consisting of

1. Concepts and definitions
2. Operational procedures
3. Empirical observations

the conclusions would *necessarily* follow, even if stated in probability terms. By our definition, then, logic is *deductive,* and science exists in a deductive form. This means, simply, that *however it was that the scientist reaches his conclusions, they must be put into deductive form.*

This is easily seen if the theory is so far advanced as to permit a predictive statement, *e.g.,* "If A, then B; I observe A, and hence I predict B." This is the classical form of scientific theory, though not all current theory is stated in such formalistic terms.

The deductive form of a solution to an *ad hoc* problem is not so clearly seen. "Ad Hoc" means "to that," *i.e.,* one has a set of problematic data which he seeks to explain. He develops an hypothesis which, "after the facts," are in the form "if A (his explanation) then B (his problem)." But the development of a hypothetical solution to an *ad hoc* problem does not constitute a test of the hypothesis. When the hypothesis is directly tested, it is put in the form, "if A (the hypothesis), then B (observations similar to those which gave rise to the original problem)."

Of course, a test of a hypothesis may fail, and the scientist may reformulate his hypothesis in terms of his new findings. Such a reformulation is, essentially, *ad hoc:* the reformulated hypothesis must again be subject to test. The goal, however, is always to be able to state one's findings in the classical "if A, then B" form.

Because of the logical form which hypotheses tend to take, it is much easier to discuss how to test them than it is to show how to derive them. Formally, the issue is often put as "deductive logic vs inductive logic." In this form, "deductive logic" is defined as 'going from generals to particulars" while "inductive logic" is defined as "going from particulars to generals." We simply cannot say how one decides what general conception will permit subsequent inference of the particulars; there seems to be some sort of intellectual "leap" in the process. Once the formulation has been made, it is easily subjected to deductive test.

Perhaps the best formulation of the issue, at the present stage of the student's knowledge, is to admit that what is often called "induction" is the same thing as the "art in science." From our definition of logic, such leaps are not purely deductive; for if it were, the new formulation exists in the premises and is not, strictly speaking, really "new." Nor are we alone in the argument; Russell [8] argues that even "mathematical induction" is really a matter of definition.

It is sometimes held that statistical inference is "inductive". To anticipate subsequent terminology, inferences from a sample about a population from which the sample is drawn is sometimes called "induction".[9] This is largely a semantic issue. By our rather strict definition of logic, statistical inference is deductive. Using our definition, it is easy to verify the deductive nature of any statistical assertion.

For example, the average (or mean) is computed as the sum of the quantities in question divided by the number of objects measured. This computation can be written as a set of premises: "if the first object is, say, 10 years old, the second is 12, and the third is 11, then the total is thirty three years. Since there are three objects, the conclusion is that the average age is 11 years." By immediate generalization, it can be seen that any equation or formula can similarly be written as a set of premises and a conclusion.

This implies two things. First, we must distinguish between the logical form of our argument and the temporal sequence of knowledge. We might not have known the average age of the group prior to the computation of the formula. But we did know the logical structure of the argument from which we could infer the average had we been given the necessary premises. We ought not confuse the solution of *ad hoc* problems with the logical structure of science.

Second, we must note that statistical formulas are themselves forms of argument and hence formal solutions to problems. Therefore, the scientist must first show that a given statistical equation is structurally isomorphic with the theoretical problem before he uses it. Otherwise, he may be forcing conclusions onto his data, and may be solving a problem different from the one he faces.

Moreover, logic itself does not prescribe which premises are to be admitted into the argument. Logic merely allows us to say whether or not the conclusions are warranted. The promiscuous use of equations, while possibly satisfying some existent technical fad, is not basically science. The logic of inquiry is not merely the application of techniques. Logic may guide the research, and offers a guard against incorrect in-

---

[8] Bertrand Russell, *Introduction to Mathematical Philosophy* (London: George Allen & Unwin, Ltd., 1948), pp. 20 ff.

[9] Margaret J. Hagood and Daniel O. Price, *Statistics for Sociologists* (NY: Henry Holt & Co. Rev. Ed., 1952), pp. 185 ff.

ference. Form should never be mistaken for content; and content is largely a theoretical issue.

Nor should the student easily accept the issue as "qualitative *versus* quantitative logic," as though one had a choice in which type of logic he would utilize. The fact that mathematical equations could be written, in a cumbersome way, as a set of premises and conclusions, seems to suggest that mathematics depends upon and does not negate the so-called qualitative logic. To the extent that this is true, the proper issue of logic seems to rest upon a consideration of the problem to be solved and which logical postulates are satisfied by the data necessary to solve the problem.

Instead of selecting some technique (which, as we saw, assumes an argument) and seeking some problem which allows one to use the technique, one should first understand this problem and let that decide what argument is necessary. When the data involved permit the use of a mathematical argument, then, of course, it should be used. But if the logical level of abstraction is such as to make a mathematical (i.e., numerical) argument meaningless, then some other form of argument should be used.

At the same time, unless one knows the structure of a given argument, he is not likely to use it, even if his problem does call for it. It is not likely that each of us could, or would, invent statistical arguments as the need arises. Rather, it seems necessary for us to learn different *forms* of inference in order that we will properly be prepared to use them when occasion arises. One should also recognize, however, that the decision to use one technique or another, one logic or another, depends as much on the current state of theory as it does on purely formal grounds. This being so, one is guarded against making logic the sole consideration of science. Logic may, by analogy, be the skeleton, but the other tissues and whatever *elan vital* there is seems to come from the broader aspects of theory.

4. Steps in Scientific Research

For purposes of analysis, we will separate some of the more important 'steps' in scientific research. It should be recognized, however, that the distinction between them is not as clear-cut as this presentation may insinuate. As a matter of fact, and as the student gains experience in research he will bear this out, one tends to "jump back and forth" from one step to another. Thus, while the temporal order of research is pretty much as given, the fact remains that "steps in scientific research" is a somewhat idealized account of how the scientist actually does his work.

(1). Selection of problem area. This aspect of research is often a question of motivation and interest; many "accidental" things go into the selection of a problem area. The possibility of obtaining prestige, security, or even the solution of a personal problem, may determine the area in which the scientist is interested. We cannot deny the importance of such highly private considerations; but science is public. These "ought not"

become a part of science itself. Often, however, these private things later hinder the research, intruding to bias the results. This is simply true. The scientist must always be on guard against such factors and seek self-consciously to overcome them or their effects.

(2). Acquaintance with current theory and knowledge in the area. Science is on-going, and after the scientist is aware of his problem area, he must continuously seek to know and understand the theory and problems of that area. Ordinarily, this part can be largely conducted in a library, as one would be reading the current literature on the area in question.

(3). Definition of the problem. This is the most crucial phase of inquiry, although it does not ordinarily come about in a clean-cut way. Indeed, as one is getting acquainted with current knowledge, he will be formulating his problem. Due to the possible motivational factors in selecting the area, or, possibly, to inadequacy of contemporary theory, he may poorly state his problem.

Just as there are various levels of abstraction of the propositions of science, so are there various levels of problems. Each level, presumably, can be solved in its own way: the solution of an empirical problem does not necessarily solve a highly abstract one. One should not imagine, then, that the formulation of a problem is an easy task. Nor are there any formal rules for telling one how to go about stating a problem. Stating a problem in such a way as to permit a solution is a most difficult task. It is critical to subsequent research; for only as the problem is clearly apprehended is there a possibility for the development of an adequate theory.

(4). Development of hypotheses. The hypothesis is, as we said earlier, a possible solution to a problem. Its source may be that of a "hunch" or "shrewd guess" by the scientist; or it may have been deduced from current theory. That is, if the theory is correct then other things ought to follow, one of which is the hypothesis in question.

Clearly, the development of hypotheses is not independent of the formulation of the problem and may be related to the phase of getting acquainted with current knowledge in an area. One important thing to remember is that good theory is abstract and tends to be general. Hence more than one hypothesis can be deduced from it. Thus, one cannot say *a priori* just what hypothesis will flow from a theory. Many will; and which ones are selected for test is often as much a function of the personality of the scientist as it is of the theory.

If correctly considered, the hypothesis tells what data the scientist is to gather and what to omit. Obviously, in a given piece of research, one does not look at all possible data, even at all data relevant to the field of inquiry. As a trivial example, in a study of occupational success, atmospheric information is seldom considered and the signs of the zodiac are almost ignored. Such information could be included: sociological hypotheses, however, exclude such data and hence they are not incorporated into that science.

(5). Development of the formal argument. Given the statement of the problem, and the hypothetical solution to the problem, how can one prove that the hypothesis (a) is 'true' and (b) does in fact solve the problem? One must, then, decide precisely how the hypothesis is to be tested, what data one needs and what alternatives exist. In the fact of possible alternative findings, one ought to decide how one will argue in the face of each alternative. If one will use a statistical argument, he would at this point determine what tables he will use.

(6). Delineation of the source of data. The hypothesis tells what data are needed, and the structure of the argument tells what form they should be in. Whether one will directly observe, will interview, give a paper-and-pencil test, use official documents, library materials, or what, must now be decided. Each source of data is liable to errors peculiar to itself; some, as secondary sources, have errors twice compounded. Many problems call for more than one source of data, particularly as the hypotheses get to be more complex. At any rate, the scientist must make certain that the data needed are available, or can become available. Clearly, if the data necessary to a test of one's hypothesis cannot be obtained, the hypothesis in question must go begging.

(7). Creation of the instrument. Presumably, the research is at the point where the scientist knows what data he needs and what form they are to take. The immediate task is to develop an instrument which will get him the data he wants in the form he wants. The instrument may be a questionnaire, interview, recording device, or whatever. Often, the scientist will be dealing with theoretical classes of things and faces the difficult task of properly identifying empirical members of such classes.

It is at this point that the "operationalism" of science is of critical importance. For the instrument will be part of the operations to be performed in the acquisition of data. All of the difficulties in going from abstract theoretical definitions to concrete empirical entities must at this point be squarely faced. Again, we recall that the theoretical class may tend to be abstract and general; if so, apparently more than one identification can be made to get members of that class. The question then arises, should other identifications also be made?

To illustrate the issue, suppose we wanted an instrument dealing with "neurotic personalities"; suppose, further, that an observer was simply called upon to record observed behavior. We might desire information regarding the subject's continuous washing his hands. But neuroticism is manifest by other behaviors: do we record them all? Or only some? If only some, how do we choose which?

Recall that there were differing levels of problems. Each would have its own hypothetical solution. Each hypothesis will contain some content material, such that the level of abstractness of the hypothesis in question will go a long way in answering these questions.

Thus, the instrument ought to give us the data called for by the hypothesis to be tested, and should be in the form which will allow us to come to a rigorous conclusion as to whether or not the hypothesis is true, and if true, if it solves the problem. We should not, however, think that operational definitions are the equivalent of theoretical definitions. We must recognize the fact that theoretical definitions must be such that an instrument can be created which will give the class empirical members, otherwise they cannot be used in research. We cannot avoid the necessity of making operational definitions; however, we must recognize the logical priority of theoretical ones and avoid the error of equating the two.

(8). Writing a "dummy argument." Often there are flaws or unanticipated gaps in one's argument. Sometimes further data are needed, or unneeded data are being gathered. It is a good device, in guarding against such flaws to write up the argument in terms of the data you expect to find. It may be held that such an action will predispose a person to certain findings and hence bias the study. The fact is, any scientist has some notion of what he is going to find. The suggestion is to formalize this and to see if, at this point in the research, correctable gaps exist. Much subsequent anguish and activity can be forestalled by such a simple device as this.

(9). Pretest of the instrument, and possible revision. No one ought to engage in full-scale research, expending the time and money available for research, unless he has knowledge that his instrument does in fact give him the data he thinks it will. In questionnaires, for example, the wording of the questions is often misleading to certain segments of the sample. It is generally better to try the instrument out and see if it works on a small scale rather than assume that no errors exist. He who creates an instrument may be too close to it to see the changes which later develop, unless he has properly pre-tested it before wide-scale usage.

(10). Formal acquisition of data. After the instrument has been created, and the source known to be available, the task is simply that of gathering the material—applying the instrument.

(11). Analysis of the data. With the method for using the data already known, a large part of analysis is somewhat routine. Often, however, some unanticipated results emerge,[10] and the data behave differently from the hypothetical solution. The scientist, if he seeks to revise his hypothesis, is essentially faced with an *ad hoc* problem. Except for the fact that he is limited to the data at hand, this situation generally calls for a reformulation of the problem, and the reformulation of hypotheses.

(12). Formal write-up of conclusions reached. This is the last step, but an important one. The write up, generally, will be *in the form of an argument*. It will become a part of the intellectual heritage of the science

---

[10] Robert K. Merton, "The Bearing of Empirical Research upon the Development of Social Theory," *American Sociological Review,* 13 (October, 1948.) pp. 505-515.

in question. Subsequent researchers will read it, in "getting acquainted with the current theory and knowledge." The fact that it is in the *form* of an argument may present some difficulty to the future researchers. The temporal sequence of research is not necessarily the same as the sequence of propositions in an argument.[11]

5. Scientific Attitude

The scientist is often pictured as being detached and aloof. Often, he is allegedly disinterested in the world about him and is completely absorbed by his experiments. We would hesitate to claim that these are necessary conditions for scientific behavior. It is true that the scientist is "passionately logical"—*i. e.,* will accept the consequences of scientific discovery even if it makes him emotionally uncomfortable.

For our purposes, however, we will choose to emphasize the *scepticism* upon which science rests. Descartes is supposed to have finally concluded, "I doubt therefore I am." [12] Weber argues that the scientist is committed to the situation of being proved wrong: every known theory has undergone change and modification.[13]

Recall that science has complete control over its propositions. In the so-called "induction," we held that some intellectual "leaps" take place. We admit that much research is often guided by hunches, guesses and "intuition." But science does not trust such sources. These are always subjected to empirical test.

Science, in its published form, is in the form of an argument. Whatever the source of the scientist's ideas, they are put in propositional form and tested. This is true even if the hypothesis is the logically necessary conclusion from the data as given. Science does not mistrust "intuition" alone; science mistrusts "logic" as well. No matter how rigorous the inference, the basic notion always is, "well, now, let's see if that's true."

This does not imply that the scientist believes nothing. He has a fundamental faith in "scientific methodology"—even while questioning some particular technique. He may never state it, but the scientist develops a philosophy upon which his whole conception of science rests. Many of his assumptions he takes on faith, unswervingly, unquestioningly, blindly: particularly, if he denies any philosophic connection.

One issue that often brings out passionate discourse in those scientists who are otherwise detached and aloof is the question as to whether the "laws" discerned by science constitute a part of the "real world," or whether the real world can be described by atomic empirical observations and the "laws" are the products of orderly *human* minds.

The issue is illustrated in an anecdote about three baseball umpires who were arguing about their job. Each called balls and strikes; each

---

[11] See Chapter 5 on Experimentation.
[12] This is often written as "I think, therefore I am."
[13] "Science as a Vocation," in *From Max Weber: Essays in Sociology,* ed. & trans. by H. H. Gerth and C. W. Mills (NY: Oxford U. Press, 1946.)

was bragging as to who did the best job. Said one: "I call them as I see them—and no one can do better than that." The second retorted, "That's nothing; I call them as they are." The third paused a moment, and finally added: "They ain't nothing until I call them—and then that's what they are."

Each umpire represents a different school of philosophy. The scientist virtually asks himself the same question, and the responses are as varied. To some, we describe uniformities of behavior as we observe them; to others (egotistically, perhaps) science does indeed manage to describe the world as it is; to still others, scientific laws are merely the products of shrewd men.

We will not take issue with any of our umpiring friends. We will note, however, that in any case, statements of uniformities of behavior are reducible to propositional form, stand in logical relations to each other, subject to empirical test. Regardless of the philosophy adopted, certain things are common to scientific activity: the rigorous empirical test of inferences—and hunches.

6. Science, Values, and Value-Judgments

It is commonplace to say that the "values" which a people hold are a proper subject for sociological inquiry. It is also commonplace to say that the private value-judgments of an individual ought not intrude onto scientific findings. A large portion of methodological activity has been in minimizing the effect of personal value-judgments. When the value-judgment adheres to a cultural entity the existence of the value-judgment may be harder to detect than when the position is held simply by an individual.

One difficulty with value-judgments is that they are largely private, and not shared by the entire group of scientists. This privacy may be a function of geographic area, of historical period, or both. To whatever extent the value-judgment is uniquely a function of the time-space location of the scientist, its presence would limit and restrict the generality which scientific theory seeks.

This is not to say that "no value judgments" are permitted to a science. No *private* ones are admissable, but certain public ones seem to be necessary for a proper functioning of a group of scientists. The most commonly held value is that knowledge itself is good: Scientific knowledge need not be practical, in the sense of immediate application. The scientist may be privately motivated to reduce human suffering (or, according to his philosophy, to increase it), or to gain wealth, or whatever. Science is indifferent to such values—knowledge, alone, and for its own sake, is the goal.

However, we may assume that the scientist is acquiring knowledge which is a form of human behavior. If we did not make this assumption, we would need somehow to get the scientist to act. Changing the situation changes the problem: what value-judgment must be made once the act is begun? The basic value seems to be what is normally meant by "intellectual honesty." This value seems to be fundamental to all research, and in particular, to the publication of research. In the public nature of science, since it is essentially propositional in character, one scientist must believe in the intellectual honesty of the other. Unless this value is met, it seems unlikely that one could seek knowledge, or truth.

To determine the significance of intellectual honesty as a fundamental scientific value, the student should play around with the consequences to science if it were denied. Suppose the researcher could select his cases as he wanted them to, or to say they were whatever he wanted them to be. Clearly, science would be reduced to individual dream-worlds. This, however, contradicts a basic assumption about the knowable real-world of science. Intellectual honesty seems to be even more important than "knowledge for its own sake" as a value. It would be possible to say that, ultimately, all knowledge must be usable, and still science could continue pretty much as it has in the past. But to admit dishonesty as a legitimate type of scientific behavior would contradict the goal and characteristics of science.

It is more or less commonplace to point out that science is indifferent to how it will be used. Whether knowledge will be used for social "good" or "evil" is not up to science to decide—since, among other reasons, science cannot decide what constitutes "social goodness." Whether nuclear energy is to be used for peace or war is a question of how scientific knowledge is to be used. Its answer comes from an ethical source rather than a scientific one. The scientist as a citizen may be highly concerned with how his knowledge is to be used; but as a scientist, he is strangely silent.

It is not so commonplace, however, to raise the question as to "who will use" scientific knowledge. The position that science is indifferent to this question also is not as clear as in answer to "how" science will be used. If the variable in question can be manipulated solely by a social entity greater than the individual, then "who" can possibly use the knowledge seems to contain value-premises. If scientific knowledge can be applied only by a group, we are then denying the individual a certain amount of freedom. Rather, perhaps, we are ultimately forced to say, as did Rousseau, that if there are those who do not wish to be free, we will force them to be free.

If the knowledge gained by science can be used only by a group, the decision to use that knowledge—even if made through a democratic process—could easily work against those who were opposed to its application.

The general position which science takes is that it is indifferent to its use. It need not be used at all, except to further research. "Who" uses knowledge is relevant only if we first assume that knowledge will be used. The assumption that knowledge will be used is based upon an action premise, and not one of inquiry.

This is not to say that science is free from the consequences of the type of theory developed. Whether or not the scientist is morally responsible for the consequences of the application of his knowledge is an ethical judgment, and the student should determine his own position on the matter. The critical issue is the addition of premises which warrant an activity other than an intellectual one.

When the scientist decides to play the role of a teacher, he is making ethical assumptions about knowledge and who should learn it. When he decides to publish, *i.e.,* to share, his knowledge, he is making assumptions about a behavior other than an intellectual one. In so doing, his values are held in public view and are subject to public scrutiny. Further, we must recognize a social hierarchy of values. It is not particularly surprising to find certain social values limiting others. In the case at hand, certain social values for societal survival certainly limit the value that scientific knowledge should be available to whomever wants it. This is another form of the question "who should use scientific knowledge?"

7. Summary

Science is related to philosophy in at least three ways: (a) in basic conceptions of "reality"; (b) in basic conceptions of knowledge and (c) in basic ethical judgments. Without trying to impose any philosophical orientation upon the student, we notice that modifications of assumptions in these three areas lead to further modifications in science.

We must recognize that science comes to us in propositional form. This leads us to consider other general characteristics of science: (1) It is concerned with a real world. (2) It is logical. (3) To get content into logical forms, science is operational. (4) Science is public in the sense of not allowing private biases as a part of science. (5) Science is problem-solving. (6) It tends to be abstract and (7) towards a system. No research stands by itself: Science is on-going.

The characteristics of science lead to major analytically distinct steps (though there is, empirically, some "interaction" between them). One first selects the problem area; this is largely a matter of individual motivation. Then one becomes acquainted with the current theory and knowledge in that area in order to define the problem. Formally one proposes solutions to the problem in the form of hypotheses and develops instruments to get the proper data. These will be cast in a specified form of argument and will be obtainable from a known source. After the data are gathered they are, of course, submitted to analysis. Surprising results, or modifications of hypotheses, lead to *ad hoc* problems and *ad hoc* hypotheses.

Science is geared to change. Accepted beliefs of today may be rejected tomorrow—and re-accepted the next. This gives rise to, and reinforces, the sceptical attitude. Science does not trust "intuition"—though it utilizes hunches, shrewd guesses, etc. It does not trust logical inference—everything is put to test.

Value-judgments, as matters of private convictions, are not a part of science, though they may be proper subjects for scientific analysis. There is, however, a fundamental value-orientation of science. And that is summarized in the concept "intellectual honesty." Intellectual honesty is the *sine qua non* of science. The contradiction of it destroys the basis of science. It follows that whatever social forces impinge upon intellectual honesty impinge also upon the scientific mind.

SELECTED REFERENCES

Kaufman, Felix, *Methodology of the Social Sciences* (New York: Oxford University Press, 1944).

MacIver, Robert M., *Social Causation* (New York: Ginn & Co., 1942).

Ramsperger, Albert G., *Philosophies of Science* (New York: F. S. Crofts & Co., 1942).

Russell, Bertrand, *Human Knowledge: Its Scope and Limits* (New York: Simon & Schuster, 1948).

Searles, Herbert L., *Logic and Scientific Methods* (New York: The Ronald Press Co., 1948).

Chapter 2

SCIENCE AND CONCEPTS*

1. Introduction

THE systematic characteristics of science, and scientific inquiry, have been described in the previous chapter. Science is a form of inquiry which has as its objectives the description of particular phenomena in the world of our experience, and the establishment of general principles which will allow for the explanation and prediction of these phenomena. It is the purpose of this chapter to examine the nature and function of concepts in the scientific endeavor.

The use of concepts is not, of course, peculiar to science. Concepts are just as much a part of John Doe's communication and language equipment as they are a basic element of the scientific method. Witness the use of such common sense concepts as "wise-man," "honest-man," "religious-man," etc. One further example should be sufficient to point out the use of concepts by Homo sapiens in general—take the concept mass. The ordinary person usually implies nothing more that the idea of bulk in his usage of this term. However, anyone who has had elementary physics knows that the scientist attaches a different meaning than that of the layman. Thus to the physicist the concept mass involves weight, force, acceleration, inertia and gravity. Further, the physicist is interested in the specific relationships among these factors. For instance, force is equal to the product of the mass of the body and the acceleration of the body or $F = MA$. Mass then is equal to the ratio F/A. Thus, the scientist's use of the concept is such that its essential characteristics are expressed in terms which may be measured either directly or indirectly. But, more about the likeness and difference of common-sense concepts and scientific concepts later.

It should be recalled that this chapter was introduced by calling attention to two main objectives of science, namely, description and explanation. Now, once we have posed a problem in scientific explanation, and it has been settled as to how we are to observe the phenomenon about which the problem is stated, there is still the problem of how we are going to interpret what we observe. Thus it is the scientist's task to make theoretical sense out of his observations. This is quite often a most difficult task, since it essentially means *choosing the right concepts* to interpret what we observe. Therefore, it is obvious that the problem of the *reliability* and *validity* of concepts is central to science. Concepts are central not only from the point of view of the validity of the interpretation made upon the scientific observations, but the concepts which

* Written by John T. Doby.

a researcher begins a study with largely determine the type of data to be *selected* for observation and testing.

The following example should make this point clear. Prior to the *Concept* of the mosquito as the carrier agent of malaria one concept as to the cause of this malady was "bad air." Thus the data selected for observation and study concerned the presence of "bad air." However, with the new concept of the mosquito as a factor related to malaria in human beings, then the data selected for study represented the new idea of a carrier agent.

With this general background as to the nature and function of concepts, we now turn our attention to the specific problems of this chapter. What is the nature and function of concepts in science and how are concepts in science formed? The first of these problems is treated in this chapter under the general heading: the function of concepts in science. The second is the process of conceptual formation, and is treated under the heading, The Conceptual Process.

2. The Function of Concepts

As indicated above the purpose of this chapter is primarily to show the role of concepts in scientific procedure, so that the student may come to understand more clearly their functions. Therefore, such polemics as to whether the concept is "real or nominal, whether abstraction is a process of disclosing reality or of distorting reality, whether the universe is being or pure idea" will not concern us here.

Psychological Aspects of Conception. The individual, in adjusting himself in his environment, uses his sensory capacity to become aware of certain aspects of the world which confront him. These specialized sense organs permit us to sift out some of the welter of stimuli with which the world is filled, and enable us to respond *specifically* to some of its aspects. This selection of a few impressions which have relevance for us from a mass of impressions, and the organization of these into one primary image, we call *perception*. Perceiving then is a way of ordering the environment by playing up certain features and playing down others.

While perception serves to facilitate behavior it, however, does not allow us to circumvent all obstacles as this example will show. There are many situations in which perception is insufficient, or one is not able to perceive all the relevant elements in a situation. One then has to act on the basis of *conception* by making certain assumptions. A striking example of the blocking of perception, and the need for conception is afforded in the following quotation from *The Evolution of Physics* by Einstein and Infeld. To be more precise one would say that the following is an example of the postulational characteristic of science.

> In our endeavor to understand reality we are somewhat like
> a man trying to understand the mechanism of a closed watch.
> He sees the face and the moving hands, even hears its ticking,
> but he has no way of opening the case. If he is ingenious he

may form some pictures of a mechanism which could be responsible for all the things he observes, but he may never be
quite sure his picture is the only one which could explain his
observations. He will never be able to compare his picture with
the real mechanism and he cannot even imagine the possibility
or the meaning of such a comparison. But he certainly believes
that, as his knowledge increases, his picture of reality will become simpler and simpler and will explain a wider and wider
range of his sensuous impressions.[1]

However, if he is sufficiently clever he *can* circumvent the obstacles to
perception through ingenious conception. In such a case conception
serves the same purpose as perception, that is, it permits adjustment or
provides a new orientation. It should be emphasized that there is a
mutual or reciprocal relationship between perception and conception,
i.e., perception aids conception and the new-formed concepts feed back
into perception, thus giving old precepts a new perspective.

The above should suffice to show the relationship between the concept
and perception. However, the concept is not only an aid to perception,
but it is also a *way of conceiving*.

It is this aspect of the concept which we are most interested in. The
history of science is replete with examples where certain individuals
when confronted with puzzling situations or phenomena have in their
efforts to understand them suggested the *existence of something not
directly perceived*. As examples of this one needs only to think of
bacteria, atom, gene, electricity, motive and attitude.

This idea of the concept as a way of conceiving the nature of phenomena
is most effectively expressed in a passage by Herbert Blumer.

> Perhaps it might be better to say that, on the basis of given
> tangible perceptual experiences which were puzzling, certain
> individuals fashioned constructs which would give these experi-
> ences an understandable character. As far as I can see, scientific
> concepts come into existence in this way. They refer to some-
> thing whose existence we presume, but whose character we do
> not fully understand. They originate as conceptions occasioned
> by a series of perceptual experiences of a puzzling character
> which need to be bridged by a wider perspective. I hasten to
> add that the concept does not merely suppose the existence
> of something which bridges perceptual experiences, but it im-
> plies that this thing has a nature or certain character.[2]

The above point by Blumer that concepts are not just a way of
conceiving, but also have a *content* which is conceived is a further aspect
worthy of elaboration. The concept permits one to catch and hold some

---

[1] Albert Einstein and Leopold Infeld, *The Evolution of Physics* (New York:
Simon and Schuster, 1938), p. 33. Reprinted by permission.
[2] Herbert Blumer, "Science Without Concepts," p. 3, unpublished mimeographed
copy of address given before the Ninth Annual Institute of Social Research, University of Chicago, Aug. 20-23, 1930).

content of experience. For example, the young child as his command of language increases, begins to use words which stand for some common property of a number of objects, acts, persons, situations, etc. He at first is only able to specify *particular* objects or things. This is because our perceptual world is one of particulars, for although conception is always involved, it is conception working through particulars. Thus the young child may be able to name correctly such animals as horse, dog, cat, mouse, but it is not until sometime later that he is able to group all these animate objects under the single *unifying* concept of animal. That is to say, that the abstraction of experience from the world of particulars, and the holding on to it, is possible only through conceptualizing and necessitates, ultimately, a concept.

This process of developing concepts by learning to group objects in terms of some isolated common property is called *abstraction*. A good example of this is to be found in Biology in the abstraction of the common properties of plants and animal life. By identifying the isolated particulars of experience one is then able to group them in terms of their common content and characteristics. However, if this conception is to be held on to, it must be given a name, a sign, or an identifying symbol. Three developments of paramount importance for science are then made possible by the above process of abstraction: (1) the common content conceived out of the mass of particulars may become the object of separate investigation and study, (2) it may become the experience of others, since it may be identified by a language or symbols which are the common property of others and thus making possible collective action, (3) it makes possible the unity and systematic nature of science by linking together the particular elements and ideas in a pattern. Science gets its systematic nature through the coherence of its concepts.

One or two examples will suffice to show this idea. Think for a moment of the concepts of motion, mass, inertia, and force. These are concepts that are interrelated and linked. Together they have formed a pattern which has guided research in physics. The same is true of the concepts of heredity, chromosome and gene in genetics, and institution, status, role, and attitude in sociology. This development of concepts in science prevents the work of individual scientists from being just a series of discrete and separate studies by providing organic connection between studies through the organization and reorganization of experience which without the aid of concepts to represent the previous experience would not be possible.

The main points which have been made so far in connection with the psychological aspects of concepts may now be briefly summarized. (1) the scientific concept, as a way of conceiving, enables one to picture and present that which cannot be seen or directly perceived. In other words it enables one to circumvent problems of perceptual experience. (2) The content of the scientific concept consists of an abstracted relation which becomes the subject of additional study. (3) The concept, because of its verbal or symbolic nature, may be shared, thus it permits collective or serial activity in scientific procedure. (4) The interrelations of scientific concepts make possible the systematic structure of science. With this general background of what the psychological aspects of concepts permit in scientific research, let us now look more specifically at what the concept *does* in science.

Specifically considered what do scientific concepts enable the scientist to do? Assuming as we did above that the main objective of science is to explain phenomena by establishing predictable cause-effect relationships, then what part do concepts play in this process? Certainly the aim of any scientific concept is to account for scientific observations as completely and as economically as possible. Observation in science follows certain rules or procedures which permit the observer and/or other observers to determine the validity and reliability of the observations made. In other words, scientific observations are guided and controlled as anyone who has ever conducted a laboratory experiment can testify. But what *does* the guiding or what are the "seeing eyes"? It is perhaps common knowledge that Pasteur in his study of the causes of certain diseases was guided by his proverb, "seek the microbe." That is he had a concept of microscopic or infinitely small organisms as disease bearing organisms, and he used this concept to guide and order his research. Following this as most everyone knows, the mysteries of fermentation, anthrax, septicema and hydrophobia yielded to the new approach made possible by his concept of microscopic organisms. Thus we can say that the *first* function of the concept is to *guide* research by providing a *point of departure or point of view*. A little reflection upon the results of Pasteur's work will show us that his concept of the microbe provided him with a way of looking at his problem and this resulted in the bringing of new facts into existence. That is to say, that concepts provide a way of looking at things and also a way of bringing invisible relationships into existence. In Pasteur's case the particular invisible relationship brought into conscious existence was the relationship of bacteria to disease.[3]

The next illustration is drawn from Blumer and it affords a rather impressive picture of how conceptions guide and direct research. "Through conception objects may be perceived in new relations, which is paramount to saying that the perceptual world becomes reorganized. It is well to bear in mind that in the process new problems may arise, new techniques may appear, and new interpretations may suggest themselves. An entire new field may open up; scientific energy may be released in new productive ways. As I see it, this has been the experience of science on the adaptation of a new orientation or, what is equivalent, on the adaptation of a new conceptual framework. A conspicuous case which may be given in illustration is the origin of modern physics. The work of Galileo is usually chosen, with good reason, as marking the change from the meta-

---

[3] We are not concerned here with the historical fact of who first conceived the idea, whether Fracastoro, Leeuwenhock or some other, but as an example of the idea.

physical preoccupation of the medieval logicians to the scientific endeavors of modern scientists. This work is significant not only for the introduction of experimental technique but also for the development of new concepts which became the basis for the new attack of modern physics. These concepts are familiar. Mass, motion, inertia, force, came to take the place of the concepts of medieval logicians: essence, quality, substance, potentiality. They provided a new perspective; they opened up a new field of endeavor. They raised new problems and suggested new techniques; they sensitized perception to new relations and guided it along new directions; they made experimentation possible, and ultimately they yielded new forms of control. A similar picture, I suppose, is being presented in contemporary physics in the new orientation and conceptual framework surrounding the work in relativity and quantum relations."[4]

It is of interest to note how the conceptual point of view determines the data to be selected for the scientific research in the social and psychological sciences. One striking example is the "individualistic or psychologistic" approach and the "group mind or sociologistic" approach to the study of human behavior. As Blumer says perhaps "the milling and halting condition of our own science does not come directly from the inadequacy of our techniques, as almost everyone contends, but from the inadequacy of our point of view."[5]

Let us turn now to the *second* function of the concept. If the reader will recall Einstein's example of the observer trying to understand the working mechanism of a closed watch and his inability to perceive directly this mechanism, and the consequent necessity to perceive indirectly *via* conception, he shall then be in position to deduce the second function of the concept. In other words, if the observer were not able to conceive of say, gears, wheels, springs, etc., he would not be able to *pursue* the task of explaining the operation of the watch. Thus activity would be prevented. But with aid of the concept the impediment to activity is removed. Therefore, the *second* function of concepts is that they are instrumental to activity in that they liberate action. This function of the concept is often expressed by the phrase, "the concept is a tool." We might summarize the above two functions jointly as follows: Conception, in filling the deficiency in perception, not only provides a point of departure or view and releases activity, but directs such activity with varying degrees of effectiveness. The success of the activity is, of course, dependent upon the validity of the concept. However, the concept as a tool is at first crude, as are all tools in their beginning stage of development. Later, like polished and perfected tools, it may become refined and its use standardized. This process of refinement and standardization takes place through use and subsequent experimentation or study.

---

[4] Herbert Blumer, *op. cit.,* p. 9.
[5] *Loc. Cit.*

A *third* function of the concept arises out of the consequences in practice of the above two. To understand this one must realize or recall that the concept was formulated out of observation in connection with a problem, and that it provided a point of view toward solving the problem, and also to some extent directed the problem solving activity. Now, once one has formulated and used concepts in connection with one kind of problem he can by reasoning visualize *new problems* and procedures which transcend the immediate problems which gave rise to the concept. That is to say, one may by deduction generalize new applications of the concept to new problems. Thus the third function of the concept is its *deductive consequences*.

An illustration or two of this character of the concept should suffice to make clear this function. Prior to 1900 all efforts to formulate a law of radiation in terms of varying wave length and temperature had failed. Max Planck made an effort to patch up or remedy those attempts by making an assumption that radiant energy is emitted *not* in a continuous or unbroken stream but in broken, discrete or discontinuous bits which he termed *quanta*. This concept enabled him to formulate a mathematical equation which described the results of experiments in radiation with complete accuracy. Later, in 1905 Einstein took Planck's quanta concept and postulated that all forms of radiant energy—light, heat, X-rays, etc.—actually travel through space in separate and discontinuous quanta. Einstein's refinement and deduction from Planck's concept later led to practical applications in the form of radar and television.

Another and outstanding illustration taken from Blumer should suffice to convey the idea of the deductive function of concepts in science. He takes as an example the concept of the number system. "The historians of mathematics have made it clear that the early concepts of number arose out of practical experience and were tied to it. Certain developments, which we need not consider here, permitted the use of number concepts in other than mere utilitarian ways. Deductive consequences of number concepts were perceived, and the implications of their alignment and interrelation with one another have given rise to the huge complex structure of modern mathematics, seemingly endless in growth. This growth has proceeded not always in empirical but in logical fashion, and seemingly has raced far ahead of experience. Thus formulas for numerical functions have been worked out which may lie idle for decades before gaining practical use. But if the structure of mathematics may grow logically and not empirically, outdistancing actual experience, its interesting feature is that it ties back so successfully into actual experience. So clean cut has been this application to experience and so productive of control that it has given rise recurrently to views that the cosmos was numerical. Without doubt, all science on its deductive side seeks to approximate the ideal character of mathematics. Although no science has enjoyed more than partial success in this effort, the attempt signifies an appreciation of the deductive values of concepts."[6]

Finally, attention should also be called to the fact that the deductive nature of concepts supplies not only to new or future conditions or *prediction,* but also to the past or *post-diction:* for example, geology, archaeology, paleontology, and historical sociology. A great deal will later be made of this point in Chapter 7.

This brief consideration of the functions of concepts in science leads us to the question: what is the general applicable form in which concepts function in science? In other words what is the general conceptual process? This question is easy to ask, but rather difficult to answer, since the answer involves a number of interrelated ideas.

3. The Conceptual Process

We may begin our discussion with a short summary of the functions of concepts. The reader will recall that concepts serve to remove the blocks to perception, to guide observation, and to reveal by deduction new facts. Our task now is to see how concepts function as a part of the process of scientific problem-solving.

In general the first step to the solution of any problem, whether practical or theoretical, is the initial formulation of the problem either from some *actual* baffling observation or observations or from some *hypothetically* deduced situation in terms of existing theory. Perhaps some explanation should be made as to just what is meant by a scientific problem in the above sense. For purposes of exposition, we may say that when the scientist observes a type of behavior which he cannot explain by existing theory then a problem may be said to exist. For example, cancer is a type of disease for which present medical theory does not seem to have, as yet, an explanation. This, of course, is an actual or empirical problem. The other or hypothetical type of problem is more often of the laboratory type. Dr. Einstein is noted for his great ability in stating hypothetical problems which when solved would provide a test for a theory or an hypothesis. As an example, let us cite Einstein's hypothetical example of a connection between general relativity theory and geometry. "Let us begin with the description of a world in which only two-dimensional and not, as in ours, three-dimensional creatures live. The movies have accustomed us to two-dimensional creatures acting on a two-dimensional screen. Now let us imagine that these shadow figures, that is, the actors on the screen really do exist, that they have the power of thought, that they can create their own science, that for them a two-dimensional screen stands for geometrical space. These creatures are unable to imagine, in a concrete way, a three-dimensional space just as we are unable to imagine a world of four dimensions. They can deflect a straight line; they know what a circle is, but they are unable to construct a sphere, because this would mean forsaking their two-

---

[6] *Ibid.,* p. 11.

dimensional screen. We are in a similar position. We are able to deflect and curve lines and surfaces, but we can scarcely picture a deflected and curved four-dimensional space.

"By living, thinking, and experimenting, our shadow figures could eventually master the knowledge of the two-dimensional Euclidean geom-- etry. Thus, they could prove, for example, that the sum of the angles in a triangle is 180 degrees. They could construct two circles with a common center, one very small, the other large. They would find that the ratio of the circumferences of two such circles is equal to the ratio of their radii, a result again characteristic of Euclidean geometry. If the screen were infinitely great, these shadow beings would find that once having started a journey straight ahead, they would never return to their point of departure.

"Let us now imagine these two-dimensional creatures living in changed conditions. Let us imagine that someone from the outside, the "third dimension," transfers them from the screen to the surface of a sphere with a very great radius. If these shadows are very small in relation to the whole surface, if they have no means of distant communication and cannot move very far, then they will not be aware of any change. The sum or angles in small triangles still amounts to 180 degrees. Two small circles with a common center still show that the ratio of their radii and circumferences are equal. A journey along a straight line never leads them back to the starting point. But let these shadow beings, in the course of time, develop their theoretical and technical knowledge. Let them find means of communications which will enable them to cover large distances swiftly. They will then find, that starting on a journey straight ahead, they ultimately return to their point of departure. "Straight ahead" means along the great circle of the sphere. They will also find that the ratio of two circles with a common center is not equal to the ratio of the radii, if one of the radii is small and the other great.

"If our two-dimensional creatures are conservative, if they have learned the Euclidean geometry for generations past when they could not travel far and when this geometry fitted the facts observed, they will certainly make every possible effort to hold onto it, despite the evidence of their measurements. They could try to make physics bear the burden of these discrepancies. They could seek some physical reasons, say temperature differences, deforming the lines and causing deviation from Euclidean geometry. But sooner or later, they must find out that there is a much more logical and convincing way of describing these occurrences. They will eventually understand that their world is a finite one, with different geometrical principles from those they learned. They will understand that in spite of their inability to imagine it, their world is the two-dimensional surface of a sphere. They will soon learn new principles of geometry, which though differing from the Euclidean can, nevertheless, be formulated in an equally consistent and logical way for their two-dimensional world. For the new generation brought up with a knowledge of the geometry of the sphere, the old Euclidean geometry will seem more complicated and artificial since it does not fit the facts observed." [7]

While the situation of two-dimensional creatures on a two-dimensional surface was hypothetically conceived in relation to these same creatures on a three dimensional surface the principles involved were not hypothetical, but instead were a part of a body of knowledge called geometry.

Inasmuch as the above illustration was somewhat lengthy, we should perhaps re-establish the point in question, namely, that the first step involved in the building of concepts is the awareness of a problem stemming from an actual empirical or hypothetically conceived situation. For example, our two-dimensional creatures referred to above would in the three-dimensional situation have eventually revised their concept of lines to include not only flat surfaces but curved surfaces as well.

4. Logical and Methological Problems in Concept Formation

Before we begin with the next step in concept formation a few words should be said concerning the special nature of scientific concepts as over and against common sense concepts. First, scientific knowledge requires that all statements of science be capable of being tested by reference to evidence which is public, that which can be secured by different observers, and the evidence is independent of the observers. To this end, data which are to serve as scientific evidence should be described by concepts whose use by scientists is marked by a high degree of uniformity and precision. The vocabulary of everyday discourse does not exhibit such precision and uniformity; so, science has evolved a system of concepts which is suited for the°formulation of general explanatory and predictive principles. However, certain connections do obtain between common sense concepts and their scientific counterparts. If it is intended that science systematize the data of our experience, then this is possible only if scientific principles have a bearing upon, and are conceptually connected with the language which has been established by common observation. Consequently there exist certain connections between the technical terms of empirical science and the vocabulary of everyday experience. However, the scientific *meaning* of scientific concepts in terms of their definition and use are quite different from the same aspects of these terms when used in the everyday language. This does not imply, however, that the scientific definition is any better than the common sense one. For scientific purposes certainly the scientific definition is better, but for everyday personal relations the common sense term is better.

It must be realized that scientific concepts are derived and defined for scientific purposes *per se*. Thus the scientific concept is defined in such a way as to yield a uniformity and precision in usage which permits measurement and experimentation for the purpose of establishing explanatory and predictive principles in the form of general laws or

[7] Albert Einstein and Leopold Infeld, *op. cit.*, pp. 235-238.

theories. For example, it is sufficient for the man on the street to refer to pressure as meaning force. In general no further specification would be necessary. However, for the physicist he would specify whether he was referring to solids or liquids. If liquids then his general definition would be $P = \dfrac{F}{A}$, where F is the force on a surface in a direction perpendicular to the surface, and A is the area of the surface.

In the initial phases of research, and in the early stages of a scientific discipline like psychology and sociology the concepts are often characterized by observational terms which are found in the everyday language, and which have an immediate empirical referent. Such concepts as motive, trait, emotion, status and role are examples of the above. A difficulty of such concepts is that they yield a low level of generalization, *i.e.,* they generally do not have much systematic import, and are really not explanatory concepts at all, but rather descriptive labels. However, as research progresses and as a scientific discipline becomes more advanced, then its concepts become more general in nature, and further removed from direct observational and empirical referents. Modern physics is a case in point where its concepts are so far removed from direct observation that their empirical referents have to be inferred. These highly abstract terms are sometimes referred to as theoretical constructs for which some experts would claim are "mere fictions." However, the inability to formulate them entirely in observation terms is not necessarily justification for labeling them as "fictions to which nothing corresponds in experience." Our sensory experience appears to be very limited indeed, while such concepts as "electron," "proton," cosmic ray, and gene have been very useful in enabling the scientist to interpret and organize the data of direct observation by means of a uniform and comprehensive system which permits explanation and prediction irrespective of the number of logical operations the concepts are removed from *direct* observation.[8]

To summarize: In exploratory research and in the early stages of development of a scientific field, science will often have to use the vocabulary of conversational language with all its difficulties for this pursuit. But with the development of more precise means of observation both direct and indirect, and the accumulation or more adequate data thereby, science has to modify its concepts. The resultant picture of nature as yielded by the revised concepts is one which is much different from the picture provided by everyday experience and direct observation. In respect to this changing picture of reality Einstein remarked: "Insofar as mathematics is about reality it is not certain, and insofar as it is certain it is not about reality." The fact that scientific concepts and common sense concepts describe the same referents in different ways, and the fact that scientific concepts change in meaning and definition

---

[8] For a discussion of concepts of a similar nature in the social sciences see Chapter 7 on Constructive Typology in Social Research.

as new data is added is a source of confusion to the student and researcher. However, it need not be once we realize this problem in concept formation.

The next difficulty considered in concept formation had to do with the systematic nature of concepts and science. For instance, science aims toward ever simpler systems of explanation of its observations. Consequently concepts have to be considered in terms of their logical relationships to other concepts. This is especially true when scientific theory deals as it often does with things that have not been directly observed. It is also true with those concepts which deal with the *relations* between things rather than the things or referents themselves. Nevertheless, it is of the greatest importance for conceptual clarity that the ultimate phenomenon or empirical referent of a concept be determinable, irrespective of the number of logical operations the concept is removed from its final referent. Indeed as Hempel says, "the entire history of scientific endeavor appears to show that in our world comprehensive, simple, and dependable principles for the explanation and prediction of observable phenomena cannot be obtained by merely summarizing and inductively generalizing observational findings. A hypothetico-deductive-observational procedure is called for and indeed is followed in the more advanced branches of science: Guided by his knowledge of observational data, the scientist has to invent a set of concepts—theoretical constructs, which lack immediate experiential significance, a system of hypotheses couched in terms of them, and an interpretation for the resulting theoretical network; and all *this in a manner which will establish explanatory and predictive connections between the data of direct observations.*"[9]

How does one go about overcoming the above mentioned difficulties in concept formation? Assuming, of course, that there is no substitute for ingenuity and a thorough knowledge of one's field, then the problem is simply one of knowing the procedures and principles of concept formation. This is the task to which we now turn.

5. Principles of Concept Formation

The reader will recall that concepts function in science (1) to remove blocks to perception, (2) to guide or direct observation, (3) to reveal new facts by the process of deduction. Without attempting to assess the relative importance of each of these functions, it is, however, desirable to call attention to a particular aspect of Number 2.

Recall the example of early research in malaria where the concept of the causal source of malaria was "bad air." Consequently the observations made, and the data collected were made and collected in relation to "bad air." Note that the concept of "bad air" led the investigator to look in the wrong place for the answer to his problem. This is a

[9] Carl G. Hempel, "Fundamentals of Concept Formation in Empirical Science," *International Encyclopedia of Unified Science,* Vol. 11, Number 7 (The University of Chicago Press, 1952), pp. 36-37. Italics mine.

frequent error in a beginning science and a most damaging one. Needless to say, data selected on the basis of inadequate, ambiguous or invalid concepts result in inadequate and invalid theory. Therefore, if the goal of science is a body of theory which yields adequate empirical explanations, then a particular science in pursuit of such a goal must of necessity be guided by *valid and precise concepts*.

While a definition of concept has been implied from the context of the discussion in the first part of the chapter, it is now necessary to provide a more explicit definition. For our purposes, we may regard a concept as a shorthand representation of a variety of facts, *i.e.,* a basic idea of what something in general is. Roughly, it subsumes a number of facts, and events under one general idea. The word dog does not refer to any particular dog. However, it is sufficient to call up a reasonable good image of the main characteristics of any dog. While the concept animal is still more abstract and may call forth an image of almost any animal, it, nevertheless, separates animals from plants.

With this general background as to the nature and function of concepts, we now turn our attention to a consideration of some principles of concept formation.[10]

As indicated previously, we may assume that in general there are two main sources of concepts. First, from deduction, *i. e.,* we may deduce a new concept from the existent body of theory in the field. Second, from observation, *i. e.,* we may from several observations of particular instances of behavior formulate a general concept embracing these. Nevertheless, whatever the source of the concept if it is to be of value to science it must meet certain requirements. Among these are: (1) it must refer to what is common to a class of data, by specific reference to the common property or properties, *i.e.,* the concept must *prescribe what* to look for, (2) it must guide and direct research along fruitful channels, *i. e.,* it must have value for theory.

These requirements are so important that some elaboration seems necessary. Recall again, the function of concepts in science, especially the one which referred to the removal of blocks to perception. First, it is obvious that an ambiguous concept, or one whose properties are not clearly prescribed would frustrate or impede contact with the empirical world rather than remove blocks to perception.

Second, the concept should tie in to the theory of the field in such a way as to suggest new or additional principles, rather than to stall thinking with a kind of "first cause" block.

The concepts of attitude, motive, and emotion in sociology and psychology are good examples of the first, or ambiguous concepts which frustrate contact with the empirical world. That is their properties as presently used are so vague or ambiguous as to block perception, rather than to liberate it. In respect to the second requirement of suggesting new

---

[10] *Methods and techniques* for formulating and deriving concepts will be discussed in Chapters 4, 5, 6, and 7.

principles or theory rather than stalling thinking, we have only to refer to such concepts as innate disposition, drives, and instincts as being good examples of theoretically sterile concepts in the behavioral sciences. In addition to their vagueness, such concepts do not permit a functional tie-in with the principles of learning, but instead suggest a kind of "hereditary given" which blocks thinking with a kind of "first cause."

It is, of course, recognized that one generally does not start out with clear-cut and definitive concepts. If not, then the problem becomes that of refining the concepts by more adequate study of the empirical facts to which they refer.[11] It is not the purpose of this chapter to discuss the techniques for concept formation and refinement but rather to consider concepts in terms of their logical and methodological aspects. It is, however, desirable to further consider certain logical principles for concept formation and refinement. This will be done by a brief analysis of the logic of classification, ordering and measurement.

The first step in concept formation is the formulation of a problem and *observation* of the "facts," "data," or "events." The reader is again reminded that observation usually involves more than mere sense perceptions, since observation usually involves some degree of interpretation and inference. Scientific observation lies somewhere between the extremes of objectivity and subjectivity—it is inevitably selective to some extent, for not all facts are relevant or ascertainable; nevertheless, it seeks to avoid bias. Preliminary observation in a new field may be merely exploratory for the purpose of locating the problem, but beyond this stage it is guided by some elementary theory, and is, therefore, to that extent selective. In fields where research is somewhat advanced the careful scientific observer will be guided by the accumulated body of knowledge in his field, and, therefore, will know how and where to look for what is relevant to the problem. He will be aware of the distinction between observations as such and inferences made from them. He will carefully make the observations by means of instruments of observation, and, if possible will experimentally vary the observations for purpose of clarifying and verifying his observations.[12]

To summarize: observation is a necessary means to concept formation, but it is not sufficient. It is necessary in that the scientist must have accurate raw data from which to build a conceptualization by subsequent treatment of *classification,* of *comparative ordering,* and of *measurement.* It is not intended to imply by the listing order of the above three techniques of concept formation that one has to go through these three stages before one comes out with a concept. Quite the opposite may be true; that is, one may arrive at a concept by either of these techniques; however, subsequent analysis of a concept may require all three of the above for purposes of refinement. When such is the case, however, the

---

[11] As indicated previously this is done by the methods and techniques described in Part II of this text.

[12] Controlled Observation is discussed in Chapters 4 and 5.

definition of the concept usually changes. For instance, the definition which was adequate for classification or ranking purposes may not be adequate for measurement purposes.[13] In the following section we shall briefly consider classification.

Classification. Closely connected with observation, yet a step beyond it, is the systematic classification of objects, data, and events as a type of scientific concept formation.

Generally speaking a classification of the objects or data in a given category (such as societies, bacteria, chemical compounds, etc.) is effected by laying down a set of two or more criteria such that every element of the category satisfies exactly one of those criteria. Each criterion determines a certain class, namely, the class of all objects or events in the category which satisfy the criterion. If each object in the category actually satisfies exactly one of the criteria, then the classes thus determined are mutually exclusive, and they are jointly exhaustive of the category. The points to watch in classification are careful, objective definition of the several classes in terms of criteria that are independent of the observer, and that the objects to be classified are easily recognizable by other competent observers in order to permit some measure of the reliability of the classification.

The general rules governing logical division are also applicable to classification, although they cannot be so rigidly followed.[14] Logically, any classification should be based on the same criterion throughout. Also, any classification should be totally inclusive of the category defined and exclusive of all other categories to prevent overlapping. The above rule of inclusiveness and exclusiveness in classification is an ideal which may be only partially achieved in growing and dynamic fields such as the social sciences, biology and zoology. Generally complete classification is not possible until the science has become quite systematic and the laws governing the evolutionary processes are known, and hence the objects or members of the class are known. The excellence of a scientific classification is measured by the discovery of *essential or basic properties,* so that knowledge of the presence of a given property holds implications regarding the presence of other properties, ultimately resulting in a large degree of systematic relationship. Classification of this degree of coherence is exemplified by the periodic table in chemistry.

As an example of the technique of classification as a type of concept formation Hempel cites one anthropometric classification of human skulls, the resultant concept being the cephalic index. The classification is based on the following criteria, C_1 to C_5: "C_1: The cephalic index, $c(x)$, of skull x is 75 or less; or, $c(x) \leq 75$; C_2: $75 < c(x)$

[13] Thomas C. McCormick, *Elementary Social Statistics* (New York: McGraw-Hill, 1941), p. 21.
[14] See "Logical Division and Classification" in any text in logic, e. g., H. L. Searles, *Logic and Scientific Methods* (New York: The Ronald Press, 1948), pp. 46-49.

≤ 77.6; C_3: $77.6 < c(x) \leq 80$; C_4: $80 < c(x) \leq 83$; C_5: $83 < c(x)$.

"The properties determined by these criteria are referred to respectively, as (1) dolichocephaly, (2) subdolicocephaly, (3) mesaticephaly, (4) subbrachycephaly, and (5) brachycephaly. In this case the requirements of exclusiveness and exhaustiveness are satisfied simply as a logical consequence of the determining criteria; for, by definition, the cephalic index of any skull is a positive number, and every positive number falls into exactly one of the five intervals referred to by the criteria (C_1 to C_5). An analogous observation applies, in particular to all those dichotomous classifications which are determined by some property concept and its denial such as the division of integers into those which are and into those which are not integral multiples of 2, of chemical compounds into organic and inorganic, and of bacteria into Gram-positive and Gram-negative." [15]

A concept may be vague and in need of clarification by analysis in which case the ordinary procedures described in Chapters 4, 5 and 6 below would be used. That is, analysis may be needed to enable one to get hold of some specific or more familiar aspect of a concept in order to give a clue to the less-known aspects. In which case the analysis may be of physical wholes in terms of their component parts, or it may be of their qualities or both. An example of the former would be an organ and cell analysis as in biology, while the latter would be an analysis of the qualities and attributes of these parts such as size, structure, color etc.

It is often considered of greater significance for science where at least one of the conditions of exclusiveness and exhaustiveness in classification is satisfied not simply as a matter of definition or logical consequence of the determining criteria, but as a matter of empirical fact. This implies an empirical law and thus gives some measure of systematic coherence to the classificatory concepts involved. Thus, *e.g.,* the division of mankind into races on the basis of some primary biological characteristics or the division of humans into males and females, or the marriage institution into monogamy, polygamy and polyandry. These are not logically exhaustive, but the extent to which they are factually so, they possess systematic importance. Such Classification is sometimes referred to as *natural classification*. It is, however, in reference to *classes* of objects rather than individual objects. That is, the above type of classification takes the form of "characteristic A belongs to the things of class B," which implies that characteristic A invariably is associated with class B either on logical grounds or as a matter of fact. It does not say that objects can be individually described, and then divided into groups forming a natural classification.

To summarize, we may say that a classificatory concept represents a characteristic which any object in the category under consideration must

---

[15] Carl G. Hempel, *op. cit.,* p. 51.

either have or not have; if its meaning is precise, it divides the category into two mutually exclusive classes. The properties or attributes of these concepts may be analyzed experimentally and/or by correlation analyses to determine other characteristics which they are associated with. Classificatory concepts are generally used for the description of observational findings, and for the formulation of initial empirical generalizations. But with the necessity for a more precise and theoretically fruitful set of concepts, classificatory concepts are replaced by other types, which make it possible to deal with degrees of characteristics in terms of gradation and variations. That is, instead of the "either-or" nature of classificatory concepts, these other types of concepts represent terms of "more or less," and metrical terms of a quantitative nature which attributes to each item in the category a certain real number or numbers. This brings us to the next type of concept formation, namely, that of comparative ordering.

Comparative Ordering. The idea of the comparative concept is fairly simple. It consists of determining for any two objects in a given category whether they are the same in respect to some characteristic, and, if not, which of them has more or less of the characteristic. For instance, in respect to mineral objects a comparative concept of hardness could be arrived at for any two minerals within a category by determining whether they are of equal hardness, and if not which of them is less hard. To derive a genuine comparative concept it must be possible to arrange the object or elements of a given category in serial order, in which an object or element *precedes* another if it is smaller than another, whereas objects of equal characteristics coincide, *i. e.,* share the same place. Thus, we see that to meet the requirements of the comparative concept any two elements or objects of a category must be comparable in regard to the attribute under consideration; that is, they must either have it to the same extent, or one must have it to a lesser extent than the other.

In the social sciences two frequently used means for comparative concept formation are ranking and rating. By ranking it is meant that a number of objects or elements are ordered in terms of amount. For example, we consider person A more intelligent than person B, B more intelligent than C, and so on. As soon as the instances of the element are ranked they become capable of some statistical treatment, especially rank correlation. Ranking is, of course, ordinal in character rather than cardinal. That is, the rank assigned an element or object within a category will depend not only on the object, but also on the category within which it is ranked. Thus, a person's rank height will depend to some extent upon the group within which he is being compared, but the number representing the measure of his height will not.

Rating is the classification of objects, items or elements, into ascending, or ordered classes. An odd division of classes is usually followed in order to allow for a median class. Thus a person may be rated in terms of body physique as slim, medium, or fat, or in terms of intelligence as mentally defective, feeble-minded, dull, slow, normal, superior, or very superior. The means by which the ranking and rating is carried out is very important. For instance, the use of humans as instruments for comparison or observation has many disadvantages in terms of precision and reliability. The use of impersonal or mechanical instruments where possible is to be preferred, since those are less subject to observer bias.

While the idea of more or less of a certain attribute is an improvement over the "either . . . or" type of concept in simple classifications one, nevertheless, often needs to know how much more or how much less an object has of a certain attribute. Thus, in psychology instead of classifying attitudes as favorable or unfavorable Thurstone has developed an attitude scale, and in physics the distinciton of hot, cold, etc., is re- placed by the concept of temperature in degrees centigrade. Such con- cepts are called quantitative or measurement concepts and this brings us to the third or last type of concept formation to be considered here.

Quantitative or Metrical Concepts. To begin with we shall refer to quantitative or metrical concepts as those concepts which attribute to each item or object in their category a certain real number or numbers. Con- cepts such as height in feet, length in centimeters, time duration in sec- onds, will be called quantitative concepts. Quantitative concepts provide a greater descriptive flexibility and subtlety in meaning as compared with classificatory or non-metrical concepts. Thus, *e. g.,* to assert that one car was moving at a "moderate speed," while another was moving at a very "high speed," yields some distinction, but it does not show their relative position in the sense that a speed of 40 miles per hour is one-half of 80 miles per hour. This advantage of quantitative concepts is much like that obtained by the use of numerals rather than proper names in naming streets and houses. Numerals indicate direction and spatial relationships which are not reflected by proper names.[16]

The greater descriptive flexibility of quantitative concepts makes for greater flexibility in the formulation of more systematic. general laws. Hempel cites a good example.

> By means of classificatory terms, we might formulate laws such as this: "When iron is warm, it is gray; when it gets hot, it turns red; when it gets very hot, it turns white," whereas with the help of ordering terms of the metrical type it is possible to formulate vastly more subtle and precise laws which express the energy of radiation in different wave lengths as a mathe- matical function of the temperature.[17]

This greater precision and flexibility of laws in physics awaited a set of fundamental quantitative concepts in physics and it may safely be said that such concepts in sociology and psychology are still awaited, though prog- ress in that direction is being made.

---

[16] Carl G. Hempel, *op. cit.,* p. 51.
[17] *Loc. Cit.*

Finally, the introduction of *fundamental* quantitative concepts make possible an extensive application of the concepts and theories of higher mathematics. This makes possible the determination and expression of general laws or principles in the form of functional relationships between different quantities. Such concepts permit not only the *establishment of relationships,* but also the *amount of the relationship.*

In the following, we shall provide a brief introduction as to how quantitative concepts are formed. Counting and measuring are extensions of observational and inductive methods for the purpose of exactness and precision; however, no amount of counting and measuring can substitute for the need of accuracy and precision in the initial stage of observation.

We express much faith in measurement, largely because of the great success achieved in developing standards for measuring mass, time, space, temperature, etc. in the physical sciences. However, different objects, processes, and qualities exist in different degrees of availability to observation and control, and measurement is more difficult in respect to some qualities and processes than others.

The simplest form of measurement is counting, or simple enumeration of individual items or units as they occur. It consists of assigning a number unit to each item or object in a one-to-one relationship which may then be placed in serial order and treated by the familiar methods of arithmetic. As in classification the individual items of a category must be discrete, so that one may know exactly what it is being counted. If the concept is not sufficiently recognizable for its instances to be counted, one may assume that further efforts toward a more reliable definition should be made before further scientific manipulation is attempted.

Campbell[18] distinguishes two ways of forming metrical or quantitative concepts, namely, *fundamental measurement and derived measurement;* we shall limit our consideration of measurement to a brief introduction of these two. Less technical terms for labeling these two types of measurement would be direct and indirect measurement, respectively. There is hardly any fundamental or direct measurement in the social sciences to date, and not much in the physical sciences. Fundamental measurement is illustrated by the measurement of mass, length, weight and time, and these only when applying to relatively medium-sized objects, speeds, etc. It consists of two steps: *first,* the specifying of a comparative concept, which determines a nonmetrical order; and *second,* the metrifying of that order by the introduction of numerical values. To illustrate, let us cite the old balance type of scale.[19] It consists of a balance and an arbitrarily chosen standard or weight. If, when an object is placed on one end of the beam and the standard or weight on the other, they

[18] Norman R. Campbell, *Physics: the Elements,* part 11 (Cambridge, University Press, 1920).
[19] The problem of scalars and scale construction in the social sciences will be treated in Chapter 6.

balance, they are said to be equal. If the standard end goes down, it is said to be heavier, and if it goes up, it is said to be lighter. It can then be said that if A is heavier than B, and B than C, then A is heavier than C. Also, if A is equal in weight to X, and B is equal in weight to Y, A and B taken together at one end of the scale will balance X and Y at the other, *i.e.* the quality of weight is additive.

We may specify more specifically the requirements as indicated in the above example. It will be recalled that fundamental measurement is accomplished by specifying a serial order as in the above, and then metrifying that order. What is meant by metrifying is indicated as follows:

Let A and B above be two relations which determine a serial order for a given category or class. This order has been metricized if a standard or criteria has been specified which assigns to each element or item in the class exactly one real number, in such a manner that the following conditions are satisfied for all the elements of the class: let x and y be two elements of the relations A and B of the above class of weights, now:

If xAy, then $f(x) = f(y)$
If xBy, then $f(x) < f(y)$

Any function f, which assigns to every element x of a given class or category exactly one real-number value, $f(x)$, will be said to constitute a quantitative concept. For example, force and acceleration are functions which when described in terms of the ratio of force/acceleration give us the quantitative concept of mass. The principal condition for fundamental measurement is that the qualities be *additive*.[20] The requirement for additiveness is that the units or items within a class being measured be objective in the sense that they have the same meaning for all. Thus it is meaningful to say that A, who weighs 180 pounds, is twice as heavy as B, who weighs 90 pounds, or the difference in value between units 3 and 4 on a scale is the same as the difference between 7 and 8 on the scale. This requirement is difficult to meet in the physical sciences, and it is more difficult in the behavioral sciences because of the frequent inability to observe directly the nature of the qualities. It is also difficult in relativistic physics, *i.e.,* measurement in modern physics is more of an indirect type.

A quantity is additive whenever there exists an operational interpretation for the numerical addition of the scale values of two different objects which belong to the same category or class of objects. That is $a + b = b + a$, thus a quantity is additive relatively to a combining operation if $\Sigma(x + y) = \Sigma x + \Sigma y$, whenever x, y, and combined x, y belong to the category within which the quantity is defined. However, it should be observed that quantities are not combined in a series just for the sake of combining them; they are combined only when such combin-

---

[20] For a detailed discussion of measurement see Norman R. Campbell, *An Account of the Principles of Measurement* (Longman, Green & Co., N. Y., 1928), and S. S. Stevens, *Handbook of Experimental Psychology* (John Wiley, N. Y., 1951).

ing or addition will result or give rise to a simple and fruitful concept or theory. In this sense fundamental measurement is not the end result of science, but is itself a means or way of defining, describing, and explaining. But in dealing directly with homogenous units as in fundamental measurement, it often occurs that we need to measure elements or relations of these units which are not amenable to the procedure of direct measurement, in which case some other procedure is necessary. We refer to this type of measurement as *derived measurement*.

Derived Measurement. By derived measurement is meant the determination of one quantitative concept by means of other quantitative concepts.[21] Thus the concept of density is derived by relating mass and volume, and temperature by relating pressure and volume. Measurement makes sense, of course, only if the same process or property is being measured at different positions on the scale, and in different objects or individuals. Thus, the minimum assumption underlying scaling is that a given property or characteristic in different individuals or objects is an identical process that varies along an identical dimension or dimensions. The concepts have to be broken down to parts that are equal and interchangeable for the purpose in hand.

If by derived measurement is meant the determination of a quantitative concept by means of criteria which presupposes at least one previous scale of measurement, then how are derived measurements performed? We shall consider two procedures by which measurement may be accomplished; Hempel labels these derived measurement by *stipulation* and derived measurement by *law*.[22] Thus by stipulating that water freezes at zero degrees centigrade, and boils at 100 degrees at altitude of sea-level, we have a scale which measures temperature at or between these two points. To illustrate again, the average speed of an automobile is by definition or stipulation the quotient of the distance covered and the length of time involved. The concept of I. Q. is derived by the same process, *i.e.*, the stipulated ratio of $\frac{\text{M. A.}}{\text{C. A.}}$. Thus the determination or stipulation of another or "new" quantity by means of other quantities, which are already available, is *derived measurement by stipulation*.

Derived measurement by law, on the other hand, does not introduce an additional or "new" quantity, but instead is a different or alternative way of measuring one that has already been introduced. This is done by the use of some principle or law which represents the quantity in question as a mathematical function of other quantities, for which methods of measurement have already been determined. Thus certain laws of trigonometry make it possible to determine the distances of inaccessible points as functions of other distances which are accessible to more direct measurement. For example, when the rectangular coordinates of a given point are specified, its radius vector can always be determined

---

[21] For example, the coefficient of correlation and regression in Chapter 4.
[22] Carl G. Hempel, *op. cit.*, p. 70.

by the theorem of Pythagoras, $r^2 = x^2 + y^2$; $r = \sqrt{x^2 + y^2}$. As one further illustration, we cite the familiar sign "caution—radar speed control," where certain laws of physics make it possible to use sound or radar echoes for measuring spatial distances by the measurement of time lapses. The above two methods may, of course, be combined, thus extending the rules of measurement for a given quantity.

All attempts to measure an intangible quality, must, of course, be indirect in nature. However, there must be provided at least a partial empirical referent or interpretation for the quantity or for certain of its properties, so that we may know what to expect from Y when the scale registers a certain value of X. It should also be noted, that irrespective of the quantitative precision of the concept it is useless for science unless it has theoretical importance and systematically relates to other concepts.

Thus the principles governing the formulation of quantitative concepts represent complex and ever tentative modifications of initial observational criteria; modifications which are determined by the objective of obtaining a theoretical system that is simple and has great explanatory and predictive power. To that extent concept formation and theory go hand in hand.

The reader will recall that one of the main functions of concepts in science was the deductive function of the concept which enabled the scientist to predict the existence of additional or unknown properties within a class. Also, in the preceding paragraph it was concluded that concepts represent a process of abstraction which yields a theoretical system of some degree of explanatory and predictive power. This obviously leads to the following question: What is meant by explanation and prediction in science? The answer to this question is the problem of the next chapter.

6. Summary

We saw that concepts provide the foundation for the development of scientific theory by serving as a guide to the empirical world. Concepts function in research by (1) providing a point of departure or point of view, (2) liberating scientific research by removing blocks to perception, (3) permitting the deduction of new problems and facts.

Concepts, facts and theory interplay, *i.e.*, concepts and theory guide research in the search of new facts. New facts give rise to new concepts and theories, and new concepts and theories cause old concepts and old facts to take on new meaning. This interplay is the means by which science develops.

Finally, we formulated certain principles to guide the forming and development of concepts. Namely, they must refer to what is common to a class of data, by specific reference to the common property or properties, *i.e.*, they must prescribe what to look for, and where to look. For example, the properties referred to by the concept of heredity are the genes and chromosomes. Second, concepts must guide and direct research along fruitful channels, *i.e.,* they must have value for theory.

SELECTED REFERENCES

Adler, Franz, "Operational Definitions in Sociology," *American Journal of Sociology,* Vol. 52, number 5 (1947), pp. 438-444.

Bergmann, Gustav, and Kenneth W. Spence, "Operationism and Theory Construction" in Melvin H. Marx, *Phychological Theory* (New York: Macmillan, 1951), pp. 54-66.

Campbell, Norman R., *An Account of the Principles of Measurement* (New York: Longman, Green, and Co., 1928).

Cohen, Morris R., and Ernest Nagel, *An Introduction to Logic and Scientific Method* (New York: Harcourt, Brace, 1934).

Hempel, Carl G., "Fundamentals of Concept Formation in Empirical Science," *International Encyclopedia of Unified Science,* Vol II, number 7 (The University of Chicago Press, 1952).

Langer, Suzanne K., *Philosophy in a New Key* (New York: Penguin Press, 1942).

Stouffer, Samuel, *et al., Measurement and Prediction* (Princeton: Princeton University Press, 1950).

Woodger, J. H., "The Technique of Theory Construction," *International Encyclopedia of Unified Science,* Vol. II, number 5 (The University of Chicago Press, 1939).

Chapter 3

SCIENCE AND PREDICTION*

1. Introduction

ONE of the major ideas considered in the preceding chapter was the necessity for ordering and interpreting the data or "facts" observed by the researcher. While Joe Blow may contend that "the facts speak for themselves," the scientist knows that they do not. It is the function of concepts and theory to provide the data with their meaning. It may be said that facts come into existence through the use of concepts and theory. It should be pointed out, however, that the classifying and interpreting of data are only a part of the scientific process. The goal of scientific activity per se is the development of new theory. Since this chapter concludes our consideration of the logic and procedural rules of science, then logically speaking, the propositions in this chapter should relate to the final product or aim of science. As we shall see below this is indeed the case. We may now formally pose the problem of this chapter. Namely, what is the relation of prediction to science; and under what conditions are warranted predictions made?

The reader will also recall that concepts and theory give direction to the search for data. If we regard science as a form of inquiry, then scientific activity has as its point of departure a problem to explain, or a set of observations that demand explanation. The researcher formulates hypotheses (*i.e.,* possible explanations) either directly from the observations made or deductively from an existing body of theory or both. The hypotheses state what we are looking for. The initial unsolved or heterogeneous observations constitute the problematic data, *i.e.,* the data to be explained. The hypotheses state or define the data to be selected for explanation of the problematic data. The process of explanation then consists of establishing a relation between the class of data called problematic, and the other data which we shall call "explanatory data." At this point in the procedure there is no knowledge as to whether the hypothesis or hypotheses are correct. "Sooner or later, in the course of inquiry, the scientist reaches a decision; to be verifiable, it must be communicable. This means that he must have rules by which he is justified in arriving at his decision. At that point when the scientist is justifying his decision, he is no longer engaged in inquiry, but in an argument. The decision he has reached must be the logical consequent of earlier propositions."[1] The understanding of how scientific decisions are

---

* Written by John T. Doby.
[1] Roy G. Francis, "Prediction as a Sociological Operation" (Unpublished Ph.D. dissertation, The University of Wisconsin, Madison, 1950), p. 5.

45

reached leads to a consideration of the meaning and nature of scientific explanation and prediction.

2. The Meaning of Prediction in Science

In approaching the problem of the meaning of prediction in science, we shall first distinguish between *qua-scientific* decisions and *quasi-scientific* decisions. By qua-scientific decisions we mean decisions belonging to science *per se*. For example, the assertion or hypothesis that there exists a relationship between a certain type or certain types of viroses and cancer in human beings is a decision which would belong to science *per se*. Assuming that the decision would be made in the affirmative, and the type and nature of the virus, and its connection with the effect, cancer, was known, then the connection would be formulated into a theory and become part of the body of knowledge called science. However, by quasi-scientific decisions, we mean decisions that are made in the manner of science, but that do *not* belong to science. That is, decisions of this nature use the *means* of science, but not its *goals*. To illustrate, we cite the example above which asserted an hypothetical relationship between a virus and cancer. Now, suppose the same researcher who made the above hypothetical discovery were to perfect by scientific means a chemical to combat the cancer effect; the decision involved here would be "like science" rather than "belonging to science." While prediction may be involved in both qua-scientific decisions and quasi-scientific decisions, it is predictive activity in respect to qua-scientific decisions with which we are concerned here. In other words we are concerned with predictions which test hypotheses. The hypotheses underlying the predictions if confirmed become a part of the *body of science*. The hypotheses underlying quasi-scientific prediction, if confirmed become a part of the body of knowledge called *technology*.

Before we begin our analysis of the meaning of predictive activity in science it is desirable to make one further distinction, *i.e.*, the distinction between empirical laws and theoretical laws from which predictions are based.

By somewhat oversimplifying the idea, it is sufficient for our purpose here to say that empirical laws refer to finite observable characteristics, and are, therefore, restricted in the number of characteristics they can discriminiate. The fact that water boils at 100 degrees centigrade at an altitude of sea level is an example of an empirical law, whereas theoretical laws refer to an infinite number of characteristics and values. Thus they are of the nature of universal propositions. For example the "law" of inertia in physics which states that matter will remain at rest unless some force acts upon it, follows from the definition of force as *that which produces motion*. That is, the law is a universal proposition derived from the postulates and definitions. As such this type of law is the result of logical syntax of the language, and is not directly dependent upon any empirical reference.

The student should not be tempted to think that theoretical laws, because of their greater degree of abstraction are not as important as empirical laws. In fact without these theoretical laws it would be impossible to apply the principles of higher mathematics in science. For example the concepts of limit, continuum, derivative and integral would be unavailable. The importance of the distinction between theoretical and empirical laws is to avoid the frequent confusion between rules of procedure in research in contrast to deductive logic. In other words these theoretical laws are not laws describing actual or concrete phenomena, but rules or prescriptions for scientific procedure concerned with actual phenomena.[2] Consequently there is some question as to how theoretical laws are affected by the invalidation of correlated empirical laws.

The reader will recall from Chapters 1 and 2 that science was regarded as a form of inquiry which has as its objectives the description of particular phenomena in the world of our experience, and the establishment of general principles which will allow for the explanation and prediction of these phenomena. This being so, we may assert that the goal of *science* is a system of verifiable propositions about empirical phenomena. This, however, says nothing about the goal of the *scientist,* nor is that of any concern here.

We therefore assert that a scientist may engage in scientific activity . . . that is, may seek to establish verifiable propositions about empirical phenomena . . . for a variety of motives. . . . Whatever his reason, he still seeks such propositions. And as far as his scientific activity[3] is concerned, the *predictability* of his proposition is a test of its correctness.[4] We may conclude that it is the criterion of predictability which largely enables the scientist to come to a decision about some proposition. Prediction in science involves the specifying of what to do if we wish to observe a certain relationship. A predictive statement asserts, "since such and such, then something else." In this respect Kaufmann says, "from an empirical law combined with a pertinent statement of fact a prediction can be deduced.[5] This is tantamount to saying that an underlying causal law exists, such that if A is the cause of B, then in a given instance of A one may estimate that some determined future time B will exist also.

From this we may conclude that a predictive statement means the following: *first,* an hypothetical statement of relationships; *second,* an observation of an existing datum contained in the premise of the hypothetical proposition; and *third,* an estimation of some future consequent which is the logical conclusion of the relation between the proposition and the existent datum. When viewed in the light of the above, it is obvious that a prediction tests an hypothesis. We do not wish to imply the notion of "prediction for prediction's sake," nor do we believe that

---

[2] See Einstein and Infeld, *op. cit.,* and Felix Kaufmann, *Methodology of the Social Sciences* (Oxford University Press, N. Y., 1944), p. 87.

[3] In the sense of belonging to science.

[4] Roy G. Francis, *op. cit.,* pp. 24-25. Italics mine.

[5] Felix Kaufmann, *op. cit.,* p. 93.

the above does imply such. However, the type of relationships tested by predictive statements should be made more explicit. To do this we shall give a brief but specific discussion of the function of prediction in science.

3. Function of Prediction in Science

The initial phase of scientific inquiry is the formulation and careful definition of the problem. Actually one may begin by simply exploring a set of crude observations for the purpose of determining the problem. But once the problem has been determined, and its hypothetical explanation has been formulated, the scientific argument or prediction part of the research has as its empirical point of departure the hypothetical explanation. This is obvious once we realize that we do not make scientific *predictions* about already verified propositions. If the proposition in question were already verified, then it would already be contained in the science, and could simply be deduced at the time the question is posed. This would be explanation rather than prediction, since explanation does not involve any scientific decision[6] if both *law* and *fact* (major and minor premise) are established. However, scientific decisions are required if one or both of the premises are yet to be verified.[7]

The establishment of a solution to a scientific problem requires a chain of steps of which the formulation of the problem and the conclusion are only two, namely, the beginning and the end. The hypothesis is a provisional explanation put forward upon the basis of accumulated knowledge for the guidance of the research. It performs this function by asserting a relationship between two classes of independently defined data, previously referred to as "problematic data" and "explanatory data." For instance one may assert a relationship between the weight of a class of individuals, and their diet. The validity and the amount of the relationship would then be confirmed or refuted by experimental and/or statistical test of the hypothesis. To be incorporated into science the hypothesis must assert some meaningful relationship which possesses theoretical or empirical power of explanation. Thus, the kind of propositions which science seeks are those which assert the existence, description, and amount of relationship between two or more different classes of data. The correctness of these assertions determines the validity of the predictions. Failure to predict correctly, therefore, means that the asserted relationship was not true as stated. Therefore, the scientific *function* of prediction is that of testing hypotheses. And it is the function of the hypothesis to state a specific relationship between different classes of phenomena in such a way that this relationship can be empirically tested. That is, the hypothesis must be capable of being validated or invalidated. And finally, if it is validated it has explanatory and subsequent deductive value for science.

---

[6] In the sense of qua-scientific decision as defined above.

[7] The student should read or review chapters on propositions, inference, and the various types of syllogisms in some text on elementary logic.

A clear understanding of the meaning and significance of explanation in science is hardly possible without an understanding of the nature of scientific laws, and the notion of causality. The following will be devoted to that purpose.

4. Explanation and Casuality in Science

We have frequently referred to the goal of science[8] as that of seeking a theory in order to explain and predict. The confirmation of hypotheses by experimentation is an example of this goal. The various procedures discussed below[9] for establishing causal connections among phenomena are in effect methods of testing causal hypotheses.

Often events occur in pairs, and in such ways that if the first event occurs, the second accompanies or follows it. Thus it is often said that one event is the cause of the other if in the absence of the former the second is always absent. However, the definition of cause and effect usually has other considerations which will be more appropriately considered below. Presently it is sufficient to say that if a connection or relation between events has been observed such that when one event occurs, another necessarily follows, whereas if the first does not occur, the second will not happen, then the first event is said to be the cause of the second.[10] This definition, of course, assumes a coherence and an interdependence between things and events. This assumption of coherence and interdependence has often been referred to in terms of two kinds of conditions, namely, *necessary* conditions and *sufficient* conditions. A sufficient condition of an event is such that whenever the condition is present the event will happen. To illustrate we cite an example from Searles.

"A puncture is a sufficient condition of a flat tire, but it is not a necessary condition because the air may have escaped through the valve. . . . a necessary condition of the event is such that the event never occurs in the absence of the condition. For example, a necessary condition of life is air, for only if organisms have a supply of oxygen can they sustain life. . . . while this is a necessary condition, it is not sufficient; for, in addition, organisms need food, water, and other things. A condition is both sufficient and necessary if whenever it is present the event occurs, and whenever it is absent the event does not occur. For example, after observing the conditions surrounding the threat of inflation in wartime, we might conclude: if and only if rigid price control is enforced will we escape wartime inflation. Here we have asserted that both the sufficient and necessary conditions of escaping inflation is rigid price control."[11]

It is sufficient for our purpose here to conclude that we have explained a phenomenon when we have established the causal factors which determine the effect we have observed. However, we must warn against

---

[8] That is, of science *per se,* the goal of the scientist may be otherwise.

[9] Especially Chapters 4 and 5.

[10] See J. S. Mill, *A System of Logic* (New York: Longmans, 1930), 8th edition.

[11] Herbert L. Searles, *op. cit.,* p. 195.

thinking that since we have explained a phenomenon in the above sense that our explanation is the only true explanation. We say this in spite of the fact that we can on the basis of our causal explanation predict the effect with certainty. This is true because we are never sure that our explanation is the only explanation or even the best explanation. In fact an indefinite number of laws establishing necessary and sufficient conditions for its occurrence might be found. The reader is here asked to recall the idea in Chapter 2 that new theories cause old facts to be seen in a new light, and new facts cause old theories to take on a new meaning.

The essential point to realize in determining the meaning of "cause" 'is that we are speaking in reference to *a* cause of a given event, and not *the* cause, and that the particular cause asserted is dependent for its meaning upon the specific facts contained in the causal law. Thus in determining the meaning of "cause" explicit reference should be made to these facts. For example, if it is asserted and established that, say, social disorganization is a cause of personality disorganization, then the interpretation of this cause hinges upon the set of specific facts composing the law of social disorganization. This observation means that the researcher has in mind one or more variables, variation in which can be used to explain variation in another variable.

The "causal" variables are generally termed *independent variables,* and the variables to be explained are called *dependent variables.* If by reference to the variables of social disorganization he is able to account for, and thereby explain all the variation of the dependent variable, personality disorganization, then on the basis of the above definition of cause he is justified in asserting that social disorganization is a cause of personality disorganization. However, if the variables of social disorganization account for only a proportion of the variation in personality disorganization, then the researcher is only justified in asserting a probability relationship between social disorganization and personality disorganization.[12] In fact some experts would substitute entirely the notion of probability for the notion of cause. We merely note this in passing, since any consideration of this argument is beyond the scope of this text. However, it should be pointed out that the difficulties attendant to causal analyses are not peculiar to the social sciences alone. The problem is no different in the physical sciences.

We may briefly summarize the major ideas of the above section as follows: by explanation in science is meant the use of empirically verified propositions and facts to account for the systematic behavior between things. To accomplish this, we introduced the related notions of cause and effect. We saw that a cause is an invariable antecedent of the effect or consequent. Stated negatively, "if in one instance after the occurrence of e_1, e_2 does not occur, we can no longer call e_1 a cause of e_2."[13] Finally,

---

[12] The issue of probability statements will be considered in detail in Chapter 4.
[13] Felix Kaufmann, *op. cit.,* p. 93.

we recognized degrees of causation, and hence degrees of or partial explanation. From strict causal laws which are invariant, *i.e.,* for every instance after the occurrence of e_1, then e_2 invariably follows; too for every instance after the occurrence of e_1, then e_2 follows in a proportion which may be established.

The student has by now, no doubt, asked himself the following question: But what are the rules for establishing relationships of the above order? It is to a consideration of this question which we now turn our attention.

5. Procedural and Logical Rules

Everyone who knows baseball or football also knows that plays made by individual players while performing in these games may be assessed as good or bad plays on the basis of the logic and rules of the game. The same is true of the efforts of research workers. Given an accepted set of rules for arriving at scientific decisions, certain research can be judged good or bad.

The classical statement of these rules was formulated by John Stuart Mill in his book, *A System of Logic* in 1843.[14] These rules still remain the foundation of experimental method, although many refinements have been made. It is hardly necessary to enunciate the importance of explicit rules for any kind of activity; however, it should be said that explicit recognition of the rules of scientific method enables the researcher to proceed more soundly and effectively, and permits others to check his results.

The reader is asked to recall the idea of cause, *i.e.,* that no factor can be regarded as a cause if it is present while the effect is absent, or if it is absent while the effect is present. But how do we discover the cause of the effect? We have stressed the point several times that causal factors are not perceived as such, but are inferred. That is why several observations are necessary in order to give a sense of assurance to the inference. Greenwood cites an excellent illustration from Joseph in this connection. "A man may run around his garden on a frosty night, and next morning may find his legs stiff and his flowers blackened. From this one experience he could conclude that the frost made him stiff, and his running blackened the flowers; and again he might conclude the reverse."[15] Could he know from just one experience? He could not. He could and no doubt would on the basis of probability theory figure out how many observations he would have to make in order to have the necessary confidence in his observations.[16]

Suppose we observe an effect which we want to explain. That is, we wish to determine a cause of the effect or the event which we have

---

[14] For an interesting and detailed logical analysis of these rules see Morris R. Cohen and Ernest Nagel, *An Introduction to Logic and the Scientific Method* (New York: Harcourt, Brace & Co., 1934).

[15] Taken from Ernest Greenwood, *Experimental Sociology* (New York: King's Crown Press, 1945), p. 21.

[16] See Chapter 4 below on confidence limits.

observed. Suppose the event is a county which has an exceptionally low rate of dental decay. Now, we need to establish that when the effect occurs it is always preceded by a certain factor, *i.e.,* the effect invariably follows the factor or is invariably absent when the factor is absent. This means observing several instances of the effect and noting what single element they all have in common. This single element may probably be the cause. Taking now the illustration of the event in question, and after examining several individuals we find them to vary as to say, age, sex, and race. But they all drink water from the same source. The classification table would be as follows:

TABLE 1—ILLUSTRATING MILL'S METHOD OF AGREEMENT

Observations	Effect (no dental cavities)	Factor 1 (age)	Factor 2 (sex)	Factor 3 (race)	Factor 4 (presence of fluorine in water)
1	present	old	male	White	source A
2	present	young	female	White	source A
3	present	young	male	Negro	source A
"	"	"	"	"	"
"	"	"	"	"	"
"	"	"	"	"	"
"	"	"	"	"	"
"	"	"	"	"	"
N	present	old	female	Negro	source A

The common element which always occurs when the effect is present[17] is the presence of fluorine in the source of water. Random variation in factors 1, 2, and 3 indicates that tooth decay is not a function of those factors. Thus the cause of no tooth decay in this hypothetical county is the presence of flourine in the drinking water. Mill described the above method as follows:

"As this method proceeds by comparing different instances to ascertain in what they agree, I have termed it the Method of Agreement; and we may adopt as its regulating principle the following canon: *If two or more instances of the phenomenon under investigation have only one circumstance in common, the circumstance in which alone all the instances agree is the cause of the given phenomenon."* [18]

The discerning student has no doubt already conceived a number of weaknesses in this canon. For example, it is rare that phenomena are so simple as to have only one factor in common. Suppose the researcher isolates several common factors. Are they all causes? Or is there one which all the others may be subsumed under? A second difficulty is what assurance do we have that the factor or factors which we have established are not fortuitous factors? Maybe the real factor or at least other important factors have escaped the researcher's notice. As Green-

---

[17] The cause—effect relationship may be instantaneous, or there may be a time lapse.

[18] John Stuart Mill, *op. cit.,* p. 225.

wood says the Method of Agreement is not a method of discovery. Mill was aware of these weaknesses and formulated other canons to correct for them.

Let us assume, however, that we have by the Method of Agreement isolated all the relevant common factors. And we may for purposes of exposition further assume that one of the common factors is a basic cause. We may assume this from the procedural proposition that a cause must be a factor which is present when the effect is present. Now, assume that we had two common factors among our sample of persons with no dental decay. Besides the water consumed let us say that the other factor was regular brushing of the teeth. Now, of these two factors which is a cause: brushing of the teeth or the use of the water? How shall we answer this question? To answer this question we would find a sample of people *with* tooth decay and compare them with those *without* tooth decay. Do they both regularly brush their teeth, but drink water from different sources? If so, water is a cause, for were brushing the teeth a cause they would all be free from decay. Do they drink the same water, but some brush and some do not brush their teeth? If so, then brushing the teeth is a cause. Here we have contrasted two instances, one with and one without the same effect, and we locate a cause in the one condition wherein they differ. Of this Mill said: "Instead of comparing different instances of a phenomenon, to discover in what they agree, this method compares an instance of its occurrence with an instance of its non-occurrence, to discover in what way they differ. The canon which is the regulating principle of the Method of Difference may be expressed as follows: *If an instance in which the phenomenon under investigation occurs, and an instance in which it does not occur, have every circumstance in common save one, that one occurring only in the former; the circumstance in which alone the two instances differ is . . . the cause . . . of the phenomenon.*"[19]

Suppose our situation is complicated by a third common factor, as incidentally it often is, then what do we do? We do the same thing we did in the above case, only in this instance we find a sample of people who are the same on two of the factors, but differ on the third. The reasoning is the same as the above. For example, suppose our sample of people with no dental decay was found to consume similar water, all to brush their teeth; and let us say, all chewed tobacco. What is the cause now? Now we would have to find a sample where tooth decay was *present,* but differed in one of the above three factors. Suppose the people with tooth decay drank the same water, and all brushed their teeth, but do not chew tobacco. Then tobacco is a cause.

It is obvious that what we have done here is to select two groups who were the same in respect to two of the factors, but differ on the third. The argument being that common factors cannot account for or

---

[19] *Ibid.,* p. 256.

explain different effects. In any case one factor is left free to vary between the groups, the difference in the effects between the groups is then attributed to differences in the two groups in respect to the factor varied. This technique of equating two contrasting situations, while permitting one factor to vary is known as holding constant or controlling all relevant factors except one. Maintaining one variable free and holding constant the others enables us to determine whether the one free variable is related to the effect or not.

However, it is easy to see that as the number of our common factors increase that the difficulty in controlling them also increases. Also, in the case of matching or equating factors as in Mill's second canon, one finds that it becomes increasingly difficult to find cases that are alike in respect to all the common factors. Consequently, the size of the sample which we are studying becomes smaller and smaller until we no longer have assurance in its reliability; because the sample may be too small to be statistically reliable. At this point we would have to find ourselves a more efficient method; however, the logic would remain essentially the same. While this problem is beyond the scope of this chapter, it should be noted, however, that its solution lies in the field of mathematical measurement. That is, if you can measure the independent influences of each on the factors, then you no longer have the problem of matching them for purposes of control.[20] Also, you may control all the relevant factors between the two contrasting groups, by *randomizing* the two samples. That is, drawing the two samples in such a way that each member of the two populations from which the samples were selected had an equal probability of being included in the samples. This procedure permits a canceling out of differences between the groups, and allows the researcher to treat them as equal for purposes at hand.[21] He is then at liberty to introduce a factor to one of the groups, and withhold it from the other and then observe the results. Since the two groups are the same except for the treatment, then the effect could be attributed to the treatment.[22]

By now the introductory statement of this section concerning the importance of procedural rules in scientific research should be clear. Namely, that it is by the use of scientific rules that we are able to order our data in such a way as to permit an unequivocal decision as to the admission of a proposition into a science. This does not imply, however, that a proposition admitted at one time may not at a later time be invalidated.

The fruitfulness of a valid scientific hypothesis lies in its powers of explanation and prediction. That is, does the validated proposition allow for further fruitful scientific deductions and hence point to new scientific problems? Thus the success of a science in the explanation and prediction of the behavior in its field is a function of the amount and quality

[20] See Chapter 4 below on the regression equation.
[21] See the section on sampling theory in Chapter 4.
[22] See Chapter 5 for examples and discussion of these modern designs.

of existent theory in the field. We do not know physical data any more directly or objectively than social data, except in so far as we have developed more adequate concepts and instruments for observation and more adequate theory for explanation. The difficulties, therefore, which exist in a science of the social world, as well as a science of the physical world derive from our undeveloped techniques and instruments of observation, and the inadequacy of existent theory rather than any inherent differences in the data themselves. Nevertheless, science is the most precise means available to man for making valid and reliable decisions.

This completes our treatment of the logic of science, and it is hoped that by an understanding of the logical structure of science, and its rules of discourse, that the student will be ready and waiting to learn the methods by which this logic is carried out in actual research. Thus the task of part II of this text is to provide an introduction to the more general methods of research in use in the social and psychological sciences.

In conclusion, we wish to provide a brief summary of the main ideas introduced in this chapter.

6. Summary

We saw that scientific research was essentially a problem-solving activity. The solution to a scientific problem is dependent upon the use of correct procedural rules for research in connection with the testing of hypotheses formulated either from inductions from controlled observations or by deductions from existent theory. The validity of the hypotheses is determined by the criterion of prediction. If the predictions are actually confirmed by experiment, then the hypotheses are given the status of theory and become a part of the body of science, and the process continues through the formulation of new problems and new hypotheses. Thus the scientific role of prediction in science is that of testing hypotheses.

It then became necessary to see the prediction process in relation to the goal of science *per se*. This we formulated in terms of the existence and description of the relationship between two or more classes of data, and those asserting the amount of relationship. On the basis of the correctness of these assertions warranted predictions are made. Failure to predict correctly, therefore, means that the asserted relationship was not true as stated. Finally, we summarized the logical rules by which we arrive at the correctness of assertions. To do this we examined Mill's two main canons and briefly introduced modern versions of these.

SELECTED REFERENCES

Chapin, F. Stuart, *Experimental Designs in Sociological Research* (New York: Harper and Bros., 1947).

Cohen, Morris R., and Ernest Nagel, *An Introduction to Logic and Scientific Method* (New York: Harcourt, Brace, 1934).

Fisher, R. A., *The Design of Experiments* (Edinburg: Oliver and Boyd, 1937).

Goode, William J., and Paul K. Hatt, *Methods in Social Research* (New York: McGraw-Hill Book Co., Inc., 1952).

Greenwood, Ernest, *Experimental Sociology* (New York: King's Crown Press, 1945).

Kaufmann, Felix, *Methodology of the Social Sciences* (New York: Oxford University Press, 1944).

Lindquist, E. F., *Design and Analysis of Experiments in Psychology and Education* (New York: Houghton Mifflin Company, 1953).

Mill, John Stuart, *A System of Logic* (New York: Longmans, 1930).

Pearson, Karl, *The Grammar of Science* (London: A. and C. Black, 1911).

Part II
Scientific Methods

Chapter 4

STATISTICAL METHODS*

PART A. INTRODUCTION

1. Statistics in Research: The Problem

THE fundamental problem of empirical research is the explanation of observed variation. The variation might be in terms of quantity, as in variation of weight gained resulting from different diets. The variation might be in terms of proportions, of probabilities, as in the proportion of marriages ending in divorce. The basic element of variation as central to a research problem should never be forgotten. From it, largely, arises the need for statistics in scientific inference.

Had the traditional logic of classes been adequate to account for empirical variation, it is not likely that statistics would have arisen; or, if it had arisen, would play the role in contemporary research that it does. For that matter, a straight-forward mathematical statement of functional relations is not sufficient for empirical research since some variation around the mathematical line ordinarily exists and must be accounted for.

Another way of saying this, is to say that had all conceptual classifications resulted in completely homogeneous empirical members, there would have been little need for statistics. Let us explain what we mean by an example. If the empirical operations used in arriving at the classification of "neurotic personalities" had been such that every member of each type of neurotic personality been precisely the same as all others such that one could say, "All neurotics of type one experienced traumatic experiences as children," the so-called qualitative logic would have been sufficient for making subsequent inferences. Due either to an intrinsic variation in the real world, or to inadequate conceptualization, or to inadequate operational definitions, such statements are impossible to make. We generally are reduced to making "particular propositions," *i.e.,* "some neurotics of Type One experienced traumatic experiences as children." As we shall see, we are limited in the type of inferences possible when our premises are of this sort.

This state of affairs has led to two directions, both related to statistical inference. On the one hand, we have the development of a probability logic to enable us to come to decisions about particular propositions. On the other hand, we have an emphasis upon quantification of the basic variables. The emphasis on quantification—and the problems on quantifying social data are by no means solved—attempts two things. First, by being precise, the influence of biases on the part of the scientist are ex-

---

* Written by Roy G. Francis.

plicated and attacked. Second, clearer statements of the amount and kind of variations observed are made possible. That it is necessary to have precise data originally is easily appreciated. No statistical juggling can improve on bad or poorly defined data.

Another type of variation which flows from statistical inference is that of sampling. Recall that science trusts neither intuition nor inference. All propositions are subjected to verification. The question becomes, "will all tests of the same hypothesis give precisely the same results?" If the answer is negative (and, in fact, it is negative) we again observe a case of variation. Do the results of a series of tests differ by chance, or are the differences real? This is a basic question, which is, partially at least, solved through statistical inference.

Again, is it possible to study every instance of some problematic event or behavior? Suppose one wanted to explain neurotic behavior. Could one reasonably be expected to study every neurotic? Obviously not. Not only is the scientist limited in terms of the money and facilities available to him, but time is against him also. Even if he studied all neurotics up to some specific date, there would be subsequent cases still to occur. Hence, he can study only some of them.

That is, the scientist must study a *sample* of some population. But he wants to make inferences about the population. Will each sample give precisely the same result? Even if one knew he was studying a single population, he would observe "sampling variation"—that is, differences due entirely to the fact that a sample was studied. To distinguish between results flowing from sampling variation and from having actually studied two or more populations is a fundamental task of statistical inference.

This type of variation is critical to modern empirical science. Unless there is such uniformity (as, presumably, in certain chemical mixtures) that variation from test to test is negligible, observed variation needs to be explained. Statistical theory is simply a system of thinking, made possible by the admission of certain assumptions and postulates, which allows for rigorous inference in the case of variation. We generally study only a sample of the objects in which we are interested; sampling theory, a fundamental part of statistical theory, provides a guide in drawing inferences with scientific rigor.

2. The Logic of the Statistical Argument

One of the most potent devices of traditional logic is the two-premised argument, the syllogism. In particular, we should understand the structure of the alternative syllogism. If we have two propositions, A and B, such that they cannot be false together (admitting that they might be true together), then one can use the following form of argument:

Major premise: Either statement A or statement B is true.

Minor premise: Statement A is false.

Conclusion: Statement B is true.

If, in the minor premise, we affirmed one of the propositions, we could not conclude the falsity of the other since both could be true.

Consider, also the so-called hypothetical syllogism. Suppose we have two statements, P and Q, such that the relation of implication exists between the two. Then one could use the following form of argument:

Major premise: if P is true, then Q is true.
Minor premise: Q is false.
Conclusion: P is false.

Remember that, in the hypothetical syllogism, the truth of Q implies nothing about the truth of P, *i.e.,* the affirmation of the consequent does not imply the truth of the antecedent unless they are related strongly: if and only if P, then Q.

These two syllogisms are basic to statistical inference. Suppose we have two measures of divorce, x_1 for rural marriages and x_2 for urban marriages. Suppose, further, that these measures are not numerically identical. The question is: how can we explain our observed variation? Is it due simply to variation from sample to sample? Or is it due to "real" differences between rural and urban marriages?

The *form* of the argument is this. Set up the alternatives:

Either (A) there is only a sampling difference between the two measures, or (B) the amount of divorce is greater for one area than the other. Clearly, they cannot be false together, though one might argue that they could be true together. We are not concerned with that possibility, except to argue that we can decide between the two only through the falsification of one of the alternatives. Verification of either does not force the denial of the other.

Now we will assume that the two measures differ only to the extent of sample variation. This assumption is our premise "P" in the hypothetical syllogism. If this is true then (as we shall later learn) there is a statistic, "S", which is smaller than the number 2. This is our conclusion, "Q", in the hypothetical syllogism. If empirically, this number S is greater than 2, we have a *contradiction* and "Q" is false, hence "P" is false. But P was simply proposition A in the alternative, so that if P is false, A is false also. And we know from syllogistic argument that if A is false, the alternative B must be true.

The student should notice the difference between the form of the argument and the content of the argument. The statements "A" and "B" may or may not stand in an alternative relationship when one deals with empirical classes. The possibility of their being true or false together is a theoretical issue and must be examined prior to any test of their relationship. If this inference is not explored prior to the use of the subsequent statistical argument, the possibility of their being alternatives is an *ad hoc* problem. Of course, this state of affairs is quite common: we often use a statistical technique without being quite sure of our theoretical assumptions. After we have made our "statistical analysis" we then often look for the theoretical assumptions which must be made to warrant the techniques being used. While we do not deny that through such activity much has been learned, we wish to repeat that the *ad hoc* problem may develop, but never tests, the hypothesis in question.

The structure of the hypothetical syllogism (which is called the *null hypothesis* in statistical literature) flows from statistical theory. The main effort in this chapter will be to indicate the correctness of this type of reasoning.

3. Relation to Other Logical Forms

It is all but obvious that statistical inference is predicated on what we have called "qualitative logic." Recall [1] that we could write any formula as a system of premises and conclusions. This fact, coupled with the syllogistic structure of the statistical argument, should convince the student what we have tacitly assumed. Namely, that it is incorrect to pose the problem of "qualitative or quantitative logic."

While beyond the scope of this text, it would be possible to indicate the postulates of "categorical logic," those of "quantitative logic," and those of "probability logic." We could see that one does not deny earlier postulates, but, rather, builds on them. Instead of saying, in effect, "What logic do I prefer?" one should ask himself; what is my problem? What is my substantive hypothesis to solve that problem? What data does my hypothesis call for? *What logical postulates are met by the data needed to solve my problem?* If my data satisfy the assumptions of, say, a mathematical equation describing a functional relation, then "fit a curve" to the data. If the assumptions of statistical inference are met, then reason statistically. If only the postulates of categorical logic are satisfied, then use categorical logic. Let the problem define the logic to be used, not the converse.

Certain logical operations (*e.g.,* curve-fitting, analysis of variance, chi-square, mathematical model construction) may be the current fad. But to select first the operation, and then the data to fit it reverses the development of theory. We saw earlier, and we must repeat it again, an argument is a solution of some problem. Arbitrary use of logical operations cannot but involve arbitrary assumptions and arbitrary definitions of problems. If science is indeed problem-*solving,* then it seems necessary to spend time defining the problem in such a way that it can be solved. Only after one knows the problem ought he determine the structure of the argument he is to use.

Statistical formulas do not exhaust the ways scientists justify their conclusions. For certain types of problems, and for certain types of data, statistical formulas are apparently necessary for rigorous inference. But the burden of proof as to the applicability of the formula rests with the user. Simply because one knows some technique does not mean he must use it; the use of an equation is a decision about a proposition which must be defended before we can admit its proper place in science. The

---

[1] See Chapter 1, "The Role of Logic in Research."

student must always put scientific problems ahead of the techniques of science.

1. Collection and Classification of Data

Statistical methods are used in analyzing and in drawing inferences from a number of repetitive "events" which do not all have the same outcome. The event may be, for example, marriage and the outcome may be divorce or its absence. An event may be placing a rat in a maze, and the outcome may be the time it takes the rat to run the maze successfully. The event may be the age at which a child first responds to a smile, and the outcome may be 3 weeks, 24 days, or whatever. Two features of each situation is forced on us: first, we can observe a large number of events (of similar content) and second, there is a certain amount of variation in respect to the outcomes associated with the events in question. If there were no such variation—*i.e.,* if each event had the same outcome—there would be no statistical problem.

Statistical analysis begins with the definition and observation of "events," and the subsequent classification of them in terms of the possible outcomes. Of course, the outcomes must also be defined and operations must be performed which will allow us to classify the event properly. From our earlier discussion of scientific method, we should recall that the logical steps in inquiry involve the definition of the problem, the statement of an hypothesis to solve that problem and the creation of an instrument to obtain the necessary data. "Creating an instrument" is simply a shorthand statement of defining the operations by which the various classes of events and outcomes will have empirical members.

Of particular concern is an understanding of classification in terms of the possible outcomes; the events to be studied are ordinarily categorically defined and are shared by all objects in the inquiry. The problematic variation is in the outcomes which may be observed. The general principle is to define the outcomes in such a way that each object is a member of one and only one possible outcome class. Another way of saying this is to assert that the classification scheme must be mutually exclusive and exhaustive. Further, only one basis of classification at a time may be used. For example, if the event was, say, "occupation," one would use such classes as "lawyer," "minister," "blasksmith," and would not use "rural" since the latter refers to residence.

There are, in general, three types of possible classification systems:

Categorical. The categorical set of classes involve only the issue of whether or not the object is a member of the class. If there are two categories, we speak of a dichotomy, as, for example, "male" and "female." There may be more than two classes, as in the distribution of classes of budget expenditures.

Ordinal. If the classes are so defined that one of the outcomes is "larger" (or smaller) than another but the amount of the difference un-stated or unknown, we speak of "ordinal classes." We may, then, classify people as "old," "middle aged," and "young." The student will im-mediately perceive the possibilities for ambiguous definitions, unless the classes are defined in terms of units of time.

Cardinal (quantitative). If the membership in a class depends upon the size of the object (or the "amount"), the classes are quantitatively defined. Age, in years, is a good example, as is income. There are two basic types of cardinal data, the discrete and the continuous kind. An example of discrete data is size of family, since only integers are used to define membership. Age and income are both continuous since a decimal (or fraction) can be used to separate classes.

If the data to be used properly belong in a cardinal system, by "throw-ing away" certain information (e.g., precision as to amount of difference) we can deduce ordinal relations. Further, ordinal data can be done with-out additional knowledge; if we know only that people are, say, "old" and "young," we cannot get an ordinal system of age and, obviously, age-categories are impossible. While much statistical analysis is concerned with cardinal data, such data do not exhaust the use of statistics. Indeed, the power of statistics lies in the fact that arguments about categorical data can be rigorously made, even in the face of particular propositions.

2. Tabular and Graphic Representation of Data

Let us suppose that, for some purpose, we are studying how long it takes a group of students to complete a true-false test. It may be that, for our purposes, we operationally define time taken to complete a test as a measure of the difficulty of the test. Obviously, there are other ways to define the difficulty of a test, and there are theoretical deficiencies in the definition given. Such issues are not primarily statistical and must be decided before statistical analysis proceeds. Let us agree, for illustrat-ing statistical techniques, that we are justified in using this definition.

We first note that the *range* of time taken by the 138 students to com-plete the test is from 21 minutes to 54 minutes, *i.e.,* the smallest and largest values. The issue is: what size of *interval* should we use in defining the classes of "time taken"? We may leave the data in raw form and leave them *ungrouped*. This is the same as having classes of one member each. With 138 objects to be analyzed, 138 classes seem too many to carry around; and, clearly, if we had 1380 objects, we would need some system of reducing the number of classes.

The important thing in defining the size of the class interval is to recognize that in defining classes we will be losing a certain amount of precision. This is so, since we will treat each member of a class as though its true value equaled the mid-point of the class in question. As one would guess, the mid-point is a value half-way between the lower and upper class limits. If the data are discrete, the mid-point is obtained by adding the lower and upper limits and dividing by two. If the data are continuous, the mid-point is obtained by adding the lower limit of the interested class to the lower limit of the class just above and dividing by two. This is a device aimed at avoiding unpleasant and nonsensical decimal values for the mid-point. The number of classes, and their size, can be answered only in terms of how to reduce the difficulty in computation without distorting the data. We can give only a "rule of thumb" to resolve the issue.

The general rules follow from these considerations. We first note the range, and decide on the size of the interval; this decision fixes the number of classes as well as the "mid-points" of each class. In general, one avoids "open-end" classes as much as possible, *e.g.,* 5 years and more renders the determination of a mid-point somewhat difficult. We will go through an example to make concrete the issues involved.

The range of minutes to complete the exam was from 21 to 54 minutes, or 33 minutes. If an interval size five would not distort the data, we would have 7 classes. The smallest number was 21; if we chose, we could simply add "5" to that number and get, immediately, the lower bound for each succeeding class. Again, for convenience, we can decide to have the first class begin at 20 minutes, even though no one used precisely that time; notice, however, that the classes are quite convenient—20 to just short of 25 minutes; 25 to just short of thirty—"nice round numbers" seem easier to use than numbers like 26, 31, etc.

Having defined the classes, the next step is to classify the students into their proper classes. All those who used between 20 and 24.9 minutes belong in the first class; those who used between 25 and 29.9 belong in the next one, etc. When all have been properly classified, we can draw up a table which is one way of presenting the data.

The table will be, generally, titled—a simple declaration of the event. To the left is the "stub," in which the possible outcomes are defined. And to the right is a column showing the frequency of members of each class.

TABLE 2. TIME TAKEN TO COMPLETE A TRUE-FALSE TEST

Class interval	Mid points	Frequency
20 to 24.9	22.5	3
25 to 29.9	27.5	17
30 to 34.9	32.5	27
35 to 39.9	37.5	39
40 to 44.9	42.5	31
45 to 49.9	47.5	16
50 to 54.9	52.5	5
total		138

Source: Hypothetical

A certain amount of information is gained from the table itself. We get some "picture" of how the time used was distributed among the students of the class; and, after some experience in dealing with this kind of data, one can guess pretty closely to what the average time is. To most people, however, the numerical differences of various classes are not appreciated, unless the differences are great. Some sort of graphic presentation seems useful.

The most common graph for such data as these is the *histogram*. Along the horizontal line (or "X-axis"), we put the class intervals; and along the vertical line (or "Y-axis"), we put the frequency for each corresponding class. For each class interval, we extend a bar (equal in width to the class interval) up to the number designating the frequency of that class. The bar extends from the lower class limit to the upper class limit of each class. If we have a constant size interval for the classes, the interval can be regarded as a unit (numerically equal to one). Then the area of each bar is equal to the frequency (*i.e.,* the height times one). Since the total number is the sum of the frequencies, the area under the histogram equals the number of frequencies and can be obtained by summing the area of each bar.

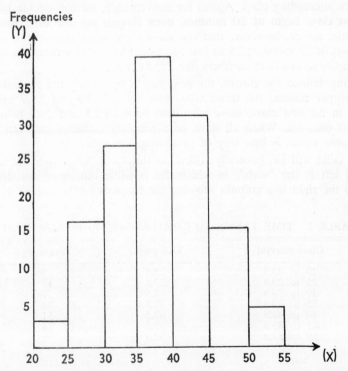

Figure 1. Histogram. Note use of class limits on x-axis. Source: Table 1.

Instead of having the frequency on the Y axis, we may put the relative frequency. This is, simply, the frequency divided by the total number.

In this case, the area of each bar represents the relative frequency of the particular class interval, and the total area of the histogram equals one.

While one gets a better picture of the distribution from the histogram, the significant point for us is the relation between the area and relative frequency. Originally, we can compute the area from knowledge of the frequency; but, subsequently a knowledge of the area allows us to infer the frequency for each class. This relation between area and relative frequency is the fundamental notion of statistical inference.

Another useful graph, and rather widely used, is the *frequency polygon*. Like the histogram, it is based on the frequency tabulation in Table 2. Unlike the histogram, the frequency polygon is constructed from the mid-points of each class. The mid-point and the relative frequency for each class determines a point (x,y). These are then connected by straight lines, as in figure 2. However, to insure that the total area under the curve [2]

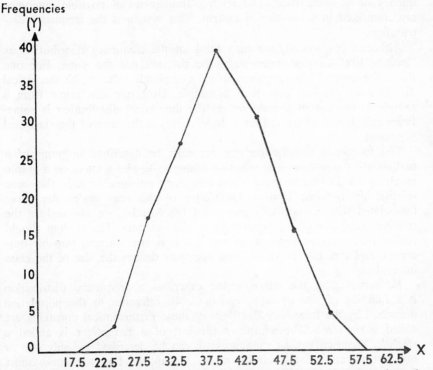

Figure 2. Frequency Polygon. Note use of mid-points and extension of graph one class above and one class below the range of the empirical data. The area of this graph equals that of Figure 1. Source: Table 2.

equals 1, the distance between each class mid-point is again regarded as a unit. Further, the line is extended from the smallest mid-point used to

---

[2] "In the case of using relative frequencies; in the case of using absolute frequencies, the total area equals the number of objects being considered, *i.e.*, N."

the mid-point of the class to the left of the smallest one with members. The line is similarly extended to the mid-point of the class next above the largest one with members. In our case, the class 15-19.9 has no members and is to the left of our smallest class. Hence, we would draw a line from the point (22.5,3) to the point (17.5,0).

Again, a knowledge of the area under the curve of the frequency polygon allows us to infer the relative frequency of the segment of the X-axis being considered.

3. The Basic Statistical Idea: the Frequency Distribution

The concept of the frequency distribution simply formalizes what we have stated in terms of the classification and tabulation of data. This involves the assumption that some causal system functions in such a way that there is associated with each possible outcome some relative frequency of its occurrence. The relative frequencies of possible outcomes are connected in some sort of system. This system is the frequency distribution.

Although heuristically we may think of the frequency distribution as "looking like" our tabulated data, the two are not the same. For one thing, the data which we gather do not completely exhaust the theoretical distribution; we deal only with a sample. How one can argue from a sample to the parent *population,* as the theoretical distribution is sometimes called, will be treated later. Indeed, this is the crux of the statistical argument.

The frequency distribution can generally be described in terms of a mathematical equation. The equation allows us to plot a curve on a graph, much as we did the histogram and frequency polygon. In fact, the same relationship obtains: from a knowledge of the area under the curve (associated with a specified segment of the X-axis), we can deduce the relative frequency of the occurrence of the outcome. The student should realize that different segments of the X-axis define different possible outcomes, and that the length of these segments defines the size of the class intervals.

Mathematically, the curve which describes a frequency distribution is a function of one or more constants. In reference to the population described by the frequency distribution, these mathematical constants are called *parameters.* The sample equivalent of a parameter is called a *statistic.* Some curves, as we suggested, can be described by only one or two parameters; others require more. It happens that the curve most frequently used in statistics, (called the normal curve) uses only two such parameters. The important point is that from a knowledge of these two parameters one can completely describe the normal curve. From our knowledge of a normal curve, we can immediately deduce the relative frequency of the various possible outcomes. Evidently, we will need to know more about these measures if we are to proceed with statistical inference.

4. Describing the Distribution

Measuring Central Tendency. When one has a set of data, such as that in Table 2, or generally speaking, cardinal data, a measure that describes, in some way, the information given is desirable. Of those which have been used, we will use mostly the arithmetic *mean,* the commonest concept of *average.*[3] This is found by summing the size of each object and dividing by the total number of objects measured. If any particular outcome occurs more than once, it is of course added as often as it occurs.

Symbolically, the mean is given by the formula

$$M = \frac{\Sigma X}{N} \qquad (1)$$

The Greek letter "Σ" (sigma) symbolizes the *operation* of summing the values designated by "X". The symbol ΣX does not mean, as might be supposed, to multiply sigma by X, but to sum all of the X values. "N" refers to the total number of frequencies. To get the mean, the sum of the X values are divided by N.

Equation (1) generally refers to ungrouped data. If any X value occurs more than once, it is convenient to write (1) as

$$M = \frac{\Sigma f X}{N} \qquad (2)$$

The symbol "f" denotes the frequency of each grouping of X values. The X values are multiplied by the corresponding frequencies and then summed. After being summed the quantities are divided by N, the total number of frequencies.

If the data are classified as those in Table 2, we do not have the "true" X-value for each object. We have classified them into intervals size five. For purposes of calculation, we treat them as if they all had the size designated by the mid-point. We will denote the mid-point as $\hat{X}$. In such a case, we write (2) as

$$M = \frac{\Sigma f \hat{X}}{N} \qquad (3)$$

---

[3] Other fairly well known measures of central tendency are the mode and the median. The mode, generally speaking, refers to the outcome which has the largest relative frequency. In the data used above, the class 35 to 39.9 is the *modal* class. Sometimes a distribution may have two classes with the same or nearly the same number of members. This is spoken of as a "bi-modal distribution" and often suggests the use of two bases of classification instead of one.

The median is a measure of position such that there are as many objects larger than the median as there are smaller. In the case of a uniform distribution (the same frequency for each class) this cuts the X-axis in half. In the normal distribution, the mean, median and the mode all define the same outcome. Unlike the mean, the mode and the median are independent of extreme values in the distribution. However, the mean is subject to algebraic manipulation and the others are not; for that reason, among others, it is preferred in the development of a theory of statistical inference.

We will illustrate the use of formula (3). Note, first, what information must be known before it can be used. We must have the mid-points of each class; we must have the frequencies of each class; we must have the product of the frequencies and the mid-points of each class. We then must sum the information gained by this multiplication process. The next step is to set up a table which will give us this information. This is done by creating a column for the different kinds of information needed.

TABLE 3.   TIME TAKEN TO COMPLETE A TRUE-FALSE TEST

Mid-points $\hat{X}$ (1)	Frequencies f (2)	f$\hat{X}$ (3)
22.5	3	67.5
27.5	17	467.5
32.5	27	877.5
37.5	39	1462.5
42.5	31	1317.5
47.5	16	760.0
52.5	5	262.5
totals	138	5215

Source: Table 2

Summing column two, we find that N = 138. Summing column three, we find that $\Sigma f\hat{X}$ = 5215.0. We simply insert this information into equation (3) and perform the indicated division. The mean is thus found to be M = $\frac{5215}{138}$ = 37.79, rounding off to two decimals.

Although the numbers used in this example were relatively simple for the calculation of the mean, an inspection of column three shows some rather large numbers. With larger numbers, or with a more complicated set of mid-points, it is easy to see that calculation of the mean by (3) could become cumbersome. A formula that lends itself to simpler calculation processes (for the more difficult the operation the greater the likelihood of error) seems to be useful.

A simpler formula results from *transforming* the $\hat{X}$ values to integers, if the size of the intervals is constant. We make this transformation by subtracting the mid-point of any convenient class, normally, the class with the greatest frequency from the mid-points of all the classes used. We then divide this difference by the size of the interval. Denoting the transformed information by the letter "d", the symbolic representation is given by

$$d = \frac{\hat{X} - A}{i} \qquad (4)$$

In Table 4, below, we have designated a column "d". Notice that certain d-values have negative algebraic signs. Thus, to get the d-value

TABLE 4. TIME TAKEN TO COMPLETE TRUE-FALSE TEST

$\hat{X}$	d	f	fd
22.5	—3	3	— 9
27.5	—2	17	—34
32.5	—1	27	—27
37.5	0	39	0
42.5	1	31	31
47.5	2	16	32
52.5	3	5	15
totals		138	+ 8

Source: Table 2

for the smallest class, letting i denote the interval (and equals 5 in this case), and choosing A = 37.5 for convenience,

$$22.5 — 37.5 = —15$$
$$—15/5 = —3$$

The algebraic signs must be retained and used in computation.

Since we have subtracted a constant value, we must add it back in our subsequent calculation of the mean. Further, we divided by another constant, i, so we must multiply our results by the same constant. Then the mean can be found by the equation

$$M = A + i \,\frac{\Sigma fd}{N} \qquad (5)$$

In Table 4, we anticipated this result. Notice, again, what information (5) calls for: we need to know the "d" values for each class; the frequencies for each class, and the product of the frequencies and the d-values for each class. Our table is constructed so as to give us this information.

$$\text{We find that } A = 37.5$$
$$i = 5.0$$
$$\Sigma fd = 8.0$$
$$N = 138.0$$

Inserting these values into (5) gives us,

$$M = 37.5 + 5 \left(\frac{8}{138}\right) = 37.79, \text{ which agrees with equation (3).}$$

Measuring Dispersion. In addition to a measure of the average value, the use of the normal curve necessitates a knowledge of the amount of variation in the distribution. The variation is measured in terms of deviation from the mean. It is called the "standard deviation." The importance of the standard deviation lies in the fact that the area of a normal curve above the X-axis in the segment comprising one standard deviation unit on each side of the mean consists of about 67% of the

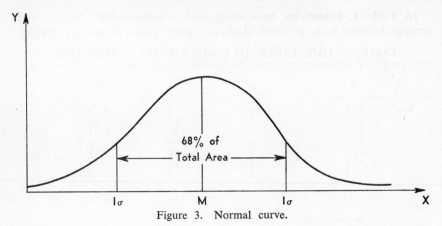

Figure 3. Normal curve.

total area under the curve. The characteristic of being able to compute the area under different segments of the normal curve—and hence the corresponding relative frequency—from a knowledge of the standard deviation is the foundation of statistical inference. The square of the standard deviation is called the *variance*.

The operational definition of the standard deviation is given in the following steps. (a) Subtract the mean from each X-(or $\hat{X}$-) value. (b) Square the differences. (c) Multiply the squared differences by the corresponding frequency (in ungrouped data the frequency equals one for each class). (d) Sum these products. (e) Divide by the total number of objects. This gives the *variance*. To get the standard deviation, step (f) is to extract the square root. These steps operationally define the standard deviation, though the conceptual definition includes its relation to the area under the curve.

Clearly, these steps can become quite cumbersome. Hence, some *computational* formulas would be useful. We will give them in the form of variance; the student should always remember to extract the square root to obtain the standard deviation.

Denoting variance by σ^2 (the "lower case" greek letter sigma), for ungrouped data

$$\sigma^2 = \frac{\Sigma X^2}{N} - M^2 \qquad (6)$$

and for grouped data,

$$\frac{\Sigma f X^2}{N} - M^2 \qquad (7)$$

When the data are arranged in classes, variance is found by

$$\frac{\Sigma f \hat{X}^2}{N} - M^2 \qquad (8)$$

and, again, $\hat{X}$ denotes the mid-point values of each class.

The student should again notice what information is called for by each equation. Illustrating the process of arithmetic computation by (8), we find we need the following information: The mid-point values for each class; the squares of these numbers; the frequencies of each class; the sum of the frequencies; the product of the class frequencies and the squares of the mid-point values; the sum of these products; and the square of the mean. We will then arrange our table so as to give us this information.

TABLE 5. TIME TAKEN TO COMPLETE TRUE-FALSE TEST

$\hat{X}$	f	f$\hat{X}$	f$\hat{X}^2$
22.5	3	67.5	1518.75
27.5	17	467.5	12856.25
32.5	27	877.5	28518.75
37.5	39	1462.5	54843.75
42.5	31	1317.5	55993.75
47.5	16	760.0	36100.00
52.5	5	262.5	13781.25
totals	138	5215.0	203612.50

Source: Table 2

By direct computation, we find the following values:

$$\Sigma f\hat{X}^2 = 203612.50$$
$$N = 138$$
$$M = 37.79$$
$$M^2 = 1428.0841$$

Inserting these values in equation (8),

$$\sigma^2 = \frac{203612.5}{138} - 1428.0841 = 47.37$$

Clearly, the computation of variance by (8) can become a cumbersome process. The numbers dealt with are large, even with these simple data. The issue of rounding off decimal places is present at each step. An easier computational formula would be useful. Analogous to equation (5) for the mean, variance can be found by

$$\sigma^2 = i^2 \left[\frac{\Sigma f d^2}{N} - \left(\frac{\Sigma f d}{N} \right)^2 \right] \tag{9}$$

where the symbols are the same as for (5). Notice that in (9) the computation does not involve the arbitrary starting point A.

Table 6, below, gives the information needed in (9).

TABLE 6. TIME TAKEN TO COMPLETE A TRUE-FALSE TEST

X	d	f	fd	fd²
22.5	—3	3	— 9	27
27.5	—2	17	—34	68
32.5	—1	27	—27	27
37.5	0	39	0	0
42.5	1	31	31	31
47.5	2	16	32	64
52.5	3	5	15	45
totals		138	+ 8	262

Source: Table 2

The information required by (9) is found to be

$$\sigma^2 = 25 \left[\frac{262}{138} - \left(\frac{8}{138} \right)^2 \right]$$

$$\sigma^2 = 47.38.$$

The difference between this value and that given by (8) is due to the rounding-off of decimal places in (8). If one used $M = 5215/138$ instead of $M = 37.79$, the two results would have been identical.

Since variance equals 47.38, the standard deviation is the square root of that number. It is found to be equal to 6.88. The area under a normal curve corresponding to the segment of the X-axis ranging from 30.91 to 44.67 is approximately 67% of the total area under the curve. A glance at Figure 2, the frequency polygon, indicates that there is a fairly close fit. The distribution in Table 1 is approximately normal.

5. Basic Ideas of Probability

To understand the mathematical conception of probability, the student must be prepared to give up some common sense ideas. For one thing, it makes no mathematical sense to discuss the probability of a unique event. The idea of re-occurrence of an event is fundamental to a precise conception of probability. In fact, we will define probability by formalizing the idea of relative frequency of an outcome. Thus, some notion of an arithmetic ratio will be present in the definition of probability. Such terms as "improbable" will at best be translated into numerically small ratios. But at what point a relative frequency is sufficiently small to allow one to talk of the "improbability" of an outcome is quite arbitrary.

Definition. If an event can occur N times, and an alternative outcome (denoted by o_i) can occur f times, the probability that o_i occurs is $p_i = f/N$. Since the outcomes are mutually exclusive and exhaustive, $\Sigma f = N$ and $\Sigma p = 1$.

In the case of a dichotomy, we ordinarily speak of *successes* and *failures*. By success we simply mean one of the two alternative outcomes, generally, the outcome of substantive theoretical interest. In this case, the probability of success is denoted by p, and the probability of a failure is denoted by q. The value of p is found by obtaining the ratio of the number of ways a success can occur to the number of ways a success can occur plus the number of ways a failure can occur. The value of q is similarly obtained.

If one is given a probability system, it is often desirable to be able to deduce the probabilities of another system comprised of various combinations of the outcomes involved in the first system. Thus, if one knows the probability that a student will complete an examination in a certain amount of time and also knows the probability a student will receive a certain grade on that examination, we may want to deduce the probability that he will finish the exam at a given time *and* receive the grade in question.

Certain rules for such inference have been derived, based on the assumption of statistical independence of the two probability systems. The inference which is drawn may then be tested empirically. Later we will learn how to be able to decide whether or not the two systems were in fact independent of each other. Evidently, such knowledge will give us a powerful device to aid in making decisions about the acceptability of certain propositions.

Rule of Addition of two mutually exclusive outcomes, A and B. If outcome A has the probability of p_1 of occurring, and outcome B has the probability of p_2 of occurring, the probability that either A or B will occur is the sum of the probabilities $p_1 + p_2$. This can be generalized to any number of mutually exclusive outcomes.

Rule of Multiplication. If outcome A has the probability p_1 of occurring, and outcome B has the probability of p_2 of occurring, with or after A in one possible way, the probability that both A and B will so occur is the product of the probabilities, $p_1 p_2$. This, too, can be generalized.

Suppose we want to obtain the probability of getting 3 heads (successes) out of a toss of 5 coins. Labeling the coins A, B, C, D, and E, we associate with each coin an outcome of interest. The outcomes for, say, A, B, and C, are successes each having a probability p. The outcomes for D and E are failures each having a probability q. Since we are interested in these outcomes occurring together, we use the Rule of Multiplication. The probability for this one set of probabilities is found by

$$P = pppqq$$

Since the p's are of the same value, and the q's are of the same value, we may write this as

$$P = p^3 q^2$$

To generalize our symbols, we will say we tossed n coins, of which r were to be heads. Obviously, there would be n-r tails. With these symbols, we would write

$$P = p^r q^{n-r}$$

If we assume that we have "true" coins, we can associate ½ with the probability p; this implies that q is also equal to ½. Then the numerical value of obtaining 3 heads in a toss of five coins *in one way* is found by

$$P = (½)^3 (½)^2 = .03125$$

In deducing such combinations of probabilities, the possible ways of arranging the outcomes in question is of some importance. This is so, since the combination of outcomes A and B, etc., can occur in more ways than one. Each way it may occur has the same probability. Rather than laboriously counting each combination, some algebraic equation would simplify the work involved.

Rule of Combination. If an event can occur n times, a successful outcome can occur r times, and a failing outcome can occur n-r times, the number of ways in which successes and n-r failures can occur without regard to order is found by the formula

$$nCr = \frac{n!}{r! \ (n-r)!}. \tag{11[4]}$$

Suppose one were tossing a set of five coins. It might be of interest to know the number of ways, say, three heads could be obtained. One way of finding out would be to identify each coin by some unbiasing mark and enumerating all possible ways of getting exactly three heads, disregarding the order in which the different coins fell. This may be a simple task with only five coins, but with larger numbers the physical counting would take considerable time. By inserting the proper values in (11), however, one could obtain the same result easily.

In this example, n = 5, r = 3, and n-r = 2. By (11), we obtain,

$$5C3 = \frac{5!}{3! \ 2!} = \frac{5 \cdot 4 \cdot 3 \cdot 2 \cdot 1}{3 \cdot 2 \cdot 1 \cdot 2 \cdot 1} = \frac{120}{12} = 10$$

Each of these different arrangements has the same probability of occurrence.

To obtain the probability of obtaining 3 heads in a toss of five coins, one must determine the probability for each of the ways in which it might occur and, in accordance with the rules of addition, to sum them. Each probability of obtaining 3 heads in a toss of 5 coins is the same. We can either add the 10 identical values, or can multiply the probability by 10.

The latter is easier, and we obtain. In symbols,

$$P = n^c r p^r q^{n-r} \tag{12}$$

---

[4] The symbol "n" is read "n factorial." This means to take the number n and multiply it successively by integers reduced by one. Thus if n equals 4, n is found by multiplying 4 times 3 times 2 times 1. By definition, O equals one.

Taking into account the 10 possible ways of getting 3 heads and 2 tails in a toss of 5 coins, we find, from (12)

$$P = 3C2p^3q^2 = 10(.013125) = .3125$$

That is, if the tossing of 5 coins were continued long enough, slightly over 31% of the time we would get 3 heads and 2 tails.

6. The Binomial Distribution and the Normal Curve

In high school algebra, we learned that we can expand the expression $(p + q)^n$. To refresh our memory, we shall expand this expression letting $n = 5$.

$$(p + q)^5 = p^5 + 5p^4q + 10p^3q^2 + 10p^2q^3 + 5pq^4 + q^5 \quad (13)$$

One of the terms in this expansion seems to be familiar: $10p^3q^2$. It looks like the expression for getting the probability of obtaining 3 heads in a toss of five coins. And so it is. The general term for the binomial expansion is the formula for getting the probability of obtaining r successes in n trials.

Formula (13) can be written as

$$(p + q)^n = \Sigma \; nCrp^rq^{n-r} \quad (14)$$

Since $p + q$ must equal one, the term on the right of (14) also equals one. This equation is important for deducing probabilities from the knowledge of p and q.

Out of n trials, r can range from 0 to n. That is, we can ask, "what is the probability of getting no sucesses in a toss of five coins?" as well as, "what is the probability of getting 5 successes in a toss of 5 coins?" There is a unique probability associated with each value of r. These are given in Table 7 below.

TABLE 7. PROBABILITY FOR GETTING r SUCCESSES OUT OF N TRIALS

r	nCr	p^r	q^{n-r}	Numerical value
0			$(\frac{1}{2})^5$	.03125
1	5	$(\frac{1}{2})$	$(\frac{1}{2})^4$	.15625
2	10	$(\frac{1}{2})^2$	$(\frac{1}{2})^3$	.31250
3	10	$(\frac{1}{2})^3$	$(\frac{1}{2})^2$	.31250
4	5	$(\frac{1}{2})^4$	$(\frac{1}{2})$	.15625
5		$(\frac{1}{2})^5$		.03125

$n=5$

An important modification of the summation operator is needed. From the knowledge given in Table 7, we may want to make some additional combinations. We might, for example, want to know the probability of obtaining either no successes or 1 success (which may be put, "the probability of no more than one success"). From the rule of addition, we simply sum the probabilities when $r = 0$ and when $r = 1$.

To show this operation in terms of Σ, we will put $r = 0$ below the summation sign to indicate the first term to be summed and the number 1 above the sign to indicate the last number to be summed, *viz.*, $\sum_{r=0}^{1} nCrp^r q^{n-r}$

Similarly, to find out the probability for obtaining 3 or more heads (at least three heads), we would put r = 3 below the summation sign and n above it.

The probabilities in Table 7 can be represented graphically. We will show them as a histogram. Recall that the relative frequency—the probability—of any r value is shown as a bar extending up from the X-axis with a width equal to the class interval. The r-values are integers: what are the class limits for the histogram? The r-values are taken as the

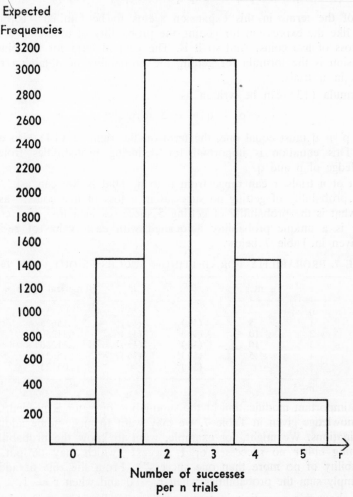

Figure 4. Histogram of Binomial for n = 5. N = 10,000.

mid-points of their respective classes. To obtain the lower class limit, we subtract .5 from the r value, and to get the upper class limit add .5 to it.

We clearly have unit widths for the class intervals. The probabilities, shown on the Y-axis, can be thought of as the heights of the bars. Again, the area in the histogram corresponds to the probability associated with a segment of the X-axis. The total area equals one.

Just as we could compute the mean and standard deviation from the data in Table Two, we can compute the two values for the binomial. To illustrate this, we must change the probabilities to frequencies. Since, by our definition, $p = f/N$, $Np = f$, where N is the number of times n coins are tossed. For convenience, let $N = 10,000$. Then we can set up a table allowing us to use (5) and (9) for the mean and standard deviation.

TABLE 8.   EXPECTED FREQUENCIES OF OBTAINING r
SUCCESSES OUT OF N TRIALS.

r	d	f	fd	fd²
0	—2	312.5	—625.0	1,250.0
1	—1	1,562.5	—1,562.5	1,562.5
2	0	3,125.0	0	0.0
3	1	3,125.0	3,125.0	3,125.0
4	2	1,562.0	3,125.0	6,250.0
5	3	312.5	937.5	2,812.5
totals		10,000.0	5,000.0	15,000.0

Inserting the proper values in our equations, we find that the mean is 2.5 heads out of a toss of 5 coins. The standard deviation (the square root of variance) is found to be approximately 1.12. Instead of using these equations, some simpler ones are available for the binomial.

$$M = np \qquad (15)$$

$$\sigma = npq \qquad (16)$$

As long as n is small, the binomial expansion is not too difficult to use to compute probabilities. When n gets large, however, the separate calculations become burdensome. However, when n gets large, the step differences of the Y-axis of a histogram gets smaller and smaller. If, say, n equals 500, a frequency polygon of the binomial expansion would be virtually a continuous curve. Indeed, a theorem of mathematical probability proves that as n gets large, the binomial approaches the normal curve. That is to say, computation of probabilities from the normal curve involves a progressively smaller error as n gets large, providing np is greater than 5.

As we indicated earlier, it will be useful to learn how to calculate probabilities from the normal curve. Recall that the area under a segment of the curve equals the probability of the outcome identified with the corresponding segment of the X-axis. Recall, also, the property of the standard deviation: transformation of the X-axis into standard deviation units allows an inference of the area covered by the segment involved.

Probabilities are calculated in terms of standard deviation units from the mean. Fortunately, areas corresponding to standard deviation units have been mathematically computed. One needs only to know how to transform the X-axis into the proper units. The transformation is quite simple. We first compute the *mean deviate* value by subtracting the point of interest on the X-axis from the mean. Then we divide this number by the standard deviation. The resulting quotient is the number of standard deviation units the original X-value is from the mean. Associated with the number is the corresponding area under the curve. This area equals the probability that an object will fall between the mean and the X-value chosen.

Symbolically, this operation is given as

$$\frac{X - M}{\sigma} \qquad (17)$$

Table 9 gives the corresponding area of the normal curve for selected values of (17). It can best be used by drawing a picture of the normal curve and

TABLE 9.   AREAS UNDER NORMAL CURVE.

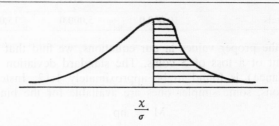

$$\frac{X}{\sigma}$$

$\frac{X}{\sigma}$	Area	$\frac{X}{\sigma}$	Area
.25	.09871	1.75	.45994
.50	.19146	2.00	.47725
.75	.27337	2.25	.48778
1.00	.34134	2.50	.49379
1.25	.39435	2.75	.49702
1.50	.43319	3.00	.49865

Reprinted with permission from Q. McNemar, *Psychological Statistics*, Copyright 1949, John Wiley & Sons, Inc., N. Y.

identifying the area we want to know. Suppose we want to know the probability of obtaining 12 or more heads out of a toss of 15 pennies. The area desired is shown in the shaded area of Figure 5,

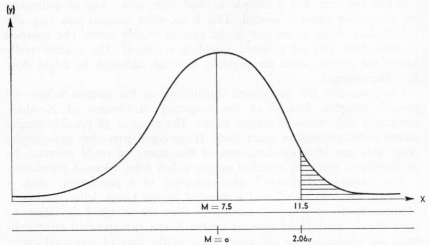

Figure 5. Normal curve showing area needed to solve the problem. Second base line indicates a transformation of the first base line to $\dfrac{x}{\sigma}$ units.

Notice that the lower limit is 11.5. Why? This is our X-value. To use (17) we need the mean and σ. M = np = (15)(½) = 7.5.

$\sigma = \sqrt{npq} = \sqrt{(15)(½)(½)} = 1.94$ approximately.

Inserting these into (17), we obtain

$$\frac{11\cdot5-7\cdot5}{1\cdot94} = \frac{4}{1\cdot94} = 2.06$$

The X-value of 11.5 falls 2.06 standard deviation units from the mean. Using Table 9, we find that the corresponding area under the curve equals .4803007 of the total area. However, the portion of the curve we wanted extends from 11.5 to "infinity." Clearly, the space from the mean to "infinity" comprises only one-half of the total area under the curve. Therefore, to obtain the area we want, we subtract .4803 from .5000. Doing this we obtain the number .0197; this is the probability that we will get 12 or more heads from a toss of 15 coins. The binomial gives .0176 for the same problem. The difference amounts to but .0021 of the total area. Even when n equals only 15, the normal curve seems to be a fairly good approximation.

7. Sampling Theory: Standard Errors and Confidence Limits

A scientist seldom, if ever, deals with a population; normally, he deals with a sample. If he does possess all the data comprising the population, the problem may lack sufficient generality to be of scientific interest. Or, as is the usual case, for one reason or another he simply does not possess all of the data.

When one only has a sample to deal with, some way of estimating the population value is needed. This is so, since samples can vary due to sampling alone, as we saw in the case of tossing coins. The question is, then, how can we measure sampling variation? The student really knows the answer, from the previous material, although he might deny it at the moment.

First, consider the population distribution of the sample values—all possible samples. Instead of the frequency distribution of X-values, consider a distribution of sample means. The mean of all possible sample means is the population mean itself. If we could transform the sample-mean axis into standard deviations of the mean, we could estimate the probability of obtaining specified sample values from a known population.

The "standard deviation," when referring to a population value, is called a "standard error" and is denoted by the Greek letter epsilon, ϵ. Mathematically, it functions exactly as does the standard deviation we have already used. If we measure on the X-axis two standard error units from the parameter, we will cover 95% of the area of a normal curve. This band covers 95% of all possible sample values.

Now, ask the question, "how often am I willing to be wrong?" We have tacitly assumed that we would be willing to be wrong 5 times in a hundred. This means that those sample values that fall beyond the band covered by two standard error units from the population mean are rejected as estimates of the parameter. The rejection would be in error 5 times in a hundred.

But we don't know the parameter value. We know only the statistic. We will use the statistics to estimate the parameters, and use an analogous argument about the confidence of our estimate. Using what are called

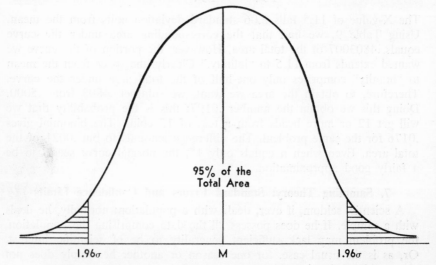

Figure 6. Normal curve showing traditional 95% confidence limits.

"95% confidence limits," we argue this way: If we measure a band around our sample mean two estimated standard errors on each side of the mean, the chances are 95 in 100 that we have included the parameter value in our estimate. Clearly, the smaller the range of tolerable error, the more confidence we have in our estimate.

The sample mean is taken as an estimate of the population mean. We need to know how to estimate the standard error. We know the standard deviation of the sample distribution. It turns out that the standard error of the mean (*i.e.,* the distribution of means) if found by

$$\epsilon_m = \frac{\sigma}{\sqrt{N}} \tag{18}$$

where σ is the sample standard deviation and N is the size of the sample. For proportions, the standard error is estimated by

$$\epsilon_p = \sqrt{\frac{pq}{n}} \tag{19}$$

It is clear that the larger the sample, the smaller the standard error, if all other assumptions have been met.

Size alone is not the criterion. Two assumptions have been made, in the argument, which must be made explicit. First, we assumed a normal distribution. In the case of means, we can find some comfort in the fact that means tend to be normally distributed even if the original distribution was not. This is true particularly in large samples. Second, we assumed *random* sampling. Random sampling means that each object in the study had an equal chance of being drawn.

It turns out, then, that the way in which a sample is taken is of fundamental importance to the inferences which are possible. To insure confidence in our knowledge, we wish to minimize the amount of sampling error. Failure to abide by the assumptions of statistical theory admits the possibility of uncontrolled error.

8. Sampling Theory: Testing Hypotheses

Instead of considering whether a statistic estimates a given parameter, consider the case of two statistics which are numerically different. This poses a problem of variation. Two major explanations can be offered. The numerical difference may be due to sampling variation. Or, the differences may be real. We must choose between the two. In Part A of this chapter, we found that the argument essentially involves an alternative syllogism; the student should review that discussion.

We will justify the test of the null hypothesis which asserts that sampling variation is a sufficient explanation for the observed difference. Assume that this is true. This implies that all *pairs* of samples are drawn from the population and that a distribution of the differences between these pairs exists. Further, if the parent population was normally distributed, the population of differences is also normal. Since the samples are from the same population, the mean difference will be zero. If we knew the sampling error of the differences, we could transform the X-axis and measure the distance a given sample difference is from the mean in standard error units. This would allow us to assert the probability of getting a difference as large, or larger, than the one observed. If the probability is small enough, say, the arbitrary choice of five times out of a hundred, we would be justified in rejecting the hypothesis that the mean difference is zero. The transformation is called "the critical ratio." Symbolically, it is given by

$$\text{C.R.} = \frac{S_1 - S_2}{\epsilon_d} \tag{20}$$

This relationship is illustrated in Figure 7. Notice how the relation

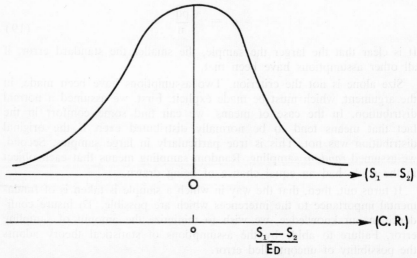

Figure 7. Illustration of a normal distribution of critical ratios. Compare with Figure 5. Note how second base line now transforms the difference between pairs of statistics into critical ratio values.

between area and probability has persisted since we first learned how to draw a histogram. We encountered the idea in the discussion of the binomial and the normal curve approximation to the binomial. We saw it again in the relation between sample values and population values. We find it again in the difference between two sample values.

Apparently, we need to know an equation for the standard error of differences. This is given as

$$\epsilon_d^2 = \epsilon_1^2 + \epsilon_2^2 - 2\, r_{12}\, \epsilon_1\, \epsilon_2 \tag{21}$$

where subscript 1 refers to one sample and subscript 2 refers to the other. Notice that a term involving a new symbol "r" is involved.

This symbol refers to a measure of correlation (see section 10 below). If the samples are drawn independently of each other, then r = 0, and (21) reduces to

$$\epsilon^2_d = \epsilon_1^2 + \epsilon_2^2 \tag{22}$$

The standard error terms to use in either (21) or (22) depend upon the type of statistic used. If one is discussing means, then the standard error of a mean is used. If the statistics refer to proportions, or relative frequencies, then the standard error of proportions is used.

We will give two illustrations of a test of the null hypothesis. The first will illustrate standard errors of proportions, and the second will illustrate a special case of the difference between correlated means. For this latter example, we will give a formula for its standard error.

Suppose we drew a random sample of 400 urban marriages, and, after 10 years of marriage, observed that .32 of these resulted in divorce. Independently, a random sample of 350 rural marriages was drawn and after an interval of 10 years, .23 ended in divorce. Is the difference of proportions of divorce due to sampling error, or is the difference "real"?

Assume that the difference comes from a population of differences with a mean equaling zero. With 95% confidence limits, this implies that the critical ratio will be smaller than 1.96, since 1.96 standard error units around the mean corresponds to 95% of the area of the normal curve. Then insert the proper numbers in (22) and determine the empirical value of the critical ratio.

We find that $S_1 = .32$; p_1 also equals .32, which implies that $q_1 = .68$; $n_1 = .400$. $S_2 = .23$, the same value being p_2. This implies that $q_2 = .77$; $n_2 = 350$. Inserting these in (20), we get

$$\text{C.R.} = \frac{.32 - .23}{\sqrt{\dfrac{(.32)\ (.68)}{400} + \dfrac{(.23)\ (.77)}{350}}}$$

$$= \frac{.09}{\sqrt{.00055}}$$

$$= 3.91$$

But this contradicts the inference that C. R. is less than 1.96. Hence the assumption that the statistics came from a common population is false. This implies that the divorce rate is higher in urban areas than in rural ones.

Suppose, for another example, we wish to find out the influence of a lecture in modifying attitudes towards defacing public property. A random sample of 10 delinquents is drawn, and an attitude test is given them regarding defacing public property. They are then given a lecture on the subject and again their attitudes are measured. Since they comprise the same group, a certain amount of correlation is obviously present, and the critical ratio formulas already given cannot be used.

A formula for the standard error of matched differences is available which does not involve the *calculation* of the amount of correlation, but which nevertheless corrects for whatever correlation there may be. In Table 10, we are given the hypothetical "before" and "after" scores on the attitudinal test. Note that one column is labeled "d", which denotes

TABLE 10.   ATTITUDE SCORES, BEFORE AND AFTER LECTURE ON DEFACING PUBLIC PROPERTY.

Individual	Score before	Score after	Difference "d"	d^2
A	8	10	—2	4
B	9	8	1	1
C	8	10	—2	4
D	6	5	1	1
E	7	7	0	0
F	5	6	—1	1
G	9	8	1	1
H	6	4	2	4
I	8	9	—1	1
J	4	6	—2	4
totals	70	73	—3	21

Sourse: Hypothetical

the numerical difference for the two scores for each person. Another column is headed "d^2" which is the square of these differences.

Directly analogous to (6), we get the sample standard deviation of the difference,

$$\sigma_d = \sqrt{\frac{\Sigma d^2 - \overline{d^2}}{N}} \qquad (23)$$

And the standard error of difference is found to be

$$\epsilon_D = \frac{\sigma_d}{\sqrt{N}} \qquad (24)$$

Notice that Table 10 is set up to give us the necessary information.

In this case, the null hypothesis asserts that the mean differences, within the 95% confidence limits, equals zero. The formula for the critical ratio is

$$C.R. = \frac{(M_1 - M_2) - O}{\dfrac{\sigma_d}{\sqrt{N}}} \qquad (25)$$

From Table 10, we get the numbers necessary to compute the critical ratio. Recall that the null hypothesis implies that the C.R. < 1.96 on the assumption that the "true value" of $\overline{d} = 0$. Simple calculation shows that, in this case, $\overline{d} = $ —.3 $\sigma_d^2 = 2.01$. Since $N = 10$, the critical ratio is given by

$$C.R. = \frac{7 - 7.3}{\sqrt{\dfrac{2.01}{10}}}$$

$$- .71$$

Now, this is certainly less than 1.96; we have not contradicted the implication of the null hypothesis. Although we have not unequivocally proved that sampling variation explains the difference between observed $\bar{d}$ value (-.3) and the assumed one ($\bar{d} = 0$), we have no better explanation. Hence, we say that "chance *can* explain the difference."

9. A χ^2 Test of the Null Hypothesis

Quite often, in social science research, the assumption of a normal distribution is not met. Further, the outcomes of the events being studied are often categorically or ordinally defined. This implies that frequencies of occurrences, rather than quantitative variation, must be explained.

To illustrate the issue, suppose one were studying the effect of educational policy on management policy in modern industry.[5] Are the higher levels of management selected from higher levels of education, or can the grade-school graduate work his way up to executive positions? To answer this question, one must be able to assert the relationship which exists between education and management levels.

In Table 11, we have *cross-tabulated* 220 employees of a hypothetical plant in regard to employment category and amount of education. There

TABLE 11. RELATION BETWEEN EMPLOYMENT CATEGORY AND AMOUNT OF EDUCATION.

Employment category	Amount of education			Raw totals
	Grade school	High school	College	
Laborer	65	50	10	125
Foreman and Supervisor	10	30	5	45
Executive	5	20	25	50
Collective totals	80	100	40	220

Source: Hypothetical.

are three columns for educational level and three rows for employment category. Is there a relationship between the two systems of outcomes, or are they independent?

If membership in the employment categories is independent of membership in educational level, then the laws of probability are sufficient to explain the observed frequencies. On the other hand, if we can contradict the laws of probability, we also contradict the assumption of statistical independence. This, in turn, implies at least some relationship between the two systems.

---

[5] Robert C. Stone, "Mobility Factors as They Affect Worker's Attitudes," *Amer. Soc. Rev.,* (February 1952), Vol. 17, No. 1, pp. 58-63.

From the Rule of Multiplication, we know that if the probability that A occurs, say, the outcome "laborer" is independent of the probability that B occurs, say, the outcome "grade school education," then the probability that the joint outcome, "grade-school education and laborer" is the product of these two probabilities. By selecting the proper column and row, we can then determine the expected probability for any "cell." A "cell" is that part of the table where a row and column overlap. Thus, the first row and the second column gives rise to the cell "high-school and laborer," etc.

The probability of any row outcome is found by dividing the row total (called the marginal total of the row) by the total number, the sum of the row totals. The probability of any column outcome is similarly found. Note that the sum of the column equals the sum of the new totals. We can symbolize any row total by n_i and a column total by n_j. Denoting the total by N, the expected probability for any cell is found by (n_i/N) (n_j/N). This in turn, can be transformed into expected frequencies, denoted by f_e, simply by multiplying the probability by N, thus

$$f_e = n_i n_j / N \qquad (26)$$

Repeated use of (26) will give us the expected frequencies for each cell in the table. If the laws of probability are sufficient to explain the observed frequencies (f_o), the differences between the f_o and the f_e values ought to fluctuate around zero. Observe that sampling variation will account for some differences from zero. How great should the variation be before we reject the laws of probability?

A statistic has been devised to answer this question. It has a chi-square (χ^2) distribution, and is, therefore, called "the chi-square test." It is found by

$$\chi^2 = \Sigma \frac{(f_o - f_e)^2}{f_e} \qquad (27)$$

Notice that if f_o equals f_e in every case, χ^2 equals zero. Table 11 has been so constructed as to give us the required information. It is based on the data given in Table 12. The sum of the last column gives us chi-

TABLE 12.　EMPLOYMENT AND EDUCATION: ARRANGED
FOR COMPUTATION OF χ^2

Observed frequencies f_o	Expected frequencies f_e	$f_o - f_e$	$(f_o - f_e)^2$	$\dfrac{(f_o - f_e)^2}{f_e}$
65	45.45	19.55	382.20	8.41
10	16.36	—6.36	40.45	2.47
5	18.19	—13.19	173.71	9.56
50	56.82	—6.82	46.51	0.82
30	20.45	9.55	91.20	4.46
20	22.73	—2.73	7.45	0.33
10	22.73	—12.72	162.05	7.13
5	8.19	—3.19	10.18	1.24
25	9.09	15.91	253.13	27.85

$$\chi^2 = 62.27$$

Source: Table 11.

square. Its calculation is simple. We record the observed frequencies, and then compute the corresponding expected frequencies. Then the difference is obtained. Since the sum of $f_o =$ the sum of f_e, the sum of the differences equals zero. Hence, the differences are squared, and these squares are divided by the corresponding expected frequencies. The sum of these last values gives us chi-square. In this case, it is found to be 62.27.

This value, 62.27, certainly differs from zero. To decide whether or not it is sufficiently different from zero, one must know the probability of obtaining a chi-square as large, or larger, through the laws of probability. Just like in testing the null hypothesis with the critical ratio, the null hypothesis is rejected if the probability of obtaining a chi-square is "sufficiently small"—say, the arbitrary 5 times in a hundred.

The probability of obtaining any size of chi-square depends upon what are called the "degrees of freedom" involved in its calculation. In the chi-square we have discussed, this refers to the table originally used. The degree of freedom may be thought of in this way. We used the marginal totals in the computation of the expected probabilities. We can, then, regard the marginal totals as being "fixed." How many cell values are independent of the marginal total? Given, say, the first cell in the first row, do we know what the other cell values must be? No, we don't, since the difference between the marginal total of the row and the first cell goes into two remaining cells. If we know the values of two cells in a three cell row, the frequencies in the third cell is also known since the three must equal the marginal total. Two of the cell values are free. The same argument applies to the columns. The question becomes, how many cells in the table are, in this sense, free? The answer is simply the product of the free cells in the row and the free cells in the column. Denoting the number of free cells in the rows by "r," and the number of free cells in the columns by "c," the degrees of freedom are computed by the equation

$$\text{d.f.} = (r\text{-}1)\ (c\text{-}1) \qquad (28)$$

In Table 13, we give the probabilities for obtaining given chi-square

TABLE 13.   SELECTED VALUES FOR X^2: .05 AND .01
LEVELS OF SIGNIFICANCE.

d.f.	.05	.01
1	3.841	6.635
2	5.991	9.210
3	7.815	11.277
4	9.488	13.277
5	11.070	15.086
6	12.592	16.812
7	14.067	18.475
8	15.507	20.090
9	16.919	21.666
10	18.307	23.209

Table 13 is abridged from Table 3 of Fisher: Statistical Methods for Research Workers published by Oliver and Boyd Ltd., Edinburgh, by permission of the author and publishers.

values to 10 different degrees of freedom. The column (1) gives the degrees of freedom, and the columns (2) and (3), designate the probabilities for obtaining the chi-squares as large or larger than the ones entered in the cells of the table. Thus, Col. (3) gives the .05 probability of obtaining chi-square values associated with various degrees of freedom. For one degree of freedom, the probability for getting a chi-square as large or larger than 3.841 is .05.

In our example, we had 3 rows and three columns. This gives by (28) 4 degrees of freedom. We find 4 in the first column of Table 13 and read under the column labeled ".05"; the entry is 9.488. We can now formally state our null hypothesis. "With four degrees of freedom, at the .05 level of confidence, if the true chi-square is zero, the empirical chi-square is less than 9.49." Our empirical value is greater than the one designated in the conclusion, and hence the premise that the true chi-square is zero is false. This implies that some relation exists between educational level and employment level.

This hypothesis, while verified, is *elliptical*. That is, a certain amount of the content is unstated. Precisely what the relationship is was not stated. Suppose, for example, that our hypothesis asserted that a specific pattern existed: that grade school graduates tended to be foremen and supervisors, and that college graduates tended to be executives. In such a case, if, say, it turned out that high school graduates tended to be executives and college graduates tended to be supervisors, we could reject the null hypothesis and still be unable to accept the alternative. This means that for a rigorous test, the content of the alternative must be stated before the test. This, in turn, means that the alternatives must have real theoretical importance prior to a test. Unless this is done, the *content* of the verified hypothesis is *ad hoc* and still must be subject to empirical verification.

10. The Idea of Correlation

The concept of correlation, or of functional relation, has a strong appeal in scientific argument. If it can be shown that one quantitative variable varies with another quantitative variable, a functional relation is said to exist between them. The simplest function is that of a straight line, *i.e.*, $Y = a + bX$, where a and b are constants.

The Line of Best Fit. In high school algebra, we met the straight line equation. Generally, the problem involved a numerical value of a and b; then the student was to determine the value of Y for given (and corresponding) values of X. Thus, a student might be given an equation like "$Y = 2 + 3X$." For a set of X values, the Y values could be readily computed, *viz.*,

X   0   1   2   3   4

Y   2   5   8   11   14

In scientific research, the hypothesis might be simply that a straight-line function exists, but the values of the constants must be computed from the data. Thus, the data for pairs of X's and Y's might be that of above, and some way for inferring the values of a and b must be known. The determination of these constant terms is the problem of "fitting a straight line" to a set of data.

The problem is solved in the following equations:

$$b = \frac{N\Sigma XY - \Sigma X\Sigma Y}{N\Sigma X^2 - (\Sigma X)^2} \tag{29}$$

$$a = M_y - bM_x \tag{30}$$

where the subscripts denote which variable is being considered. From (29), we can see how to set up a computational table for the determination of the constant terms We need (a) the sum of the X values; (b) the sum of the Y values; (c) the sum of the cross-products, *i.e.,* the sum of the values found by multiplying each X by its corresponding Y; (d) the square of the X's, and the sum of those squares. Later, we will need the square of the Y's and the sum of these squares.

Let's see whether or not (29) and (30) will give us the constant terms

TABLE 14. ILLUSTRATION OF TABLE FOR COMPUTATION OF CONSTANTS IN LINEAR EQUATION $Y = a + bX$

X^2	X	Y	XY
0	0	2	0
1	1	5	5
4	2	8	16
9	3	11	33
16	4	14	56
30	10	40	110

Source: above

of the equation from high-school algebra. Table 14 is set up to give us the required information. From the table, we find:

$$N = 5$$
$$\Sigma X = 10$$
$$\Sigma Y = 40$$
$$\Sigma XY = 110$$
$$\Sigma X^2 = 30$$

Inserting these in (29), we obtain

$$b = \frac{5\,(110) - (10)\,(40)}{5\,(30) - (10)^2} = 3$$

The mean of the Y values is easily found to be 8, and the mean of the X's is found to be 2. Inserting these, with the value of b found above, into (30), we find

$$a = 8 - (3)\,(2) = 2.$$

These values are the same ones used in the earlier example. While we haven't proved anything, particularly, the student should have confidence that the equations work. That, at least, has been verified.

The Range of Predictive Error. If a functional relation between two variables exists, and persists through historical time, the equation can be used for predictive purposes. That is, if the equation $Y = 2 + 3X$ was "true," for future values of X corresponding values of Y could be predicted. The accuracy of the prediction could be used to test the correctness of the constant terms (as well as the line itself).

The issue can, perhaps, be seen graphically. On the X-axis, the X-values are given, and similarly for the Y axis. The corresponding points for the pairs of values (X, Y) are then plotted and these points connected by a straight line. Notice, particularly, that a one-one correspondence exists between the X and Y values in the illustration.

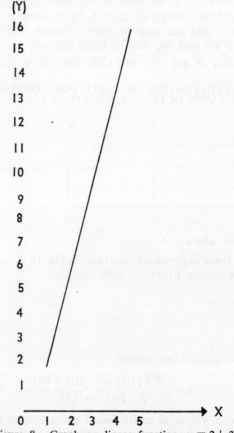

Figure 8. Graph on linear function, $y = 2 + 3x$.

In such a case, there is presumably no predictive error.

This situation seldom, if ever, exists in social science research. Generally, there is no unique correspondence between X and Y values; for any given X value, several Y values may be associated. A more realistic example would be the relationship between age at first marriage for husbands and their wives. The data would look like this:

TABLE 15. AGE AT FIRST MARRIAGE FOR TEN COUPLES

Husband X	Wife Y
18	15
21	20
22	23
23	22
25	24
25	25
27	25
30	31
30	28
35	32

Source: Hypothetical

Before we calculate the line of best fit, we could plot the paired values of X's and Y's. Letting the husbands' ages be the X values, and the wives' ages be the Y values, we would make a *scatter diagram*. Note that for any X value, more than one Y value is given. Apparently, no straight line can connect all the points.

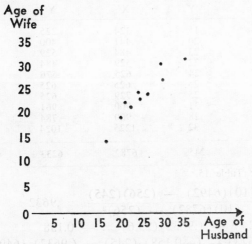

Figure 9. Scatter diagram for data in Table 14. The trend seems quite linear.

However, there seems to be a *linear trend*. The equations (29) and (30) will give the *best possible straight line* in the sense that the deviations from the empirical points to the line will be as small as possible.

We will later compute the values for a and b; now, however, we should reflect on the fact that, whatever the line will be, there will be deviations from it. This means that the equation for the line will predict only the most likely values of Y for given values of X.

Just as we sought a measure of variation around the mean, when we estimated that parameter, we would want a measure of variation around the line. Clearly the smaller the variation around the line, the smaller the predictive error. Indeed, with the proper measure of variation, we could estimate the bands around the line within which, say, 95% of the values would fall. This measure is called "scatter," and is found by the equation

$$S_y = \sqrt{\frac{\Sigma Y^2 - a\Sigma Y - b\Sigma XY}{N}} \qquad (31)$$

When (31) has been calculated, a predictive equation stating the amount of expected variation would be, for 95% confidence,

$$Y = a + bX \pm 2S$$

The calculations below use the data in Table 15 to illustrate fitting a line and estimating scatter. Note that the Table is constructed to give us all the necessary information. Since scatter involves a knowledge of the constants a and b we will compute them first.

TABLE 16. AGE AT FIRST MARRIAGE: ARRANGED TO COMPUTE LINEAR REGRESSION AND CORRELATION

Husband X	Wife Y	X^2	Y^2	XY
18	15	324	225	270
21	20	441	400	420
22	23	484	529	506
23	22	529	484	506
25	24	625	576	600
25	25	625	625	625
27	25	729	625	675
30	31	900	961	930
30	28	900	784	840
35	32	1225	1024	1120
totals 256	245	6782	6233	6492

Source: Table 15.

$$b = \frac{(10)(6492) - (256)(245)}{(10)(6782) - (256)^2} = .9632$$

$$a = 24.5 - (.9632)(25.6) = -0.158$$

$$S^2_y = \frac{6233 - (-0.158)(245) - (.9632)(6492)}{10}$$

$$= \frac{6233 + 38.7 - 6253}{10}$$

$$= 1.87; \quad s_y = \sqrt{1.87} = 1.37$$

$$\sigma_y{}^2 = \frac{6233}{10} - \frac{(245)^2}{100} = 23.05$$

$$Y = -0.158 + (.9632) \pm 2 \, (1.37)$$

It should not be imagined that a and b are always positive. They both may be negative, or one negative and one positive. When Y decreases as X increases, b, the slope of the line, will be negative.

The Amount of Correlation. We may restate the problem of correlation from prediction to explanation. In the latter case, the basic observation is twofold: first, the arithmetic mean of the Y values makes sense. That is, not only must an average be taken, but the distribution is at least approximately normal. If all of the values are bunched toward either extreme (in which case we speak of the distribution being skewed), the median or the mode may be a better average. The second aspect of the problematic observation is the variation which is present. If all of the Y values had the same value, then there would be no problem. As one would guess, the amount of variation in Y can be measured by variance.

It is this variation we seek to explain. The fundamental hypothesis of linear correlation is that the amount of variation in Y is reduced by the introduction of X. If the X value completely determined the Y value, then we would have a perfect fit. This was seen in the example of high-school algebra. If, as in the example from sociological research, the line is not perfect, but some scatter is present, then X is not the sole determinant of the Y values.

The variation of the Y values around the line is measured by scatter. Clearly, scatter measures the variation of Y not associated with X. The ratio of scatter to variance of Y is the percent of the variance of Y not associated with X. The percent of variance which is associated with X must be the difference between the percent which is not so associated and 100 percent.

Denoting the amount of correlation by r^2, the percent of the variance of Y which is associated with X is defined by

$$r^2 = \frac{1 - S_y{}^2}{\sigma_y{}^2} \qquad (32)$$

To obtain r^2, we simply insert the values for scatter and variance of Y in (32) and obtain

$$r^2 = 1 - \frac{1.87}{23.05} = .919$$

However, r^2 can be obtained from a computational formula which does not involve the actual computation of either scatter or variance of Y. Using the same symbols as before,

$$r^2 = \frac{(N\Sigma XY - \Sigma X\Sigma Y)^2}{[N\Sigma X^2 - (\Sigma X)^2] \, [N\Sigma Y^2 - (\Sigma Y)^2]} \qquad (33)$$

From Table 16, we obtain the needed numbers and compute r^2 to be, as before,

$$r^2 = \frac{[(10)(6492) - (256)(245)]^2}{[(10)(6782) - (256)^2][(10)(6233) - (245)^2]}$$

$$= \frac{(2200)^2}{(2284)(2305)}$$

$$= .919$$

11. Analysis of Variance

The Basic Problem. From our discussion of correlation, the student will recognize the general character of the problem. If we have a dependent variable which is quantitative in character, the variation present can be described in terms of variance. The problem is to explain, in some sense, the variance. Further, in linear correlation, the basic hypothesis was that the amount of variance could be effectively reduced by correlating the dependent variable with another variable X.

Recall, now, that a quantitative variable can be "reduced" to categories. Also, note that a hypothetical independent variable may, conceptually, be categorical in nature. For example, if we wanted to explain variation in delinquency rates, we may conceive of "types of childhood training" as an independent variable. Certainly, such a variable is categorical in nature. Notice, also, that we may wish to avoid the implications of linearity. We may feel that the relation between the dependent and independent variable may be curved rather than a simple straight line.

Analysis of variance is a technique which, essentially, takes into account the above possibilities. The independent variable is "categorized." Let us recall the general formula for the sum of squares used in variance. For later convenience, we will introduce some new symbols. The general symbol for each number appearing as the independent variable will be X_{ij}. The subscript "j" refers to the column of the independent variable in which the X's are cross-tabulated. The subscript "i" will refer to which one of the X's in the j column reference is being made. The mean of all X_{ij}'s will be denoted as $\overline{X}$, to distinguish it from the mean of a column which will be denoted $\overline{X}_j$.

Using these symbols, the sum of squares for variance is written

$$\Sigma (X_{ij} - \overline{X})^2 \qquad (34)$$

It is an algebraic rule that we can add zero to any quantity we want, and the quantity remains the same. If we add and subtract the same quantity, we are really adding zero to the old quantity. If we add and subtract X_j to (34), we obtain

$$\Sigma (X_{ij} - \overline{X}_j + \overline{X}_j - \overline{X})^2 \qquad (35)$$

By simple algebraic manipulation, this becomes

$$\Sigma (X_{ij} - \overline{X}_j)^2 + \Sigma (\overline{X}_j - \overline{X})^2 \qquad (36)$$

The importance of (36) lies in the fact that we can see that the total variance is made up of two sources of variance. One is the variation of the column values around the column mean. This is the term

$\Sigma (X_{1j} - \overline{X}_j)^2$ in (36). The other source is the variation of the column means around the grand mean. This is the remaining term, $\Sigma (\overline{X}_j - \overline{X})^2$, in (36).

Both of these terms can be used to estimate variance. These are only "sums of squares." When divided by the "degrees of freedom," sums of squares can be used to estimate variance, since they would be of the form of equation (6). The question becomes, "Do they estimate the same thing?" If they both estimate the same thing, then the introduction of the independent variable has not reduced the observable variance. In other words, the independent variable does not explain any of the variation in the dependent variable. On the other hand, if they are estimating different variances, then we have effectively reduced the variance in the dependent variable and the independent variable is "real."

Instead of testing for significance of differences, as one might suppose, we take a ratio of the between column estimate to the within column estimate of variance. This ratio is called the "F ratio." For given degrees of freedom, if there is no difference between the two estimates, the laws of probability will explain some variation. Hence, after selecting the level of confidence, one argues in the general null hypothesis manner, *viz.*, "For the given degrees of freedom, at the .05 level of confidence, if chance explains the difference, then the F-ratio will be less than some number."

It happens that both the numerator and denominator of the F-ratios have a chi-square distribution. The chi-square distribution is a function of the degree of freedom. For that reason, the F table must take into account the degrees of freedom of the numerator and the denominator. Certain selected values are presented in Table 17. The entire table is for the .05 level of confidence; if the F ratio is equal to or greater than the

TABLE 17. SELECTED VALUES FOR F RATIOS AT .05 LEVEL OF SIGNIFICANCE

d. f. for denominator	d. f. for numerator 1	2	3	4	5	12
1	161	200	216	225	230	244
2	18.51	19.00	19.16	19.25	19.30	19.41
3	10.13	9.55	9.28	9.12	9.01	8.74
4	7.71	6.94	6.59	6.39	6.26	5.91
5	6.61	5.79	5.41	5.19	5.05	4.68
10	4.96	4.10	3.71	3.48	3.33	2.91
15	4.54	3.68	3.29	3.06	2.90	2.48
20	4.35	3.49	3.10	2.87	2.71	2.28
24	4.26	3.40	3.01	2.78	2.62	2.18
25	4.24	3.38	2.99	2.76	2.60	2.16
30	4.17	3.32	2.92	2.69	2.53	2.09
40	4.08	3.23	2.84	2.61	2.45	2.00
60	4.00	3.15	2.76	2.52	2.37	1.92
∞	3.84	2.99	2.60	2.37	2.21	1.75

Table 17 is abridged from Table 5 of Fisher and Yates: Statistical Tables for Biological, Agricultural, and Medical Research published by Oliver and Boyd Ltd. Edinburgh, by permission of the authors and publishers.

number found, the null hypothesis is rejected. The first row of the table labeling the different columns, designates the degrees of freedom in the *numerator*. The first column, labeling the rows, designates the degrees of freedom in the *denominator*. Thus, if the numerator has 12 degrees of freedom, and the denominator has 30, the F-ratio at the 5% level is found to be 2.09.

The analysis of variance technique is not without its restrictions. These restrictions exist in the assumptions made in the derivation of the F-ratio. Of course, we did not make the derivation here; nonetheless, the assumptions must be known. The distribution of the X_{ij} values for each column is presumed to be a sample drawn from a population denoted to the jth category (column). The j samples are assumed to be random; independent of each other; normally distributed; and having the same variance. This latter assumption is called the frightful term "homoscedasticity;" since the within-column variances are averaged for all the columns, wide variation in column variances could not be tolerated.

One-Way Classification. We will here give the computational set-up for analysis of variance with one independent variable. The symbols are the same as in the preceding section. A numerical example will be given in Chapter V, section 5.[6] The dependent variable, symbolized by X_{ij}, is sorted out into m columns (*i.e.,* $j = 1, 2, . . ., m$). There are n values in each column. Thus, $N = nm$.

TABLE 18.   DUMMY TABLE FOR ANALYSIS OF VARIANCE

Treatments

1	2	. . .	m
X_{11}	X_{12}	. . .	X_{1m}
X_{21}	X_{22}	. . .	X_{2m}
"	"	. . .	"
"	"		"
"	"		"
"	"		"
X_{n1}	X_{n2}	. . .	X_{nm}
$X_{.1}$	$X_{.2}$	. . .	$X_{.m}$

Observe, in particular, the row denoting column totals, $(X_{.j})$.

For convenience, in making computations, an Analysis of Variance Table is constructed. This table indicates the source of variance, and its equational equivalent. The degrees of freedom and the mean square obtained by dividing the sum of squares by the degrees of freedom is shown. Finally, a column indicating the F-ratio to be taken is indicated. This, in turn, indicates how to set up a computational table by showing precisely what data are needed.

---

[6] To save space, a numerical example of analysis of variance is not included in this chapter. However, an example is included in the next chapter.

TABLE 19. ANALYSIS OF VARIANCE

Source	Sum of Squares	d. f.	Mean Sq.	F
Total	$\Sigma X_{ij}^2 - \dfrac{(\Sigma X_{ij})^2}{N}$	N-1		
Between	$\dfrac{\Sigma X_{\cdot j}^2}{n} - \dfrac{(\Sigma X_{ij})^2}{N}$	M-1	$\dfrac{\dfrac{\Sigma X_{\cdot j}^2}{n} - \dfrac{(\Sigma X_{ij})^2}{N}}{M-1}$	$\dfrac{\dfrac{\Sigma X_{\cdot j}^2}{n} - \dfrac{(\Sigma X_{ij})^2}{N}}{M-1}$
Within	$\dfrac{\Sigma X_{ij}^2 - \Sigma X_{\cdot j}^2}{n}$	N-M	$\dfrac{\dfrac{\Sigma X_{ij}^2 - \Sigma X_{\cdot j}^2}{n}}{N-M}$	$\dfrac{\dfrac{\Sigma X_{ij}^2 - \Sigma X_{\cdot j}^2}{n}}{N-M}$

From the analysis of variance table, we see we need (a) the square of each item summed $(\Sigma X_{ij})^2$; (b) the sum of each item squared (ΣX_{ij}^2); (c) the square of each column total summed for the m columns $(\Sigma X_{\cdot j}^2)$; (d) the number of items in each column (n); (e) and the total number in the table (N).

The computational table would then be:

TABLE 20. COMPUTATIONAL TABLE FOR ANALYSIS OF VARIANCE

Treatments

	1		2		. . .	m	
	X_{11}	X_{11}^2	X_{12}	X_{12}^2	. . .	X_{1m}	X_{1m}^2
	X_{21}	X_{21}^2	X_{22}	X_{22}^2	. . .	X_{2m}	X_{2m}^2
	"	"	"	"		"	"
	"	"	"	"		"	"
	"	"	"	"		"	"
	"	"	"	"		"	"
Column totals	$X_{\cdot 1}$	$(X^2)_{\cdot 1}$	$X_{\cdot 2}$	$(X^2)_{\cdot 2}$		$X_{\cdot m}$	$(X)^2_{\cdot m}$
Square of $X_{\cdot j}$	$(X_{\cdot 1})^2$		$(X_{\cdot 2})^2$			$(X_{\cdot m})^2$	

12. Summary

We earlier learned that a major task of science was to reach a decision regarding a proposition. We now have learned that under special conditions, statistics allows us to make decisions about a particular kind of proposition. The fundamental task of statistical inference is to enable one to decide whether an observed variation is explicable by the laws of probability or must be explained by some other influencing factor.

The steps in this learning process were, despite the newness of the words and symbols, quite direct. The first task was to make a frequency distribution and to graph it. The graph has the characteristic of having correspondence. We then modified "frequency" into "relative frequency" the area and the frequency associated with that area be in one-to-one and "relative frequency" into probability. Thus a graph of probabilities would enable us to estimate probabilities.

After formally defining probability and various rules for combining probalities, we observed that the binomial p + q could be expanded into a series which could be graphed. Hence we could use the graph to estimate probabilities. Then we noted the similarity between the graph of the binomial and the normal curve. Under the general assumptions of normality and random sampling, the normal curve could be used to measure probabilities.

Thus the probable ocurrence of any statistics having a normal distribution could be estimated. Some major statistics having such a distribution are means, differences between means, proportions and differences between proportions. Knowledge of the probable occurrence of a statistic provides a basis for judging whether or not the event is too rare to be attributable to chance. This involves a prior agreement as to the range of error, or confidence limits, one wants to employ.

Two other major types of distribution, with, essentially, the same argument, are the chi-square and F distributions. The former allows one to draw inferences about a statistic called "chi-square" and the latter allows inferences about ratio of two estimations of variance. The latter estimation is fundamental to "analysis of variance."

Another significant statistical argument is that of correlation. Again, the problem is that of variation. As in analysis of variance, linear regression can start with variance as a measure of variance. Utilizing the argument of concomitant variation, the general hypothesis is that the dependent variable is a linear function of another variable. Equations for obtaining the best constants from a set of empirical data are given. Variation around the resulting line allows for two things: First, to give a range of predictive error, and second, to measure the percent of the original variance which is not associated with the introduction of the independent variable.

As a closing comment, the student should be reminded that no statistical technique can improve upon poor data. Further, each statistical equation implies a solution to some problem. Prior to using any statistic, one must make certain that the problem solved by the equation is relevant to the research problem at hand.

SELECTED REFERENCES

Clark, Charles E., *An Introduction to Statistics* (New York: John Wiley & Sons, 1953).

Hagood, Margaret J. and Price, Daniel O., *Statistics for Sociologists* (New York: Henry Holt & Co., rev. ed., 1952).

Jackson, Robert W. B. and Johnson, Palmer O., *Introduction to Statistical Methods* (New York: Prentice-Hall, Inc., 1953).

Lev, Joseph and Walker, Helen M., *Statistical Inference* (New York: Henry Holt & Co., 1953).

McCormick, Thomas C., *Elementary Social Statistics* (New York: McGraw-Hill Book Co., 1941).

Chapter 5

PRINCIPLES OF EXPERIMENTATION*

1. Definition and Problem

SOCIAL scientists have reacted variously to the word "experiment." Some, shocked, perhaps, by an invidious surrender to the assumptions and formulation of physical sciences, have retreated with rather ignoble flopping of academic regalia. Others, stimulated by the social rewards in the form of prestige and monetary support for research, have cast envious glances at the spotless white gowns of the biologist, the bubbling test-tubes of the chemist and the wonderful mechanical paraphernalia of the physicist. Neither baleful glances nor lecherous leers at the figure of Experimentation can properly resolve the issue. Like a third group of social scientists—growing, possibly, in numbers and influence—we should examine the logical role of experimentation, its place in research, the limitations of the argument, and the conditions under which it seems applicable in social inquiry.

In short, experimentation is here to stay. It has something to offer. It is not the end-all of science; astronomy has done quite well without it. Good research is possible without it. Yet, under proper conditions, experimentation permits rigorous and convincing arguments. We use it where it fits, and avoid it where it doesn't.

There is nothing particularly mysterious about experimentation. It is simply a part of a general scientific framework. Science attempts to obtain a theory from which hypothetical deductions can be tested; the experiment is simply a way in which a hypothesis may be tested. Contrasted with hypothesis testing by field observations, the experiment is characterized by a maximization of control over the various variables involved in the test.

While a certain amount of trial and error is empirically involved in early attempts at experimentation, trial and error does not define the experiment. Indeed, scientific experimentation tries to minimize the trial and error activities of the scientist. In the place of merely "seeing what happens if we do so and so," the rigorous experimenter deduces as many potential consequences as his theory allows. He then proceeds to determine the relative likelihood of the various consequences of his manipulations.

Another contrast with observational research is that in observational research one necessarily encounters as many factors as empirically exist. In experimentation, the goal is to vary only the critical variables and to

---

* Written by Roy G. Francis.

101

control ("hold constant") other variables of theoretical interest. Many experiments, as a matter of fact, are designed to permit the manipulation of a single variable.

The formal structure of the hypothetical proposition, "if A, then B," can be used to characterize the sort of propositions which science, in general, seeks to validate. The "A" part of the hypothesis is seldom a single factor; rather, it is often a set of conditions. Experimentation seeks to control the variables such that it is first possible to assert that "A" is indeed present.

Recall that the predictive argument was of the form "If A, then B; I 'create' A; hence I predict B." Above, the "creation of A" involves all of the operations performed in the experiment.

Notice, however, that nothing is said, in this form, of the negation of "A." If it turns out that one could also say "if 'not A,' then B," the experiment has not proved anything. Hence the experiment goes beyond a merely predictive hypothesis. Generally, the experiment will in some sense include a "control group." A control group is one in which the theoretical antecedent is negated. Thus many experiments involve operations identifying the antecedent and operations identifying its negation. When this is so, the "if A, then B" statement must be amended. The "premise" then includes the operations identifying both the antecedent and its negation.[1] In this respect, the experiment epitomizes scientific prediction.

Notice one last contrast with observational research. In that type of inquiry one often temporarily begins with a set of observations requiring explanation. The premise is discerned after the problematic consequence is observed. That is, one begins with the "B" part of the hypothesis, and hopes to be able to connect it with the "A" part. In experimentation, however, the temporal sequence of knowledge is the same as the logical sequence of the argument. From one's theory, one can deduce what the "A'" conditions must be; these are then re-created under controlled conditions. Then, this sequence of time and with passage of time, one observes whether or not the predicted consequence occurs.

This identity between the temporal sequence of knowledge and the logical sequence of the argument gives rise to the power of the experiment as a scientific test of hypotheses. It also raises the central problem: how to secure sufficient control to enable one to infer that the identity exists. How to insure the re-creation of the theoretical premise is the critical issue in experimentation.

2. The Logic of Experimentation

The logic of experimentation is a straightforward extension of the general scientific argument. Adding the fact of manipulating the explanatory variables, one seeks to observe a connection between the explanation

[1] S. A. Stouffer, "Some Observations on Study Design," *American Journal of Sociology,* Vol. LV, No. 4, (January, 1950), pp. 355-361.

and the problem. The traditional terminology is somewhat different (since "problematic data and explanatory data" are general terms). We often refer to the problematic data—*i.e.*, that which is to be explained—as the "consequence"; and we refer to the explanatory data as the "antecedent."

Denoting the antecedent by "A," and its absence or negation by "-A," we will similarly denote the consequent by "C" and its absence by "-C." It should be noted that these symbols and expressions are quite general. Thus, "A" may refer to a single factor, or a set of factors, or a patterning of factors. The same is true of "C." In particular, the "antecedent" refers to the whole set of operations performed in the course of the experiment, including not only the theoretical variable but the process in terms of which it has been identified. Moreover, the "consequence" may be held to include not only the specific behavior of the objects studied, but may also include the type of relationship, (*e.g.*, a linear relation with known values for the constant terms in the equation). Heuristically, however, we may regard the antecedent as defining certain conditions or factors and the consequence as the behavior we seek to explain.

We may then construct a model showing the general structure of the argument. We first build a 2 x 2 table:

	A	-A
C		
-C		

If the joint outcome C and -A has no members, this means that the consequent occurs only when the antecedent occurs; this is called "necessary conditions." This simply means that the antecedent is necessary for the occurrence of the consequent. If the joint outcome A and -C has no members, it means that while the antecedent will "produce" the consequent other things will also. We then speak of "sufficient conditions." If both of these joint outcomes have no members, we speak of "necessary and sufficient conditions."[2]

As one can imagine, the likelihood of getting zeros in these two cells is remarkably small. For one thing, the operations by which we identify the antecedents are generally not unique. That is, the same antecedent may be identified by more than one operation. But if we allow only one specific operation, then all other possible identifications occur under "-A," reducing the possibility of obtaining zero frequencies. For another thing, the relationship between the antecedents and the consequent may not be perfect. Hence some variation explicable by chance is likely to exist. It becomes obvious that a statistical argument is going to be used in experimentation.

Before proceeding to a discussion of the role of statistics in experimentation, one further point regarding the experiment must be established. The description of scientific experimentation in section 1 is, ob-

---

[2] Note the relationship of this argument with Mill's "Canons." See Chapter 3.

viously, "ideal." Researchers have often tried to conduct experiments before their theory was rigorous enough to warrant a rigorous inference either as to proper identification of the antecedent or the kind of relationship expected to emerge. Hence, we may speak of three types of experiments currently being used.

The first, and most simple, is that experiment which seeks only to answer questions. This is not too far removed from trial-and-error experimentation. In this case, one simply asks, "What will happen if I do so and so?" Clearly, nothing is being tested in this type of activity. It may give rise to a fruitful hypothesis; it may, on the other hand, involve a great waste of time and money.

The second type of experiment involves the test of an elliptical hypothesis. You recall that the elliptical hypothesis omits certain elements of content, presumably until after the experiment is completed. Quite often the elliptical hypothesis is the null hypothesis which simply asserts that the hypothetical antecedent is no different from its negation in producing the consequent.

The third main type of experiment involves a specific hypothesis. Of course, the amount of specificity varies from one experiment to another. Since this type of hypothesis is the most easily falsified, it is also the most rigorous test. When one can predict within a relatively small range of statistical error, the argument is not only tightened, it is more convincing as well.

This third type of experiment is, perhaps, the most desired in scientific research. Currently, however, it is engaged in less frequently than the second type. Nonetheless, it is the goal; and the first two types of experiments must be regarded as steps towards the third.

3. Statistics in Experimental Design

The critical experiment in which one spectacular result is completely convincing of the vertification of the hypothesis is virtually non-existent. The test of any experiment rests, by and large, upon the replication of the entire set of operations. The repetition of any test, unless a perfect relationship exists, generally involves the possibility of sampling error. This being so, the statistical rejection of chance as an explanation is fundamental to experimental inference.[3]

At the same time, the statistical argument must be fully considered before the experiments are to take place. Some years ago, the author was asked to give some advice to a physiologist who was engaged in an experiment on cats. The general hypothesis was that electric stimulation of different sections of the brain would result in different reactions in heartbeat and respiration of the cat in question. The preparation of each cat for the test was a tedious job; about one cat a day could be prepared and used in the experiment. By the time the advice was sought, some 400

---

[3] Cf. C. West Churchman, *Theory of Experimental Inference* (NY: Macmillan Co., 1948).

cats had been used up. After the data had been classified, some statistical design was sought.

By then, it was too late to develop a rigorous statistical argument. The categories were not designed to permit statistical analysis. The various controls were lacking in rigor. The basic assumptions of statistical inference were unknown and hence ignored. At best, some simple frequency analysis could be safely used. From the point of view of rigorous experimentation, no general inferences could be drawn. Some descriptive statements about a particular group of dissected cats was all that was possible. The moral is quite clear: the statistical design must be incorporated into the general system of operations to be performed.

Recall the argument given in the preceding chapter: a statistical formula represents the solution of some problem. Unless the problem solved is in fact the one faced by the experimenter, gratuitous use of statistics is misleading. This is not to say that there is absolutely no value to the *ad hoc* application of a statistical argument. But it does mean that the chances for meeting the assumptions of statistical inference are minimized if these assumptions are not explicitly a part of the experimental design.

Perhaps the simplest statistical argument which could fit an experimental design would involve the simple dichotomy of "success" and "failure" regarding the identification of the possible outcomes of the consequent. The antecedent would, of course, be the "experimental group" which is subject to some experience; its negation would be a "control group" which is subjected to some experience; its negation would be a "control group" not subjected to the experience. If, prior to the experiment, both groups are independent random samples from the same population, the statistical design would be the critical ratio of proportions. Of course, since frequencies of outcomes are involved, a chi-square test of a 2 x 2 table could be used.

If the consequential behavior varies in amount, a simple experimental design would involve differences in mean amounts before the experiment and after.[4] The "Control group" would be a random sample whose problematic behavior is measured before the experiment. The "experimental group" would be the same group measured after the experience. Now, a certain amount (though unknown) of correlation will exist since the same people occur in both the control and experimental groups. Hence, the standard error formula would have to take the correlation into account. Formula (24) in chapter 4, it will be recalled, does take the correlation into account.

So far, the experimental argument has been relatively simple: the comparison of one presumed antecedent against its negation or absence. However, the same problematic behavior could be differentially related to a set of possible antecedents. For convenience, let us call the "set of antecedents" "treatments."

The experiment will then proceed in this way. The problematic data

---

[4] See Chapter 4.

are essentially quantitative. Corresponding to each treatment, a random sample is drawn either from a parent population which has not been subjected to the treatments, or from an original sample so drawn. Each sample is then subjected to the treatment designated in the design. Then each object is measured in respect to the problematic data. If the consequence of each treatment differs from all the rest, then the arithmetic means of the several treatments ought to be significantly different from each other. It would be possible to test the difference between all possible pairs of means. Clearly, that kind of analysis would be rather difficult and time consuming.

A more direct approach would be to ask whether the variation of the treatment means around the grand mean estimates the same variance as does the variation of the dependent variable around each treatment mean. If the two sources of variation estimate the same thing, then the treatments make no real difference. If, however, the two sources are estimating different kinds of variance, then the treatments have been differentially effective. This can be tested by the F-ratio of analysis of variance.

We will proceed to give a numerical example.

It is known that performance level, as identified by measuring the time taken to complete a uniform task, is a variable. The problem is to explain, as much as possible, this variation. The statistical explanation is of the form of reduction of variance. Accordingly, we seek to determine if performance under different controlled conditions results in any explanation of the variation.

The experimental design is simple and straightforward. The problematic data consists of the time taken by school children to solve a relatively simple puzzle. The "treatments" consist of four conditions under which the puzzle-solving activity is to take place. Group A will consist of those children who have been given instruction on how to solve a similar type of puzzle. This instruction is "treatment A." Group B will consist of those who have simply been asked to solve the puzzle, but no instructions have been given. Group C will consist of those who have been given the instruction in treatment A, and, in addition, are promised a reward if they can

TABLE 21. TIME TAKEN IN MINUTES TO COMPLETE SIMPLE PUZZLE
UNDER SELECTED CONDITIONS

With Instruction (A)	Merely Asked to Solve Puzzle (B)	Instructions Plus Rewards (C)	Distractions Present (D)
5	6	3	9
8	10	5	12
10	12	4	12
7	9	7	8
8	10	6	10
5	8	8	11
10	9	5	10

Source: Hypothetical.

solve the puzzle. Group D will consist of those who are not only not instructed, but are subjected to certain mild distractions (*i.e.,* doors opening and closing, people talking, etc.). The entire group is a random sample of 28 school children drawn from a class of 156 5th graders. They are randomly assorted to the four groups, each having seven children.

The number in Table 21, below, represents the number of minutes taken by each child to complete the puzzle. Notice that the column sums vary, apparently considerably. The legitimacy of analysis of variance seems obvious.[5] To refresh our memory, the computational formulas for analysis of variance are given in Table 22. This is simply a reproduction of the table given in the preceding chapter.

TABLE 22. ANALYSIS OF VARIANCE

Source	Sum of Sqs.	d. f.	Mean Sq.	F
Total	$\Sigma X_{i^2j} - \dfrac{(\Sigma X_{ij})^2}{N}$	N-1		
Between	$\dfrac{\Sigma X._{j}^2}{n} - \dfrac{(\Sigma X_{ij})^2}{N}$	M-1	$\dfrac{\dfrac{\Sigma X._{j}^2}{n} - \dfrac{(\Sigma X_{ij})^2}{N}}{M-1}$	$\dfrac{\dfrac{\Sigma X._{j}^2}{n} - \dfrac{(\Sigma X_{ij})^2}{N}}{M-1}$
Within	$\dfrac{\Sigma X_{i^2j} - \Sigma X._{j}^2}{n}$	N-M	$\dfrac{\Sigma X_{i^2j} - \Sigma X._{j}^2}{\dfrac{n}{N-M}}$	$\dfrac{\Sigma X_{i^2j} - \Sigma X._{j}^2}{\dfrac{n}{N-M}}$

To facilitate the computation, we will construct a table which will give us the needed information. This is given in Table 23 below. Notice that

TABLE 23. TIME TAKEN TO COMPLETE PUZZLE, ARRANGED TO FACILITATE COMPUTATIONS

	A		B		C		D	
	X	X^2	X	X^2	X	X^2	X	X^2
	5	25	6	36	3	9	9	81
	8	64	10	100	5	25	12	144
	10	100	12	144	4	16	12	144
	7	49	9	81	7	49	8	64
	8	64	10	100	6	36	10	100
	5	25	8	64	8	64	11	121
	10	100	9	81	5	25	10	100
Totals	53	427	64	606	38	224	72	754
$(\Sigma X)^2$	2809		4096		1444		5184	

Source: Table I.

under each treatment we have a column labeled "X" and "X^2." Direct computation gives us the following results:

---

[5] For a test of homoscedasticity, Wilfrid J. Dixon and Frank J. Massey, Jr., *Introduction to Statistical Analysis.* (N.Y.: McGraw-Hill Book Co., 1951), p. 147.

$$\Sigma \ X_{1j} = 227$$
$$\Sigma \ X^2{}_{ij} = 2011$$
$$\Sigma(\Sigma \ X_{ij})^2 = 13,533$$
$$(\Sigma \ X_{ij})^2 = 51,529$$

Since there are four columns, $m = 4$. Inserting these into the equations given in Table 22 above, we find

TABLE 24. ANALYSIS OF VARIANCE, NUMERICAL EXAMPLE.

Source	Sum of Sqs.	d.f.	Mean Sq.	F
Between	$\dfrac{13533}{7} - \dfrac{51529}{28}$	3	$\dfrac{92.96}{3} = 30.99$	30.99
Within	$2011 - \dfrac{13533}{7}$	24	$\dfrac{77.72}{24} = 3.24$	3.24

Note that $\Sigma \ (\Sigma X_{1j})^2$ can be used to denote $\Sigma X.^2{}_j$

Thus, with the between column mean square in the numerator, and the within column mean square in the denominator,

$$F = 30.99/3.24 = 9.86$$

With 3 degrees of freedom for the numerator and 24 degrees of freedom for the denominator, we find from Table 16, p. 94, supra, that the probability of obtaining an F-ratio as large or larger than 3.01 is .05. Our formal null hypothesis would be, "If chance explains the differences in means squares, at the 5% level of confidence, the F-ratio will be less than 3.01." Since ours is much larger than that, we reject the null hypothesis. This, in turn, implies that the column means differ significantly and, hence, that level of performance varies according to the conditions under which the activity takes place.

4. Experimental Design: The Control of Variables

The results in our hypothetical experiment seem quite conclusive. Certainly, the results conform to our expectation. We may, in order to clarify the issue of controlling variables, ask if we did have sufficient control to place any confidence upon the operations performed.

In regards to our problematic data, *i.e.*, the level of performance, we may wonder whether recording the data in terms of minutes taken to solve the puzzle was sufficient. That is, is "time taken to solve the puzzle" a sufficient identification of performance level? Ought we not include the number of false-starts, the incorrect solutions tried? Does the person who tries several false solutions quickly have the same performance level as the one who tries only one but who takes as much total time? Have "trial and error" solutions to the problem been sufficiently controlled, or do we have reason to infer they make no difference to the outcome?

Further, no one is particularly interested in the solution of puzzles as such; we wish to generalize to a theoretical construct "performance level." In a general theoretical sense, have we properly identified our problems? Keeping the same sorts of treatments, would we get the same results if we changed our identification of performance? All these questions must be carefully considered before we can have any faith in the outcome of the experiment.

In reference to our "treatment," we may ask the same general questions: (a) have we properly identified the variables we think are important and (b) have we properly controlled other variables which might be present? For example, does past experience with puzzles of this type have any effect on performance? Judging from our own experiment (Treatments A and B differ by the former having instructions which the latter did not), prior knowledge of the task is exceedingly important. Have we controlled past experience? What about general intelligence? Does this make a difference? We are tempted to say that it *obviously* does. Has it been controlled? Other relevant factors are just as easily thought of; the student should consider as many as he can.

The main principle of control which we employed was that of *randomization*. We selected our primary sample by random means and sorted out the four treatment groups randomly. This means that we hoped that the presence of these other factors appear equally in all four groups. This is a rather large order, in view of having four groups of only seven in each group. Moreover, the population from which the original sample was drawn is itself limited. If, for example, past experience with puzzles is partly a function of the social class of the child, and if, ecologically, different schools service different social classes, we would lose control through the sample we took.

Randomization is the fundamental control in experimentation in the social sciences. Whenever we reach the point of being unable to further control the variables in question, we resort to randomization. The main justification is a theorem in mathematical statistics which shows that the means of a large number of samples of a large set of variables tend to be normally distributed even if the original variables were not.[6] This theorem is appealed to when the error is considered a consequence of a large number of uncontrolled factors. The difficulty lies in knowing what "a large number of uncontrolled factors" really means. Then, too, the possibility of correlation between the factors (as between social class and past experience) rules our "randomization" since correlation negates the inference of statistical independence.

Some control exists in *matching* for factors. One way is to select the experimental groups in such a way that each group has the same number of members having, say, past experience with puzzles, certain levels of

---

[6] This theorem is generally called the Central Limit Theorem. See Alexander Mood, *Introduction to the Theory of Statistics,* (N.Y.: McGraw-Hill Book Co., Inc., 1950), p. 136 ff.

intelligence, etc. Another way is to match individuals for these characteristics. That is, if a member of group A has a high level of intelligence, comes from a certain social class, has a certain amount of past experience, each of the other groups should have a member with the same characteristics. Clearly, this kind of matching is more rigorous than the group matching; it is also more time consuming and more costly. Further, either kind of matching introduces correlation between the several groups and complicates the statistical argument.

If the potentially interfering factors are subject to physical manipulation, we may speak of *"equalizing"* them. In our example, it might be true that the relative amount of light is a significant variable. This could be controlled by keeeping the amount of light *constant*,[7] *i.e.,* the same amount of light for each group. Holding the influence of interfering variables constant is a principle second to randomization in experimental design.

The reason for holding certain variables constant is quite apparent: it reduces the complexity of the design, and clarifies the statement of relationships   which can be made. Instead of having to compare the experimental results simultaneously for differing levels of the interfering variable (*e.g.,* differing amounts of light) the relationship is described for only one level (*e.g.,* the constant amount of light used). Of course, the generality of the experiment might be reduced; in effect, one buys rigor at the expense of generality.

Thus, one of the main controls in experimental design consists of holding variables constant, where possible. If the problem, or data, is such as to make that infeasible, the objects studied are matched for the several interfering variables. This matching may either be in terms of the experimental groups, or by individuals in the different groups. When the possibility for holding the variables constant, or for matching them, is no longer real—increased rigor may lead to a complex design if a larger number of variables are considered simultaneously—one employs the principle of randomization.

The control of variables in experimental research is a difficult task. One must not only have a clear conception of what variables are related to the problem; one must also know how to identify the variables empirically. Since there is an element of fadism connected with experimentation, we should be reminded that the operation identifying the variable ought not be equated with the variable itself. Two dangers exist in the equating of operational and theoretical definitions.

On the one hand, it may lead to over-generalization of the results. If, in particular, the explanatory antecedent is defined operationally by a specific operation but retains a general "name," one might draw false

---

[7] An advanced statistical technique for "holding variables constant" is that of multiple and partial correlation. See Mordecai Ezekiel, *Methods of Correlation Analysis,* (N.Y.: John Wiley & Sons, Inc., second edition, 1941).

inferences about instances of the antecedent when identifiable by other operations. On the other hand, restricting the argument simply to the operational definition can lead to sterile results. In particular, the operation may properly identify an antecedent, but because of its restricted utility, be of little theoretical importance.

5. Experimental Design: Learning Theory

While most contemporary research in learning theory generally involves highly complex statistical arguments, we will illustrate only the most simple kind of experimentation from learning theory. It will be recalled that an elementary form of experimentation is designed simply to answer a question.

One of the basic tenets of physiological learning theory is the assumption of random behavior on the part of a subject learning some particular type of activity. Indeed, many formulations of learning theory emphasize the reduction of error in the process of learning. Reduction of error, as a measure of learning, makes sense only if the initial stages of the activity were of a trial-and-error sort.

Consequently, it becomes important to know if the amount of random behavior is a function of controllable conditions, or if it is a *constant* "force." When the conception of "drive" was introduced to explain "motivation" for the reduction of error, the question was raised "is the amount of 'drive' related to the amount of 'random behavior' of the subject being studied?" If the answer was "yes," then the amount of "drive" would have to be controlled in future experiments.

To answer the question, a relatively simple experiment was designed.[8] The subjects were white rats. The variable "drive" was operationally defined in terms of hunger. Accordingly, 17 white rats were recently fed, and 17 were hungry. The "maze" was simply marked off with an equal number of squares;; no "goal" (*i.e.,* nothing to reduce the drive) was present. The only behavior possible was "random behavior." The rats were alternatively set in the "maze" (*i.e.,* a fed rat followed by a hungry rat). The concept "random behavior" was measured by counting the number of squares the rats entered. Thus, operationally, the more squares the rat entered, the greater its "random behavior." It turned out that the average number of squares entered by the fed rat was 26.7; while an average of 42.9 squares were entered by the hungry rats. From this, the conclusion was that the amount of random activity varies with the amount of "drive."

Notice the way in which "controls" were used. (1) The "drive" was directly manipulated by giving or withholding food. (2) The possibility of drive reduction as an explanation was controlled through the absence

[8] J. F. Dashiell, "A Quantitative Demonstration of Animal Drive," *J. Comp. Psychol,* 1925, 5, pp. 205-208.

of any "goal" directly connected with the drive.[9] (3) The alternation of hungry and fed rats randomizes the sequence of the activity. (4) A genetic assumption about the "intelligence" of rats is at least partially controlled by a random sorting of the original 34 rats into the two groups.

6. Experimental Design: Social Psychological Theory

The concept "frame of refereence" has a wide currency in social psychological theory. For the most part, the inference of a frame of reference was an *"ad hoc"* one—used "after the fact" to account for certain types of behavior. In other words, the temporal sequence of knowledge reversed the logical sequence of the argument. The logical form went something like: "If frame of reference X, then behavior B," but the temporal sequence was to discern 'frame of reference X' after observing 'behavior B'. To gain a more rigorous foundation for the concept, it was desired to develop a "frame of reference" under controlled conditions, *i.e.,* experimentally.

To control the possibility of potentially intruding factors, *e.g.,* the possibility of a pre-existing frame of reference), the basic condition was to insure an absence of a frame of reference. The knowledge of auto-kinetic phenomena led to the experimental design. It was long known that a fixed light in an otherwise darkened space gave the appearance of motion. Since no physical position could be attached to the space of motion, no ordinary frame of reference could be employed.

Three hypotheses occurred to Professor Muzafer Sherif.[10] One was that an individual, after a number of trials, would eventually hit upon a projected norm of the amount of movement, and that this norm would result from a basis of judgment subjectively defined. That is, in the absence of an external frame of reference, a subjective one would be evolved. The proof would lie in the existence of a consistent pattern of estimation of motion; erratic judgments would falsify the hypothesis.

The second hypothesis was that a group of individuals would neither give a hodgepodge of individual judgments, but would show a group consensus. If the latter were true, and we could argue that a group norm had been established, what would be the effect of the group norm on individual judgments? The third hypothesis was that the group norm would persist and become the frame of reference for the individual judgment. The verification of this hypothesis warrants the inference that a frame of reference had been produced under controlled conditions.

---

[9] Had the subjects been human beings, the amount of "random activity" may have been a type of drive-reduction, *i.e.,* in certain situations a social value, and hence a drive, to "do something" exists. This implies a conviction that "some activity is better than nothing," even if the activity is logically unrelated to other goals or wishes. An example may be found in the experience of many soldiers during the World War II who, in critical front-line actions, preferred to be doing something to relatively pure idleness. This preference was made even if the only inferential result was the reduction of tension. In other words, human beings might not always behave like white rats in essentially the same experimental set-up.

[10] Mazafer Sherif and Hadley Cantril, *The Psychology of Ego-Involvements*, (N.Y.: John Wiley & Sons, 1947), p. 52 ff.

Accordingly, a darkened room was chosen, and the stimulus light (five meters from the subjects) was a tiny point of light controlled by a shutter operated by the experimenter. One group of individuals were first tested for individual judgments. A second group consisted of individuals without previous experience, but who were to arrive at a group judgment. Later, some of these were to make individual judgments. A third group consisted of those who had made individual judgments and who later made group judgments.

Briefly, the data tended to verify the major hypotheses. To be sure, there was considerable fluctuations. In the group situations, however, much of the fluctuation was a group phenomenon: the norms differed for each session, perhaps, but it was the group which fluctuated.

Despite the schematic presentation of this design, it is possible to discuss ways in which one could increase the amount of control over the behavior of the subjects. For one thing, in the group situation, the personalities of the subjects have been uncontrolled. If personality can be typed along a leader-follower continuum, the composition of the groups in terms of this variable could conceivably result in changes of the resultant norms. That is, if a group consisted of "followers," the emergent norm might have a different pattern than if the group consisted of both "leaders" and "followers."[11] As an exercise, the reader should consider other possible variables and decide how these may be controlled in future research designs.

7. Experimental Design: Sociological Theory

If group A believes that group B is interfering with the attainment of its goals, are hostilities likely to break out between them? Admitting the possibility of a "precipitating factor," most sociologists would agree that hostilities are likely. Can this point be experimentally demonstrated?

To demonstrate the correctness of the statement, several things must be experimentally created. The individuals selected to comprise the groups must not merely be a congregation of discrete personalities, but must be members of a social group. That is, there must be some structure, some identity of self, and a "consciousness of kind." Further, the belief that B is interfering with A must be subject to experimental control. In other words, the members of group A ought not begin with the notion that group B is "against them." Finally, the precipitating factor must be subjected to control by the experimenter. Granting the experimental creation of the two groups and the experimental creation of inter-group tensions, it is possible that hostilities could begin without the intervention of the experimenter. In this case, however, the precise situation leading to hostilities would not be well enough known to permit rigorous inference.

[11] At the time this was being written (1953), further research in this problem area, particularly in an attempt to be more rigorous statistically, was being pursued by the staff of the Urban Life Research Institute at Tulane University. It is not, obviously, a dead problem.

To determine whether or not such an experiment was feasible, Sherif[12] made a study on a group of 24 boys from the lower-middle class income group in the New Haven area. The deliberate attempt was made to secure a homogeneity of background: similarity of religious affiliation (19 belonging to the same denomination), educational experience and backgrounds. None were behavior problems, all more or less "normal," with about average I.Q. The boys were enrolled in a summer camp.

The initial stage of the experiment allowed the boys to develop their own friendship patterns. In the second stage, when the two groups were to be "created," the friendship patterns were deliberately broken: 65% of those who were put in the "Bulldogs" group preferred friends who were put in the "Red Devils" group, and vice versa. Thus, later hostilities between the two groups would have to overcome those friendship feelings which had not been "controlled" in any way. Later on, some 95% of the Red Devils were to prefer boys from that group for friends; this compares with the 35% at the beginning of stage II.

Stage II, then, can be called the stage of in-group formation. Activities of the boys were designed to create a feeling of group membership and identity of the group as such. Opportunities were created in which the individual participants could "show their stuff," and in that way be accepted as worthwhile members of the groups. Rewards were made on a group basis, rather than to individual stars. In this period, leadership patterns emerged, and data were carefully recorded which permit the inference of group solidarity.

In stage III, open competition between the groups was fostered. Ball games, and tugs-of-war were engaged in. While the Bulldogs tended to win, the Red Devils developed group rationalizations for their losses. A general pattern of prejudice developed, and the conception of the Bulldogs as "cheaters" typified the attitude of the Red Devils.

Certain frustrating experiences were carefully manipulated by the experimenters, so designed that the "blame" would fall on the other group. Towards the end of the experiment, a big party was held for the two groups. Half of the food was slightly damaged (*e.g.,* the cake crushed), and the Red Devils, being allowed to eat first, were told to take their share. They took the good food. When the Bulldogs entered, they saw the damaged goods, and attributed it to the other group. Some wanted to fight immediately, but they decided to eat what they could. They retired to a corner and began to hurl insults at the Red Devils. When the Red Devils went to leave, one Bulldog was seen putting an empty ice cream carton on the Red Devils' table. This lead to physical contact, and one Bulldog opened a knife and had to be restrained.

This led to a series of raids and fights between the two groups which had to be stopped. Though the experiment had ended with the production

---

[12] Muzafer Sherif, "A Preliminary Experimental Study of Intergroup Relations," Chapter 17 of *Social Psychology at the Crossroads,* edited by John H. Rohrer and Muzafer Sherif. (N.Y.: Harper & Bros., 1951).

of open hostilities, those in charge of the study then attempted to minimize the extent of the conflict. To some extent, they were successful.
But on the last night, the two groups wanted to be by themselves "for
the last time."

This study shows quite clearly that by careful manipulation, true
social groups can be formed. It is also possible to instill beliefs in the
minds of group members antagonistic to members of the out-group.
Moreover, open hostilities can be produced under controlled conditions.

One striking thing about the study is the attempt at control over
variables. Notice, for example, that none of the boys were "behavior
problems"; yet the pattern of physical fighting and even drawing a
knife resulted from the hostile attitudes. Note, also, the careful way in
which a potentially interfering variable was put to good use in the design.
The original friendship patterns were broken and surmounted. Despite
earlier feelings of friendship, *group* antagonism was indeed possible. Had
the two groups been originally composed of these "natural friendships,"
the strength of the experiment would have been weakened.

Of course, some basic elements were not controlled. As Sherif points
out all of these boys came from a culture which accepts and emphasizes
the competitive role in society. Whether the same results could have
been obtained from a sample of boys drawn from a non-competitive
culture could not be answered by this experiment.

8. Experimental Design: Communication Theory

Does the "pressure" of members of a group to communicate to other
members of the group about some item, say x, increase with increases
in the cohesiveness of the group? Assuming, for the argument, that all
other factors are either constant or irrelevant, the answer seems to be
yes. We may have begged the question insofar as the item x may be
concerned: it may be such an irrelevant item that there never is any
"pressure" to communicate about it. Or, the mores of the group may be
such as to exclude communication about the item, irrespective of the
amount of cohesiveness or, perhaps, lack of cohesiveness might bring
about discussion, *i.e.,* communication. An example would be "sex" in
the Victorian family group.

Limiting our concern, then, to topics which are of generic interest
to the group, we might wish to demonstrate the affirmative answer to
our question. That is, we may phrase the question as an hypothesis and
strive to test it experimentally. This was done by members of the Research Center for Group Dynamics, Institute of Social Research, at the
University of Michigan.[13] They defined "cohesiveness of a group" as
"the resultant of all the forces acting on the members to remain in the
group."[14] They further identified the significant forces as the attractiveness

---

[13] Leon Festinger, Kurt Back, and others, *Theory and Experiment in Social Communication,* Ann Arbor, Michigan, Research Center for Group Dynamics, Institute for Social Research, 1950.

[14] *Ibid.,* p. 7.

of the group in terms of the prestige of the group, the personal attraction of the members, and the activities engaged in. In any experimental test of their hypothesis, these "forces" must be controlled and, if possible, measured in some way.

The action to be engaged in by the participants consisted of (1) looking at a set of pictures. The participants were paired, and each pair member got a slightly different set of pictures. They were separately to (2) write a story about these pictures and, subsequently, were to (3) discuss their story with their pair partner for possible revisions. The experimenters were then to trace the patterns of agreement and direction of influence which occurred.

The operational definition for the three measures of cohesiveness are, essentially, these: (a) The personal attractiveness of the members was dichotomized into "low" and "high" cohesiveness. Those in the "low" category were given the usual instructions and then some comment on how they had tried to match group members to get compatible people together, but in this case, they could only get the main points. Those in the "high" category were told that the pair matched very high and that the two would like each other a lot.

(b) The attractiveness of the activity of the group was also dichotomized into "low" and "high" categories. Those in the low cohesiveness category were told they were to use their imagination and to strive for a high score. Those in the "high" cohesiveness category were promised a reward. Both groups were told that they could not be matched on personality factors, except that the main objections had been met. The third force, (c) the attractiveness of the prestige of the group, was also dichotomized into low and high categories. In the "low" category, the comments were of the order that their lab instructors had said they would be particularly good material for a good group. For the "high" category, they were told that they had all of the qualifications which were needed for success in the task and that this pair should be the best group, and could be used as a model in subsequent instruction.

Table 25, below, gives the mean number of changes in the stories which were influenced by the partner. It is seen that, in each type of "force," there were more changes in the high cohesiveness category than in the low one, just as one would expect by the hypothesis. The question

TABLE 25. MEAN NUMBER OF CHANGES IN STORIES WHICH WERE INFLUENCED BY THE PARTNER

	Nature of Attraction To Group		
	Personal Attraction	Task Direction	Group Prestige
Low Cohesive Pairs	7.9	8.9	6.7
High Cohesive Pairs	10.5	11.0	8.3

Source: Adapted from *Ibid.*, p. 31, with verbal permission of senior author.

becomes, is this a significant finding, or is this a chance relationship? The question was answered by use of analysis of variance. These means were different at about the 10% level of significance. This implies that if we were using the 5% level, we could not reject chance.

We are not so much interested here in the fact that the significance level in support of the hypothesis was not reached as we are in an assessment of the operations performed. We might first question the existence of a "group" in a sociological sense. The simple fact of taking two people in the same room and have them talk about a common subject does not necessarily imply that a group exists. One might arbitrarily define a group to include such a situation; but science is public and the term "group" must be defined in other than idiosyncratic fashion.

We might also question the validity of the operations defining the various "forces resulting in the members remaining in the group." It might well be that the variable which the experimenters were really measuring was the psychological dimension of "suggestibility" rather than the sociological one of group cohesiveness. Certainly, one could argue just as plausibly in favor of "suggestibility" as one could for "cohesiveness." The alternative arguments appear equally strong. As a result, we must admit that the results from this experiment are not very conclusive. Insofar as the operations do measure the variables in question, we can have confidence in the direction of the findings. But, on the contrary, insofar as the operations fail to measure the variables in question, we must question the findings.

The purpose of the criticism is not to suggest the fundamental inadequacy of the experimental method in testing hypotheses such as these. The logic of experimentation is untouched by the criticisms offered. Rather, we seek to point out, and the authors of the volume cited certainly agree, that experimentation is a difficult task. Particularly difficult is the development of a set of operations upon which general agreement can be obtained. The fact that agreement about the operations is lacking is not, methodologically, a deterent to future experimentation. One can, if not ego-involved in the particular experimental design, learn much from failure and criticism. The subsequent experimenter, at least, can face up to some of the criticims of which the original experimenter was unaware.

9. Some Limits on Experimentation

The experiment is a very convincing argument. The logical sequence and the temporal sequence of the argument are the same. A temporal fact is built into the design: first one creates the antecedent and then one observes the consequent. This temporal sequence serves to distinguish relationships which can be called "associational" from those which can be termed "causal." By illustration, the relationship between hair color and eye color is associational; presumably, both are a function of the same underlying genetic variable. The relation between hostile attitudes towards and outgroup and subsequent hostilities is not merely associational. The time sequence makes a difference.

However desirable experimentation may be, we must be careful not to define scientific method as experimentation. As we have indicated time and again, the critical point is the problem and the type of data necessary to solve the problem. If these are not amenable to experimentation, then other research designs are necessary.

Whether or not a problem is suited to experimentation is not merely a theoretical issue. There are many practical considerations which are involved. The data necessary to any research design must be available before the design can be carried out and if research is carried out in a social situation, that situation may prevent the acquisition of the necessary data.

In a recent study[15] direct observation of members of a bureaucracy led to the inference that the bureaucrat "individualized" (rather than "personalized") his relationships to his clients. Since the clientele proved to attach no significance to this type of behavior, the hypothesis was suggested that this behavior was a political "buffer" against negative public reaction. The hypothesis could have been tested experimentally. It is conceivable that the bureaucrats could have acted indifferently and even churlishly towards the clientele. Had the hypothesis been correct, a negative reaction should have been evidenced, perhaps by letters to editors of the local papers. However remote or likely that eventuality would have been, the manager of the office could not take that risk. A negative public reaction was precisely what he sought to avoid, even if the hypothesis had been wrong. It would have been impossible to put the claims of scientific method ahead of the claims of the office manager.

The social limitations to experimentation must be taken into account in research design. In addition to difficulty of deducing manipulable variables, which itself limits the possibility of sociological experimentation, the social situation in which the research must take place needs to be taken into account. Moreover, the social situation is not always as specific as the cited. Suppose, for example, a psychologist had a hypothesis which, if true, would render a person permanently insane. Would the social values of the American culture permit an experimental test of the hypothesis? Obviously not: the consequences to the individual compete with norms which are more basic to our culture than the norm for scientific knowledge. In contrast, perhaps, we should point out the kind of experiments on human beings were permitted during the Nazi regime in Germany. At the same time that the Nazi government permitted deprivation studies to be conducted on interned Jews, other experiments which would, if successful, contradict the ethic of racism could not be conducted.

---

[15] Reference is made to a research on bureaucracy conducted by Roy G. Francis and Robert C. Stone, under the auspices of the Urban Life Research Institute of Tulane University and will be published elsewhere.

The ethical problems underlying experimental research have other connotations. One fundamental issue is whether or not the subject has a moral right to know that he is the subject of an experiment. One by-product of the Western Electric studies[16] is the knowledge that an experimental group will often behave differently simply because it is known to be an experimental group. The study cited indicated that the experimental group had higher production levels simply because the participants knew they were "special." Thus, the knowledge that one is the subject of an experiment tends towards a bias in the results obtainable. This is not particularly surprising; but the problem it raises is not easily resolved.

There is no unique solution to the problem. Whatever answer one gives is contingent upon his own system of values, and the relative hierarchy of claims of science and other considerations. We should not expect a categorical solution, nor even a pragmatic one; the pragmatic solution is acceptable only in terms of a pragmatic ethic. It is simply an issue which the individual scientist, operating in his own social context, must work out. The solution he arrives at, however, will determine largely whether or not certain types of experiments are possible.

The limitations to social experimentation have not been exhausted in this brief summary. The student can easily discover other limitations for himself. He may also find comfort in the position that experimental designs do not exhaust scientific methodology. The old saying that astronomy has done well without experimentally producing a universe is well taken.

10. Ex Post Facto Design

Ultimately, all experiments become reduced to propositional form. The theoretical antecedents are stated propositionally. The operations by which empirical members of the theoretical antecedents are identified are similarly reduced to propositions. Propositions about the basic data are made. The conclusion is presented as a proposition. These are made a part of a logical form, and the correctness of the propositions may be communicated to other scientists, and the correctness of the inferences may be judged.

Many before-and-after events take place in the world about us. In particular, in the social world, a set of conditions is defined to be a "social problem" (*e.g.*, slum conditions after having shown to be associated with delinquency). A social policy is adopted purporting to change some of the "bad" conditions, in the hope that the "problem" is reduced. An example is low-cost housing to reduce delinquency. If the necessary data could be re-captured, this could also be reduced to propositional form, and conclusions about the effectiveness of the policy can be reached. If the policy did indeed manipulate relevant variables, the result is quite similar to a description of an experiment.

---

[16] For an account of Elton Mayo's findings in this regard see F. J. Roethlisberger and William J. Dickson, *Management and the Worker,* (Cambridge, Mass.: Harvard University Press, 1939).

These considerations prompted Professor F. Stuart Chapin to design what he called "ex post facto experiments."[17] The term "ex post facto" indicates that the "experiment" has already taken place. The "consequence" is immediately knowable, and the problem is to determine the antecedents which gave rise to the consequence. The manipulation, performed by others than the social scientist, has already taken place. But some manipulation has occurred: a time dimension is indeed present and if any relation between the manipulated variable and the consequence can be discerned, the argument is more than "merely" that of association.[18]

The initial phase in the ex post facto design would be the identification of the experimental group, *e.g.,* the group which had been admitted to a housing project. The next phase would be the identification of a control group. The control group would have to be equatable with the experimental group prior to the "experiment." Formally, this means that both groups must be random samples from the same universe. It happens, however, that the administrators of a housing project are not likely to draw subjects randomly, but will use a set of criteria which, practically, is defensible but which, scientifically, is biasing. Thus, they may have some criterion of need, with the result that only a small portion of the population of which the control group is a random sample is taken. The experimental design will have to overcome such biases.

It takes a certain amount of time for a social experiment to have an effect. Consider the problematic data as "amount of juvenile delinquency": if better housing results in lowering the amount of delinquency, it may take years before the difference is significant. During this time a certain amount of "mortality" occurs: people leaving both the project and the control group by death, migration, refusal to cooperate further in the study, etc. It also happens that the effect of mortality differs for the two groups, and that the reasons for mortality also differ. Hence, a practical problem exists in maintaining a constant equatability for the two groups.

In addition to the "gross mortality." This simply means that out of an initial number of subjects, with increasing rigor in the design, the number studied in the final analysis is sharply reduced. The problems of ex post facto design, in particular reference to "effective mortality" can be illustrated by citing a well-known experiment of this type.

One of the justifications for increasing expenditures for the school system of any locality is that the high school graduate is better prepared for economic success than those without high school training. There are other "reasons," of course, but this is a particularly critical one, *i.e.,* its consequences are "practical." We can re-state this as a formal hypothesis;

[17] F. Stuart Chapin, *Experimental Designs in Sociological Research* (N.Y.: Harper & Bros., 1947).

[18] The use of the word "experiment" has been challenged since direct manipulation by the scientist is not possible. Without clouding our thinking by introducing semantic issues, we should recognize that the same type of problem is pursued by "experimentation" and the ex post facto "experiment," namely, the addition of the time factor between the antecedent and the consequent.

or, for the sake of consistency with a statistical terminology, as a null hypothesis.

Prior to stating the hypothesis, we must clearly identify what we will mean by "economic success." Simplicity, at least, would require the single most-meaningful measure obtainable. The measure of success was to be taken in the year 1935; the impact of the depression had been fully appreciated. Since this was a critical depression year, the measure of success would be the percent of job shifts from 1926 (the year the high school graduates graduated) to 1935 that involved either an increase in salary or no change in salary as contrasted to the percent of shifts that did involve a decrease in salary. This measure of success might not be as meaningful in a period of economic growth and inflation as it was during the depression years. Whether or not a different operation identifying success during periods of inflation would give different results is a matter of further research. One persistent problem in the ex post facto design is the possible limitation inherent in the time-space matrix within which the "experiment" takes place.

The null hypothesis would be that, "other things being equal," there is no significant difference in economic success as measured between those who graduated from high school in 1926 and those who dropped out of high school in 1926 (in St. Paul, Minnesota, at least).

Out of a total group of 2127 students, 1130 graduated and 997 dropped out of school in 1926. In 1935 1194 were interviewed; the gross mortality amounted to 933 students. The hypothesis postulated an equality of conditions other than high school graduation. If the reasons for dropping out of school are correlated with economic success, then nothing new has been added by the hypothesis being tested. Accordingly, background factors known to be related to economic success must be "controlled," lest interfering variables hide or otherwise change the results.

When the experimental group and the control group were matched (on a group percentage basis) for five controls (father's occupation, parental nativity, neighborhood, age and sex), the total number of usable cases was reduced from 1194 to 400. When a sixth control, average high school grades, was added, the number of usable cases was reduced to 290. When the background factors were matched individually, 23 graduates were matched with 23 non-graduates. Evidently, effective mortality takes a big toll.

When the experimental and control groups were matched proportionately for the six control factors, 88.7% of the graduates had either an increase in salary or no change, while 83.4% of the non-graduates would similarly be judged to have had economic success. When the experimental and control groups were individually matched for the six control factors, 92% of the high school graduates had a successful economic adjustment while only 58% of the non-graduates were similarly successful. In this case, the additional labor seems to have been repaid in greater precision. However, it must be pointed out, that the relationship between high school education and economic success *might* have been shown to be smaller with more control. As Chapin comments, "Whether the analysis confirms the hypothesis or disproves it is a consideration entirely irrelevant to the experimental method."[19] The important fact is that to increase precision allows us to get closer to the underlying relationship.

11. Summary

Experimentation does not define "science"; it is possible to obtain rigorous results without it. However, experimentation seems to carry strong conviction along with rigorous proof.

Experimentation is possible when variables are amenable to control; it is desirable when time is an important dimension in the proof. Indeed, the power of experimentation resides in the correspondence of the temporal sequence of research and the logical sequence of the argument.

We have noted some elementary forms of experimentation in psychology, social psychology, sociology, and communication theory. We can notice, further, the difficulties surrounding the ways in which theoretical variables may be operationally defined. Despite the limitations known to adhere to the examples given, the difficulty of conducting an experiment should not be used to exclude experimentation from social science.

At the same time, we must be aware of certain extra-scientific limitations to experimentation. Science is conducted in a social situation; and in the social sciences the values of the broader culture prevent the utilization of many known techniques. Hence, to continue to do rigorous research we must look for ways to use the logic of experimentation without being able to use direct manipulation of our variables.

The fact that much control stems from randomization as well as manipulation led to the development of the "ex post facto design." To be sure, this is not a perfect substitute for experimentation; but it is a completely honest recognition of the social situation in which much of social science is currently being conducted.

SELECTED REFERENCES

Churchman, C. West, *Theory of Experimental Inference* (New York: Macmillan Company, 1948).
Fisher, Ronald A., *The Design of Experiments* (Edinburgh: Oliver & Boyd, 1935).
Greenwood, Ernest, *Experimental Sociology* (Morningside Heights, N. Y.: King's Crown Press, 1945).
Lacey, Oliver L., *Statistical Methods in Experimentation* (New York: Macmillan Company, 1953).

---

[19] Chapin, *op. cit.*, p. 107.

Chapter 6

SCALING TECHNIQUES IN SOCIAL RESEARCH*

SCALING techniques belong to that general field of science dealing with *the definition of concepts*. A basic problem in any research project is how to define the variable being studied. Measurement can proceed only after one has solved this problem of definition. Scaling techniques provide a valuable tool for help in *deriving definitions* and *permitting measurement* in terms of these definitions.

Let us suppose that one is faced with the problem of determining the reliability and validity of such statements as "Most factory workers are satisfied with their jobs," "Pretty girls are not very intelligent," "Inter-group contact decreases prejudice." One cannot proceed very far in research on these hypotheses without facing the problem of defining such concepts as "job satisfaction," "beauty," "intelligence," and "prejudice." Certainly one cannot hope to measure until the problem of definition has been satisfactorily solved.

How then do scaling techniques attempt to solve the problem of definition and measurement? Like most problems of definition, they proceed first by listing the characteristics of the object to be defined. This list of characteristics must then be analyzed for reliability and validity. And this is where scaling techniques come into the picture. Through the analysis of the *interrelationship* of the proposed list of defining characteristics, scaling techniques attempt to do four main things: (1) eliminate irrelevant items; (2) eliminate confusing items; (3) separate and classify items according to different dimensions; and (4) assign relative weights to the different items.

The successful operation of a scaling procedure therefore should produce for the researcher a series of items each of which has been tested for relevance to the concept being defined and for clarity of understanding. Furthermore, the various items will have been grouped or classified according to the different dimensions involved in the definition of the concept, or if it proves to contain only one definition, the uni-dimensionality of the concept will be established.

1. Basic Concepts of Scaling

At this stage it is important to understand three basic concepts or assumptions involved in most scaling procedures: (1) There exists for any object being defined or measured an unlimited number of possible characterizing or defining items. This is often referred to as the *universe of content*. (2) Any definition or measurement of this object will be

---

* Written by Edward A. Suchman and Roy G. Francis.

123

based on only a selected sample of items from this total universe. (3) A definition to permit quantitative measurement must consist of a uni-dimensional continuum.

The above three restrictions force the researcher to consider such questions as: "How shall I find items which belong to the universe of content in which I am interested?" "How broad or narrow should I make this universe of content?" "Will other social scientists accept the items I have selected as defining the concept in which I am interested?" "Do the 'manifest' or actual items I am using represent the 'latent' concept in which I am interested?" "Am I using enough items and a representative sample of items to permit me to test the reliability and validity of the proposed scale?" "Am I combining only those items that have the same meaning so that I can order along a single continuum?" 'Should I sub-divide these items into separate dimensions or factors?"

Until one has answered the above questions, one cannot proceed with assurance to "measure" individuals or objects. A ranking of individuals which is not based upon answers to the above questions may be both un-reliable and invalid. To be sure there are different degrees to which one can satisfactorily answer these questions, and in some cases one may not be able to answer all of them due to practical research considerations, or one may be forced to assume that the answers would be forthcoming satis-factorily if one had additional data, but certainly the further one proceeds actually to offer evidence in answer to these questions, the better one will have solved the problem of measurement. The systematic analysis of a series of items in an attempt to answer these questions permits one to state with greater confidence that the concept is being defined in terms of the inherent structure of the natural phenomenon and is not the result of an arbitrary and artificial classification or ordering.

2. Relation of Scaling to Other Forms of Measurement

The analysis problem one is faced with when one contemplates using scaling techniques is how to analyze simultaneously a series of observations or answers to several questions. There are three basic approaches one can use in order to analyze a series of items:

First, one can attempt to secure a uni-dimensional scale which would permit one to rank or order people according to their response on the several items involved. This problem of rank order measurement is the basic motivation for making a scale analysis. If the items form a scale, one can then score people as indicated by the scale analysis and rank them from more to less along a single continuum of meaning.

Second, one may find that the items do not fit into a single dimension but rather consist of two or more dimensions. In such a case it is impos-sible to rank individuals and one proceeds to form types or classes. These procedures are discussed in a separate chapter on typological classification.

Third, one may proceed to analyze the various items in terms of some arbitrary index or summary score. Such an index is usually a custom-made formula which permits one to summarize the responses of individuals to a series of items. Such indices usually are not based upon a logical attempt to test dimensionality as in the previous two measures.

Scale analysis then represents a decision on the part of the researcher to analyze his data in terms of logical dimensions. Usually the basis for this decision is the desire to secure a rank ordering of individuals or objects along some single continuum. The purpose of this chapter is to indicate the major forms of scaling techniques and to discuss their relative value.

3. Types of Scales

The kind of scale with which we will be concerned is usually called an "ordinal" scale. This means that the scores assigned to the various scale steps represent a rank order which permits one to say that a score of 4 is higher than a score of 2. However, such "ordinal" scales do not have any inherent metric; that is, the distance between the scores is of unknown size so that while one knows that a score of 4 is higher than a score of 2, one cannot say that a score of 4 is *twice* a score of 2. This type of rank order measurement constitutes the main bulk of "quantification" in the social sciences.

Other types of scales are the "interval" scales which permit not only the rank order of an "ordinal" scale but also offer a metric which permits one to divide the scale into equal-distant units. The highest type of scale is a "ratio" scale which not only permits a rank order with a known metric but also offers an absolute zero point along this scale offering a consistent starting point for measurement. A fourth type of scale has been called a "nominal" scale, but such a scale does not have any logical basis of measurement behind it. Such scales are basically classifications in which a number is given to the various types contained in the classification. Such numbers are usually meaningless and might better be given as letters. They permit neither a rank ordering nor a known metric.

4. Units of Scaling

While the greatest amount of attention in the development of scales has been devoted to the determination of a rank order for individuals, it is important to remember that these techniques are not limited by the type of object being measured. At the present time most of the problems in scaling are limited to the ranking of people. However, there is good reason to believe that an extension of scaling techniques to other aspects of measurement would also be beneficial.

We may classify all aspects of social existence into three general categories—people, situations or occasions, and concepts or variables. We are concerned either with the study of individuals, in which case we attempt to classify or rank people, or we may be interested in the study of situations or occasions involving a comparison or analysis of different occurrences, or, finally, we may be concerned with the analysis and comparison of different variables or concepts. *Any one of these three forms of measurement may constitute the focus of a scale analysis.*

Scale analysis is one form of multivariate analysis, that is to say that whenever we are faced with the problem of analyzing simultaneously a *number* or series of measurements either of people, situations, or concepts, we must determine some technique for studying the interrelationships of the different measures.

We may summarize the various types of measurement problems by looking at the interrelationship between the three basic aspects of measurement. First, holding our situation constant, we may scale people for a series of variables. Given a population of people who respond to a series of items, we attempt to determine the dimensionality of the items and then to rank the people according to this dimension. These are the so-called Q-scales and represent the most common type used today.

Still keeping the situation constant, we may also attempt to scale a population of variables for a collection of people. In this case our main emphasis is to rank the different variables or objects by analyzing the order they have for a group of people. The best examples of this to date are the so-called "object scales" developed by Riley at Rutgers. These scales are commonly called R-scales.

Secondly, we may hold the variable constant and study either scales of people for a population of situations, or scales of situations for a population of people. The former may be called S-scales and have recently been studied by Stouffer in an attempt to define and measure role behavior. Since roles may be defined as the behavior of an individual in different situations, this seems to be a promising development. Using a series of different situations, we now attempt to scale people according to some unidimensional aspects of role behavior (if the test succeeds in indicating such uni-dimensionality).

The scale of situations for a population of people may be called a T-scale and represents on a non-conceptual level the common measure of test-retest reliability. Holding the variable constant, we attempt to study the dimensionality of different situations for a population of people. Where this situation is a repetition of a previous one, we have the common test of reliability. However, this is a rather unimaginative and limited use of such comparative situation tests. It would be much more interesting to test a series of situations in terms of conceptual stability or dimensionality rather than purely methodological reliability. This statement of the problem seems to make better sense out of some of the current problems revolving around a distinction between reliability *vs.* meaningful change.

Finally, we may hold the people constant and study the scalability of situations for a population of variables and the scalability of variables for a population of situations. The former are commonly called O-scales and involve the problem of situational analysis wherein our concern is with the ordering of situations based upon the arrangement of variables observed in the situation. The second type, called P-scales, involves the ranking of variables based upon the measurement of these variables in different situations. These have traditionally been called trait or personality scales wherein the emphasis is upon the internal organization within a single individual of different variables under different situational conditions. This is a clinical concept implying a measure of the dimensionality of the individual's personality organization.

These various scales may be diagrammatically represented by the following model based upon these three main axes of people, situations, and variables.[1]

O & P—Sit. x Variables . People
Q & R—People x Variables . Sit.
S & T—People x Sit. . Variables

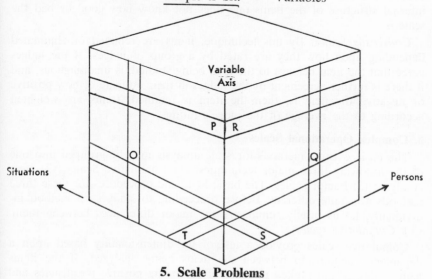

5. Scale Problems

PART A. SCALING TECHNIQUES

There are four main ways in which a scale problem can be attacked. Each of these methods, while aimed at the same general problem of developing a uni-dimensional rank order, does have a fairly different approach to the problem. It is important to recognize that these methods are all operational and subject to revision depending upon the specific problem one is attacking. If one can master the basic procedure for each of these four methods, one will be in a position to improvise a scaling technique most adequate to a particular problem.

a. Judgmental Scales

Arbitrary Scales: Before discussing these methods, it might be worthwhile to describe very quickly the many variations of scaling that are based upon arbitrary counting or weighting procedures. Quite often one will find that a scale is being used which consists of nothing more than an arbitrary addition of responses to a series of questions or items. This procedure does

---

[1] This approach was suggested by an article by R. B. Cattell, "The Three Basic Factor-Analytic Research Designs," *Psych. Bull.,* Sept. 1952. This article suggests some interesting mathematical transformations from one type of scale to another.

not constitute an adequate test of a scale but rather provides an arbitrary index which tells little about the underlying structure of the items being analyzed. Such scales are really nominal scales and do not provide any test for an underlying single continuum. This means that the researcher has no assurance that the rank order determined by the arbitrary counting procedure has reliability. Changing the weights of the items can completely change the rank order. Adding new items may have the same effect.

This does not mean that scales constructed by arbitrary counting procedures are all bad. What it does mean is that until one has studied the internal structure of the items one does not know how good or bad the scale is.

Consensus Scales: By this technique, items are retained or eliminated depending upon how they are rated by a group of judges. If the judges agree that the item belongs to the area being studied, is unambiguous, and if there is further agreement by the judges in their estimate of how positive or negative the item is, then the item is retained. Items are weighted according to the average of the judge's ratings.

b. Complex Operational Scales

The basic existing methods for scale analysis may be grouped into one of the following three major techniques: (1) Cumulative Scales; (2) Item Analysis; (3) Factor Scales. The basic logic and procedures for these three methods are quite different. Before proceeding to study each method individually, let us briefly summarize the major differences between them.

(1) Cumulative scales

Cumulative scales provide a test of uni-dimensionality based upon a dependent relationship between the items being analyzed. If the items being analyzed are ranked in order of ascending positive frequencies and descending negative frequencies, and if individuals are ranked in order of descending positive scores, the resulting pattern of responses forms a parallelogram. The presence of this pattern indicates that endorsement (or presence) of an item indicative of an extreme position should be accepted by endorsement of all items indicative of a less extreme position. Furthermore, people (or objects) occupying the same scale position should have the same response characteristics. This means that one can reproduce all responses of an individual given his scale score.

The cumulative nature of this scale is indicated by the fact that people in higher scale positions have all of the characteristics of people in lower scale positions plus at least one additional positive response. We will study this pattern in more detail when we take up the specific computational procedures.

(2) Item Analysis Techniques:

According to this technique, items are selected for inclusion in this scale dependent upon their relationship to the total score of the scale. If an item discriminates between individuals with high and low scores, the item becomes a part of the final scale series. Sometimes these items are given different weights depending upon the size of their relationship to the total scale.

(3) *Factor Scales:*

If it can be shown by a study of the intercorrelation of the items that a common factor is present which accounts for the existence of the relationship between items, then the items are said to contain a common factor. By a study of the manifest relationships between items it is possible to determine the probability that any series of items will "fit" a predetermined latent structure.

These three methods then constitute the basic forms of scale analysis existent today. While each of them attempts to solve the same problem, that is to rank individuals along a continuum depending upon their responses to a series of questions, each of them proceeds by rather different logic and technique. We will now examine each of these techniques briefly.

It is impossible in a preliminary text book to present the step by step details for each of these techniques. The student is referred to the references at the end of this chapter for computational procedures. We will present below the basic steps involved in each of the methods but cannot give enough detail to cover all specific problems.

PART B. OPERATIONAL PROCEDURES

a. Cumulative Scale

Let there be n items to which the s subjects can dichotomously respond, positively and negatively (n and s both being integers). If these items can be ordered in such a way that the positive response to the ith item implies a positive response to all succeeding items while a negative response to the ith item implies nothing about response to subsequent items, a cumulative scale may be said to exist.

The problem of arriving at the proper sequence or order of items can be approached two ways. It may be hypothesized *a priori* that the items will fall into a certain sequence. This hypothesis is most easily rejected and depends for its utility upon a strong body of theory and previous research. There are no existent examples of this kind of scale.

The second approach is an *ad hoc* one. In this case, one simply tries to get the best possible ordering out of all the response patterns which exist. This activity requires a criterion before one can agree that the best ordering has been found. Currently, this criterion is the "Coefficient of Reproducibility" and will be explained below. Right now, however, we should point out that no theoretical reason for this criterion exists. It is simply a convenient empirical "rule of thumb."

If there are n items, each having two possible responses, 2^n possible response patterns can emerge. Out of this we want only $n + 1$ patterns. These we will call "scale types" and all other we will call "non-scale types." We will describe a simple way of obtaining the best possible scale if n is small, say five or fewer.

If n is large, the operations are more complex and can become quite tedious. The student is referred to chapters two to nine in "Measurement and Prediction."[2] Those chapters were written by Louis Guttman, for whom this type of scale is often named. In it the use of Guttman's "Scalogram board" is described. Dr. Marvin Taves of the University of Minnesota has developed a "Simplified scalogram board" in which items and respondents can be treated freely and in any sequence.

Returning to the problem of developing a scale, suppose one wanted to scale "school spirit" at a hypothetical college and asked the following questions:

(1) Do you regularly attend intercollegiate debate sessions when held on this campus?

(2) Do you regularly attend theatrical performances given by the Speech Department?

(3) Do you regularly attend the concerts given by the Music Department?

(4) Do you regularly attend intercollegiate sporting events (*e.g.*, football and basketball)?

The first step would be to determine the proportion of affirmative responses to these questions. The next step is to create the initial sequence by ordering these questions from least to greatest proportion. These are shown in figure 10 below.

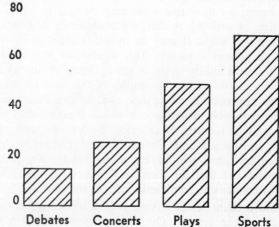

Figure 10.   Items arranged in initial sequence of percent favorable response.

[2] Samuel A. Stouffer, and others, *Measurement and Prediction.* Princeton, N. J., Princeton University Press, 1950.

The next step is to determine the existing response patterns and the number of members of each. *Fixing* the sequence as above, and denoting an affirmative response by $+$ and a negative response by $-$, we obtain the results in table 26, below.

TABLE 26. DISTRIBUTION OF RESPONSE PATTERNS
HAVING EMPIRICAL MEMBERS

Scale Type	Frequency	Non-Scale Type	Frequency
$+ + + +$	5	$+ - + +$	2
$- + + +$	8	$+ + - +$	1
		$+ - - +$	5
$- - + +$	22	$- + - +$	3
		$- + + -$	2
$- - - +$	23	$- - + -$	10
		$- + - -$	6
$- - - -$	11	$+ - - -$	1
Totals	69		31

The task is now simply to fit the "non-scale types" into the "scale types" in such a way that the amount of error is a minimum. For example, if the type $+ - + +$ were classified as belonging in type $+ + + +$, an error would be made in response to the second item, but none of the others. Had the same type ($+ - + +$) been classified as $- - + +$ there would have been an error in the first item only. Although some effort has been directed toward a unique solution to the issue of which alternative classification is right no completely satisfactory rule exists. However, had the type ($+ - + +$) been classified as $- - - +$ there would have been two errors. Clearly, if we hold as our criterion the minimization of error this would not be an admissible classification.

TABLE 27. THE COMPUTATION OF ERROR IN NEW CLASSIFICATION

	Frequency		
Scale Type Includes	Total for Type	Types With Error	Error
$+ + + +$	9		
$\quad + - + +$		3	3
$\quad + + - +$		1	1
$- + + +$	13		
$\quad - + - +$		3	3
$\quad - + + -$		2	2
$- - + +$	22	0	0
$- - - +$	28		
$\quad + - - +$		5	5
$- - - -$	28		
$\quad - - + -$		10	10
$\quad - + - -$		6	6
$\quad + - - -$		1	1
Totals	100		31

Note, that in any event, one assumes that the proper sequence of items exists. In our example, the single criterion of minimum error can be safely appealed to. But if there had been as many members of type $+ - + +$ as of type $- + + +$ the argument would be strained.

In table 27, the non-scale types are classified to the nearest scale type. Column one denotes the scale type including the former "non-scale type;" column two denotes the new frequency; column three denotes the number of predictive errors. This number of errors is the result of the following operations: (a) The number of predictive errors in each new classification of scale types is determined as before. (b) These are multiplied by the frequency of the old non-scale type, *e.g.,* putting $+ - + +$ into $+ + + +$ involves one error; $+ - + +$ had 3 members. Hence 3 predictive errors occur.

Summing the total number of errors gives us 31 misclassifications of item responses. Since each of the 100 individuals made 4 judgments, the proportion of error is 31 divided by $4(100) = 31/400 = .078$. The coefficient of reproducibility is simply this number subtracted from one, *i.e.,* $1 - .078 = .922$. This is above the rule of thumb. .90 reproducibility is the currently used criterion to judge scalability. Note, however, that 31% of the respondents were "non-scale types."

Note that, in table 27, we could have classified some non-scale types differently and obtain a different frequency distribution with the same coefficient of reproducibility. Thus type $- - + -$ which was classified as $- - - -$, with one error could have been classified as $- - + +$ with one error. Clearly the frequencies would have changed but the number of errors would remain constant. This means that, upon using a scale distribution in correlation with other variables one can obtain various results depending upon how the non-scale types were classified. The lack of a unique solution renders difficult the use of this scale to define a concept.

b. Item Analysis

It should not be imagined that "reproducibility" is a necessary aspect of measurement. Suppose one wanted to measure height by obtaining the lengths of the head, of the neck, of the trunk ,and of the legs. The sum of these would presumably give total height. Now a knowledge of total height does not imply a knowledge of the length of the separable parts. For most purposes this is an irrelevant consideration. The point, however, is clear. Reproducibility is not a necessary characteristic of measurement. Hence we are justified in assessing other types of scale construction.

One popular technique is item analysis. The argument is simple and direct. If any item has no correlation with a problematically relevant outside criterion it is rejected. For example, suppose that a scale was being developed for a study of marital adjustment. Suppose further that an item of the kind "Did you window-shop with your fiancé before marriage" was not correlated with divorce. Clearly, it would add no useful knowledge.

After a battery of items has been tested, the question becomes, "How much weight should a given item have?" This rests on the plausible grounds that the items most highly correlated with the problematic data are more important. Note that the question of weighting was irrelevant to the cumulative scale since any weighting system would have left the sequence of items unaltered. In this case, however, weighting is important.

One way of weighting items is to first obtain the amount of correlation, without extracting the square root. Then substract this number from one, and take the reciprocal of the result (*i.e.,* divide it into one). Symbolically, a weight would be obtained by $w = \dfrac{1}{1-r^2}$. As r^2 approaches one, w approaches infinity. This implies that if a single item is perfectly correlated with the problematic data further items are redundant, as r^2 approaches zero, w approaches one. If $r^2 = 0$, $w = 0$ by definition. W takes on the algebraic sign of r. Then if an individual agrees with the item in question he is given a score $= W$. If he disagrees with the item he is given a score $= (-1)(w)$. Thus, if W is negatively correlated with the criterion, and he agrees with the item, he obtains a negative score; but if he disagrees with the item, he obtains a positive score. One's total score is the sum of the scores for the n items which have been retained.

For the most part, one cannot compute a Pearsonian product—moment r for item analysis. The reason is that the responses to the item are usually dichotomous. A convenient way out is to compute ϕ^2. This is found by dividing χ^2 by N, *i.e.,* $\phi^2 = \dfrac{\chi^2}{N}$. For a 2 x 2 table—where the item and the outside criterion are both dichotomized—χ^2 can be found by $\chi^2 = \dfrac{(ad - bc)^2\,N}{(N_1 N_2)\,(_1 N_2)}$, where the letters are those found in table 28, below.

TABLE 28. A SHORT CUT—χ^2 TABLE

	Item		
	yes	no	
outside +	a	b	n_1
criterion −	c	d	n_2
	n_1	n_2	N

To illustrate with the previously mentioned example. Let the item be: "Did you discuss child-raising with your fiancé before marriage?"

Suppose that the relation between the responses to that question and divorce was as given below:

TABLE 29.   ANALYSIS OF ILLUSTRATION

	Item		
	yes	no	Total
Divorced	10	40	50
Not Divorced	90	60	150
	100	100	200

Then χ^2 would be

$$\chi^2 = \frac{[(10)(60) - (40)(90)]^2\ 200}{(100)(100)(50)(150)}$$

$$= \frac{(600 - 3600)^2\ 200}{(100)(100)(50)(150)}$$

$$= \frac{(-3000)(-3000)(200)}{(100)(100)(50)(150)}$$

$$= 24$$

This is clearly significant.

$\phi^2 = \dfrac{24}{200} = .12$, indicating low correlation. w $= \dfrac{1}{1-.12} = \dfrac{1}{.88} = 1.13$.

Since the table was constructed such that the correlation is negative, w $= -1.13$. Thus a note of caution must be sounded. The direction of correlation in 2 x 2 tables is largely a junction of the organization of the table which, in turn, is a junction of the wording of one question. Those using this technique to create a score should insure themselves that an affirmative response implies the direction of correlation which their hypothesis requires.

There are other bases for item anlysis. One such is the correlation between the response to a single item and the total score. Another involves the use of the critical ratio. The student might try to devise one of his own. In any event, each such score includes only those items which have a discriminatory power. These items are subsequently weighted according to some logical scheme.

c. Scale Construction with Factor Analysis.[3]

Suppose the solution of a research problem involved a *theoretical variable* "religiosity." The question "how can I identify objects having different amounts of this variable in the real world?" arises immediately. As a matter of fact, one could develop a set of operational measures of essentially the same variable. Thus one could argue, that each of the following measures, in part, the same thing. That is, one could assert that the

---

[3] The author thanks Dr. Marvin Taves for the use of these data and the arithmetic computations included. The materials, but not the arguments, are found in "A Study of Factors Associated with Religiosity" by Dr. Taves, *Unpublished Doctoral Dissertation,* University of Minnesota Library, 1954.

(1) amount of *religious behavior* (church attendance, office holding, contributions, etc.) is in some sense a measure of religiosity—and some irrelevant items as, say, prestige in church attendance, etc.

(2) attitudes about the church as a social institution are also measures of religiosity—plus some irrelevant items as general conservatism, liberalism, etc.

(3) beliefs about theological questions could also generate a scale of religiosity—plus some irrelevant items as the negative reaction to a disliked minister, etc.

If these operations do involve the measurement of the same underlying variable, plus things more or less unique to the operation one could obtain the amount of the basic variable in each measurement through factor analysis. We will accept, without proof, the steps involved in factor analysis and the argument that the first factor will be the underlying variable in question.

Denoting the measurements as

x_1 = religious behavior
x_2 = attitudes about the church
x_3 = theological beliefs

we first obtain the inter-correlations between these measures. Assuming, for the illustration of factor analysis, that these measures were essentially quantitative, the correlations are Pearsonian product-moment r's.

TABLE 30.   INTERCORRELATIONS BETWEEN
3 ITEM MEASURING RELIGIOSITY

	1	2	3
1	—	.54	.66
2	.54	—	.71
3	.66	.71	—

We will perform a set of operations upon this "matrix" of correlation ratios to obtain the required factor loadings of each measure. Clearly a variable is perfectly correlated with itself. Hence, we will insert one's in the main diagonal.

TABLE 31.   ILLUSTRATION OF OPERATIONS IN FACTOR ANALYSIS

		(1)	(2)	(3)	w_1	w_2	w_3	w_4
					Successive Weights			
	(1)	1.00	0.54	0.66	.93	.92	.92	.92
	(2)	0.54	1.00	0.71	.95	.94	.95	.95
	(3)	0.66	0.71	1.00	1.00	1.00	1.00	1.00
Successive	$\Sigma1$	2.20	2.25	2.37				
Summing	$\Sigma2$	2.10	2.16	2.29				
	$\Sigma3$	2.09	2.15	2.27				
	$\Sigma4$	2.09	2.16	2.28				

(a) After revising our matrix, we then sum the columns to obtain the results denoted by $\Sigma1$. (b) Divide each of these sums by the largest sum in that row. These are entered as the first weights, *i.e.* w_1 for variable (1) is $2:20/2.37 = .93$. (c Multiply col. (1) by the corresponding entry in w_1 and sum to obtain $\Sigma 2$, *viz.*, $(.93)$ (1.00) + $(.95)$ $(.54)$ + (1.00) $(.66)$ = 2.10. Repeat for col. (2), *viz.*, $(.93)(.54)$ + $(.95)(1.00)$ + $(1.00)(.71)$ = 2.16. Repeat for col. (3); in general, repeat for all remaining columns. (d) Divide each entry in $\Sigma 2$ by the largest single entry to obtain w_2.

From this point on, one successively repeats the operations to obtain the new sums, *e.g.* $\Sigma 3$, and the new weights, until "stability" is reached. Normally one continues the process until a column of weights $w_1 +_1$ is either identical with or within .001 of w_i. This is a widely used rule of thumb.

The weights in $w_1 +_1$ are proportional to the correlation coefficients of the underlying variable and these 3 measures. To obtain these coefficients one multiplies each weight in $w_1 +_1$ by

$$\sqrt{\frac{\text{largest sum of the final summations}}{\text{sum of the squares of } w_1 +_1}}$$

In this case

$$a = w_1 +_1 \left(\sqrt{\frac{2.28}{(.92)^2 + (.95)^2 + (1.00)^2}} \right)$$
$$= w_1 +_1 \ (.9107)$$

To complete the scale of religiosity, one computes the a values for each of the measures. The scale of religiosity is assumed to be a linear function of the three separate measures and is obtained by

$$R = \frac{a_1 \ (X_1 - \overline{X}_1)}{\sigma_1} + \frac{a_2 \ (X_2 - \overline{X}_2)}{\sigma_2} + \frac{a_3 \ (X_3 - \overline{X}_3)}{\sigma_3}$$

Since $\overline{X}_j$ and σ_j will be obtained for each measure and are arithmetic constants (R) can be written as

$$R = \frac{a_1 \ X_1}{\sigma_1} + \frac{a_2 \ X_2}{\sigma_2} + \frac{a_3 \ X_3}{\sigma_3} - \left(\frac{a_1 \ \overline{X}_1}{\sigma_1} + \frac{a_2 \ \overline{X}_2}{\sigma_2} + \frac{a_3 \ \overline{X}_3}{\sigma_3} \right)$$

The bracketed term will degenerate to a single constant in any emperical case; of course, if more than 3 measures were used, R would involve more terms, but the general form would persist.

6. Summary

Scaling operations have a twofold contribution. (a) By forcing one to connect concepts with the real world, they aid in arriving at precise definitions. (b) The scale then allows for a justifiable ordering in some sense of measurement.

While a naive operationalism will permit the construction of arbitrary scales, largely through circular reasoning, a type of a priori defense of scaling may be found in

(1) The cumulative scale. The fact that weights are irrelevant make this a desirable type for certain problems.

(2) Item analysis. Particularly helpful in an *ad hoc* design, or other circumstances of outside criteria; the scoring system based on weights deduced from the correlation ratio and other statistical concepts gives this type of scale a defensible base.

(3) If several measures or scales involve a single underlying variable an index or scale of this variable can be obtained through the use of factor analysis.

SELECTED REFERENCES

Cattell, Raymond B., *Factor Analysis* (New York: Harper & Brothers, 1952).

Hagood, Margaret J. and Price, Daniel O., *Statistics for Sociologists* (New York: Henry Holt & Co., rev. ed., 1952).

McNemar, Quinn, "Opinion-Attitude Methodology," *Psychological Bulletin,* Vol. 43, No. 4 (July, 1946).

Riley, Matilda White, John W. Riley, Jr., Jackson Toby, *et al., Sociological Studies in Scale Analysis* (New Brunswick: Rutgers University Press, 1954).

Stouffer, Samuel A., and others, *Measurement and Prediction* (Princeton, N. J.: Princeton University Press, 1950).

Chapter 7

CONSTRUCTIVE TYPOLOGY AND SOCIAL RESEARCH*

THE method of *constructive typology* has a long and productive history within the realm of scientific endeavor.[1] The constructed type has been a useful tool in the hands of both the scientist and historian. The device has played an undeniable role in the growth of scientific knowledge despite the fact that it has frequently been misused, misinterpreted, or not even recognized by its users. There is a truly stupendous amount of historical and scientific work that has been done wherein the constructed type has remained merely an implicit aspect of the enterprise. There has also been a great deal of historical and scientific work wherein the constructed type has been explicitly recognized and developed, but wherein the construction and adaptation of the type has not been carried out in the most rigorous and fruitful manner. On the other hand, there is an extensive body of literature accumulating that reflects the purposive attempt of researchers to maximize the *potential* of the constructive typological method.[2]

The object of this chapter is to help identify and clarify the place that constructive typology may take in the battery of approaches avail-

---

* Written by John C. McKinney.

[1] The term "constructed" type is used here in preference to the designations "ideal" and "pure" types. The terms ideal and pure have been misinterpreted so frequently that it seems advisable to follow Howard Beckers' usage and refer to these types as "constructed types." His earliest use of this label was in: "Constructive Typology in the Social Sciences," *American Sociological Review*, Vol. V (February, 1940), pp. 40-55.

[2] It is essential that the student of constructive typology acquaint himself with the work of Max Weber and Howard Becker. In particular see Max Weber, *The Theory of Social and Economic Organization*, Talcott Parsons (tr. & ed.) (New York: Oxford University Press, 1947); *From Max Weber: Essays in Sociology*, H. H. Gerth and C. W. Mills (trs. & eds.) (New York: Oxford University Press, 1946); Howard Becker, *Through Values to Social Interpretation* (Durham: Duke University Press, 1950); Howard Becker, *Systematic Sociology on the Basis of Beziehungslehre and Gebildelehre of Leopold von Wiese* (New York: John Wiley and Sons, 1932), pp. 21-23 *et passim;* Howard Becker and H. E. Barnes, *Social Thought from Lore to Science*, 2 vols., 2nd ed. (Washington, D. C.: Harren Press, 1952), pp. 779-81 *et passim,* and esp. "1951 commentary on Value-System Terminology," p. ii. Also of primary values are the sections on the "ideal type" and Max Weber" in Talcott Parsons, *The Structure of Social Action*, 2nd ed. (Glencoe, Illinois: The Free Press, 1949); and, Theodore Abel, *Systematic Sociology in Germany* (New York: Columbia University Press, 1929). For an account of typological procedure see Paul Lazarsfeld, "Some Remarks on the Typological Procedures in Social Research," *Zeitschrift für Sozialforschung*, Vol. VI (1936), pp. 119-39. For a recent excellent exposition see C. G. Hempel, Typological Methods in the Natural and Social Sciences," *Proceedings, American Philosophical Association; Eastern Division*, Vol. 1 (1952), pp. 65-86. Also relevant to the present chapter is the treatment by J. C. McKinney in "The Role of Constructive Typology in Scientific Sociological Analysis," *Social Forces*, Vol. 28 (March, 1950), pp. 235-40.

able in scientific social research. The concern here is with the applicability of the constructed type within a *scientific* frame of reference. The usage of the technique for the discipline of history is of only incidental concern here, and is treated only when the contrast of its usage assists in the clarification of the role of constructive typology in scientific social research.

The first essential is to take a suitable definition of science as the point of departure for the accomplishment of the task. This does not imply that there are not numerous satisfactory statements as to what science "is"; on the contrary, the implication is that there is considerable institutionalized agreement as to what science is; the problem is merely in selecting a definition that is in keeping with the terminology and problem at hand. Becker's conception of science as being "the systematic statement of the probability of the potential or actual recurrence of phenomena that for the purposes in hand, are regarded as identical," is suitable.[3]

Science is not only not interested in the "unique" or the "individual" as such, but is methodologically barred from dealing with them. Science is continually in search of *what is conceived of* as being the identical, the general, and recurrent aspects of the phenomena that it is concerned with. It is the assumption of science that the world in its physical, biological, and social aspects is both *intelligible* and *explicable*. It is intelligible in the sense that *uniformities* may be stated. The uniformity of nature is a basic assumption of science, and all that science can do is to demonstrate specific uniformities that justify the keeping of the assumption. The demonstration of uniformities involves the comprehension of the data of experience, which in turn involves the *conceptual* creation of order out of apparent chaos. This entails the analytic elimination of the unique, and the *construction* of a *conceptual* order of things wherein the repetitive and interrelated aspects of phenomena are exposed.

The "ordering" of data into the context of uniformities is the methodological achievement of science. Data are isolated elements in a concrete world of experienced things, and relations between things. Their isolation is methodologically overcome in the scientist's conceptual realm of construct and hypothesis. Science, in its cognitive advance, cannot stop with the data. Data are merely a phase in the attainment of scientific knowledge, and the notion that the "data speak for themselves" is nothing more than a vicious myth. However uncertain it may be of the achievement, science never stops until the data have taken on the characteristic of some sort of an ordered whole. This is necessarily a provisional and hypothetical order, but it is the only way science has of putting its objects into the context of uniformity.

The scientific search for uniformities is a selective search that neces-

---

[3] Howard Becker, *Through Values to Social Interpretation* (Durham: Duke University Press, 1950), p. 97.

šarily eliminates much of the data of experience; explicity, the unique and the irrelevant. The elimination of certain elements of data and aspects of knowledge from scientific consideration is entirely legitimate in so far as it is recognized that science does not represent the totality of knowledge—but only that part of knowledge concerned with uniformities or regularities, expressed in probability terms in the form of predictive statements. Science is geared to the prediction of what might happen under what circumstances. Consequently the scientific method is essentially hypothetical. It is a method of conceptualization wherein results are predicted on the basis of the combination of a particular set of factors under a given set of circumstances. The theoretical prediction is then justified by the results obtained. This method is obviously selective and abstractive, since one can never make a complete statement about all that is involved in anything that happens. In one sense or another everything is involved in everything that happens. To leave it at that, however, would constitute leaving the experienced world as chaos. Science conceptually eliminates this chaos by predicting and thereby tentatively *establishing the regularities and sequences involved in the uniform order of things.*

Scientific activity is largely predictive activity. A fundamental criterion of scientific statement is the degree of accuracy involved in the statement of probability relative to the actual or hypothetical occurrence of a given phenomenon when a given set of factors is present in a cluster. Scientific prediction is theoretical prediction couched in "if and when" terms. "If and when" is the theoretical proviso, and constitutes the predictive context out of which science always works. The scientist is content to say that "if and when" certain factors are combined in certain ways the results are conditionally predictable. The logic of scientific prediction then does not restrain science to the making of statements with regard to what might happen in the future. On the contrary, the restraint is one involving the "if and when" proviso. Prediction, then may be "retrospective" as well as "prospective."[4] Constructs and hypotheses may be examined by utilizing the data of history as well as that of the moment. The requirement is the finding of the situational set-ups that meet the terms of the prediction stated in "if and when" terms. The uniformities of the past are as scientifically significant as those of the present.

To achieve scientific prediction, which means the creation of order out of chaos, regularity out of diversity, general out of unique, and recurrent out of occurrent, methodology is essential. This refers to methods of observing and relating observations. It is well to remember that observation is never simply an opening of the eyes and ears and exposing one's self to what is occurring. Scientific observation is always directed by an "interest," a "problem," a "concern with an exception

---

[4] Howard Becker, "Constructive Typology in the Social Sciences," in H. E. Barnes, Howard Becker, and F. B. Becker (eds.), *Contemporary Social Theory* (New York: D. Appleton Century Company, 1940), pp. 17-46.

to a rule," a "theory," or a "conceptual scheme." *What* is to be observed is a matter of scientific interest and abstraction. *How* it is to be observed is a matter of methodology.[5]

The term method applies to any procedure that achieves some rational order or systematic pattern for diverse objects. In its scientific usage its meaning varies all the way from abstract logic to specialized techniques peculiar to a particular scientific specialty. Logic is applicable to any type of phenomena in the sense that it applies a rational order to data so that they may be comprehended within a scientific system. The "constructed type" may be identified with this general aspect of method in that it is applicable to the logical ordering of an array of discrete data. The constructed type is not confined to any particular science; it is a method that is applicable to the data of any science. The particular type-constructs as substantive entities, however, are not interchangeable among the sciences.

The constructive typological method has been used by all sciences, although not always explicitly. The scientist typically constructs the units with which he operates. This is as true of the physical as well as the social sciences. One only has to glance at any of the special sciences to realize the tremendous importance of constructs to their endeavor. For example: take away the perfect lever, the perfect gas, frictionless motion, the perfect vacuum, perfect surfaces, straight cylinders and spheres, and countless other essential notions, and see what the physicist has left. Picture economics without its "economic man" from which the classical economic theory was derived. The essential concepts of perfect competition, the perfectly mobile factors of supply and demand, the perfect monopoly, or such classificatory labels as "capitalist" and "socialist" systems, "money," "credit," or "barter" economies are all constructed types. The sociologist is dependent upon such notions as competition, conflict, accommodation, assimilation, amalgamation, individuation, socialization, superordination, subordination, exploitation, community, society, caste and class, sacred and secular, rural and urban, democracy-autocracy, charismatic leadership, legitimacy, the stranger, the social isolate, solidarity, primary group; and these and many more may be constructed types. Even the idiographic historian, whose aim is different than that of the scientist, and who is legitimately concerned with the "unique" constantly utilizes constructed types. When he talks of "epochs," "eras," and "periods" he has constructed them. When the historian speaks of "the Greek city-society," the "feudal" system, the "manorial" system, "early Protestantism," the "medieval Papacy," the "Calvinistic ethic," the "estates within the state," and countless other things he is utilizing the method of constructive typology in his own particular way.

The foregoing small sample of usage of constructs by just a few disciplines should demonstrate the point that they are both useful and inevitable. To take away constructs and constructed types from science

---

[5] See Chapter I of this work for a more extensive treatment of scientific research and knowledge.

would be tantamount to a destruction of science. The scientific method is essentially centered around constructs, and constructed types are a particular kind of construct. To say that constructed types are both necessary and useful in the comprehension of the data of experience should suffice—but it doesn't because of the manifest prevalence of misunderstanding of the method. The next task, then, is one of analyzing the character and relationship of concepts, constructs, and constructed types. The constructed type will then be appraised in terms of its *instrumental pragmatic* value for scientific social research.

1. Concepts, Constructs and Constructed Types

An initial assertion that must be demonstrated is that all concepts are constructs.[7] "Raw" experience is never *really* raw even at the moment of perception. People naturally and necessarily categorize and structure their experience in terms of *concepts*. When science begins to analyze and classify its data it is taking a definite, and formal step away from "reality" at the perceptual level. All phenomena are unique in their concrete occurrence, therefore no phenomena actually recur in their concrete wholeness. "Identity" is always "identical for the purposes at hand." To introduce *order* with its various scientific implications including prediction, the scientist ignores the unique, the extraneous, and non-recurring, and thereby departs from "reality." This departure is the necessary price he must pay for the achievement of "abstract generality." To conceptualize means to generalize to some degree. To generalize means to reduce the number of objects by conceiving of some of them as being "identical." The reduction of the number of objects reduces the number of "relationships" to be examined. Since these relationships are between conceptual elements they *always* remain hypothetical relationships.

Scientific concepts never exhaust concrete reality for they always involve selection. Concepts do not reflect the totality of "raw experience" in all its diversity and complexity, and are therefore unreal in a sense. To repeat, all concepts are generalizations and all generalization implies abstraction. The nature of this abstractive process is often ignored. Abstraction may take place in two ways, both of which contribute to the general character of the concept.[8] First, there is abstraction of the common quality from the differing particulars. Thus we ignore the ways in which "spruce," "pine," "fir," "palm," and "apple" differ from each other and grasp their generic resemblance *via* the concept of "tree." Tree is conceptual unity by means of which we grasp a multiplicity of unique aspects and comprehend them within an order. The concept is abstract in the sense that the specific differences are lost in the abstractive process.

---

[6] See Chapter II of this work for an extensive treatment of science and concepts.

[7] W. J. Goode, "A Note on the Ideal Type," *American Sociological Review,* Vol. 12, (August, 1947), pp. 473-74.

[8] For an elaboration of this idea see: A. C. Benjamin, "On Formation of Constructs," *The Monist,* Vol. 38, (April, 1928), pp. 404-11.

Second, there is abstraction in the form of selection based upon the interest of the scientist. Resemblance is usually complex and involves a plurality of simpler qualities. Consequently, the scientist is presented with a group of associated resemblances from which he can select in so far as it pertains to a particular problem. Those qualities that are abstracted from the total complex become a part of the content of the concept, whereas those that are neglected are excluded. In this process the concept has again become artificial because of its imposed limitations, omission, and exclusion. It is this aspect of abstraction, however, that enables the scientist to distinguish between essential and non-essential attributes.

To avoid vagueness, indistinctness, and complete elasticity, a concept must be *given* precision. Precision can only be given negatively by setting up artificial limits beyond which the concept has no meaning value. Consequently the very limits which give a concept precision divorce it from concrete reality. No concept is ever a perfect symbol of that which it symbolizes—for inevitably its content will be less.

It is clear, then, that concepts are constructs even when they closely reflect perceptual reality. Concepts define what is to be observed, and they are the variables between which empirical relationships are to be sought. It is the function of the concept to make explicit the character of the data subsumed under it and conversely to point up to the researcher that which is omitted.

When all concepts are seen to be constructs, and it is granted that all constructs are in one sense "creative" due to their abstractive genesis, then the way is open to move one step further and create the constructed type. Ordinary concepts are given precision as constructs through selection and limitation; constructed types are given precision through selection, limitation; and addition. The constructed type *adds* to experience either through the *junction of qualities* into a configuration that is not necessarily directly experienced or, in the emphasis and *extension of qualities* beyond their actual empirical quantitative manifestation. A constructed type is a little more out of touch with perceptual reality than other constructs are. It is determined to a greater degree by the selective and creative activity of the scientist. The primary distinction, however, is that its value as a component of knowledge is not to be measured by the accuracy of its correspondence to perceptual reality, but *in terms of its capacity to explain.* The scientific function of the constructed type is to "order" the concrete data so that they may be described in terms which make them *comparable,* so that the experience had in one case, despite its uniqueness, *may be made to reveal with some degree of probability what may be expected in others.* The constructed type is a special kind of concept especially created for predictive purposes.

The constructed type is a heuristic device. It is an abstraction taken for purposes of eliminating the research minutiae and achieving a structured order of observations that more readily lend themselves to state-ment and verification. The type is a means of reducing the diversities and complexities of phenomena to a coherently general level. It does not de-scribe or represent a concrete course of action or situation, but it does represent an objectively probable course of action.[9] The abstraction deviates from "reality" in that it accentuates to a logical extreme some attribute or group of attributes that are relevant to a problem or system of analysis.

The constructed type is a devised system of characteristics (criteria, traits, elements, attributes, aspects, etc.) not experienced directly in this form, but *useful* as a *basis* of understanding empirical reality. It is a construct made up of abstracted elements and formed into a unified conceptual pattern, wherein there may be an intensification of one or more aspects of concrete reality. The elements of the type have discoverable em-pirical referents or at least can be legitimately inferred from existent evi-dence. The constructed type is a logical expedient and does not purport to be empirically valid in the sense of retaining the unique aspects of the empirical world. The main purpose it serves is that it furnishes a means by which concrete occurrences can be compared and measured, and com-prehended within a system of general categories underlying the types.

The comparison and measurement of empirical approximations reveal nothing but deviations from the construct. Nothing but "exceptions" to the constructed types exist. This is not only to be expected but it is to be sought after for it is the basis of the value of the typological method. These deviations will be relative—to each other and to the constructed type. This procedure, then, leads to quantification in terms of *degree* of deviation. If degree of deviation is to be determined repetitively and com-paratively then the base of measurement (the type) must be held constant. The relations between the elements (criteria) of the type are *logical* rela-tions therefore they may legitimately be held constant. The type will logically contain within its structure all the essential properties or elements

---

[9] Attention should be called to the distinction between "objective probability" and "objective possibility." Howard Becker has recently emphasized the former whereas the latter is the familiar Max Weber criterion. Becker makes the follow-ing remarks: " 'Objective probability' must be distinguished from 'objective possi-bility.' " The latter can mean mere *logical* possibility; Vaihinger's fictions (The Philosophy of 'As If') are logically possible, but many of them have little or no empirical probability; *i.e.*, they can never be even remotely approximated in real life. "Some of Max Weber's less guarded methodological statements sound much like Vaihinger's: his 'objectively possible' occasionally sounds like the "purely fictional.' His actual practice belies the inferences that can be drawn from his methodological statements; no one has taken more pains to insure the 'objective probability' of his types as they are actually used. Nevertheless, Weber leaves the methodological door slightly ajar, and by stressing 'objective probability' the present writer wishes to close it against the 'pure fiction.' "The accentuation or stressing of salient features of the constructed type, and its 'closure,' is fictional only in the sense of empirically 'limited fiction.' Examina-tion of the empirical evidence must always enable the researcher to say, 'The probability that this type will ever be matched in reality is *very* slight, but the probability is not *inherently nil.*' " *Through Values to Social Interpretation* (Dur-ham: Duke University Press, 1950), p. 261.

of a concrete structure or course of action, but not necessarily in the proportion or relationship pattern of any given empirical occurrence. These properties or elements constitute the variables within the type, and they remain in a fixed invariant relationship with each other. The removal of one or more of the variables, or the alteration of the relations between them involves the creation of a new type.

Although examination of empirical cases never reveals anything more than "approximations" or "deviations" from the constructed type, it is essential that the type should be formulated as being "objectively probable." The criteria are purposively selected on the basis of empirical evidence and put into a pattern that the researcher hopes will serve as a significant base of comparison. A type implies a predictive schema. For instance, the concept of "rational man" implies the adaptation of means to ends. Granted certain ends and norms as being "given," then the test of rationality is the adequacy of selection of available means and their adaptation to the attainment of ends. Obviously no "actual" man is rational in all aspects of his behavior, and yet his behavior can be comprehended in terms of the rational schema. There is an *expectancy* of man when he is viewed as "rational man" that is only partially met by any given man. A comparison of the extent to which actual men meet the expectancy serves as the basis for explaining "difference" in their behavior.

To illustrate further, any type such as the "feudal system," "scientific man," "charismatic leader," "vacuum," or "perfect surface," on the basis of its criteria will imply a predictive schema. Feudal behavior will vary from one concrete situation to another, and yet despite these variations there is a "feudal" expectancy different from any other expectancy that enables one to comprehend the variations within the pattern. Likewise, the expectancies one has of the course of action of the charismatic leader are different than those of any other kind of leader. The scientist behaves differently than other people when he is operating as a scientist, despite the fact that there is immense variation in the behavior of scientists. One doesn't find perfect vacuums in nature, nevertheless, it is the predictive schema of the vacuum that makes empirical approximations comprehensible. The perfect surface is also a fiction, but the expectancy of perfection is what enables us to compare degrees of "roughness" as found in actual surfaces. This should suffice to establish the point that the type must be objectively probable so that it throws actual structures or courses of action into a comparative light. The type focuses on *uniformity,* and it is only through the notion of uniformity that we have comprehension of variations or deviations. Obviously any variation or deviation must be a variation or deviation from *something.* To answer the question as to what that something is, is to necessarily answer—a uniformity.

To further clarify the concept of the constructive type it is necessary to approach it from the negative point of view. Max Weber very concisely stated what a constructed type *was not*. He said of the constructed type:

> (1) It is not a hypothesis in the sense that it is a proposition about concrete reality which is concretely verifiable, and to be accepted in this sense as true if verified. In contrast to this sense of concreteness it is abstract. (2) It is not a description of reality if by this is meant a concretely existing thing or process to which it corresponds. In this sense, also it is abstract. (3) It is not an average . . . in the sense that we can say that the average man weighs one hundred and fifty pounds. (This average man is not an accentuation, or emphasis, of the considered attribute.) (4) Nor, finally, is it a formulation of the concrete things common to a class of concrete things, for instance, it can not be used in the sense that having beards is a trait common to men as distinct from women. [10]

It is possible to add the following negative limits to those of Weber. (1) The constructed type is not a homogeneous universe as that concept is ordinarily understood. The type certainly has classificatory significance but it cannot be equated with "class" because it has a configurational significance totally lacking in the "class" as a homogeneous universe. (2) The constructed type does not refer to the most common form of a phenomenon, but to the most significantly representative form. For instance, it makes sense to talk about the "economic man" despite the fact it is doubtful that the "rationality" imputed to him is the most *common* form of economic behavior. It is through the notion of rationality as the outstandingly representative form, that the non-rational forms of economic behavior are then apprehended. (3) The constructed type is not a stereotype in that the stereotype often lacks an empirical referent, and is an unplanned, affectual exaggeration that is not empirically "useful" because of a lack of explicit criteria that make it comparable to concrete cases. Also, there is never any compulsion to make empirical comparisons because the stereotype not only has an emotional base but serves as an emotional weapon. In contrast, the constructed type is a purposive, planned selection, abstraction, combination, and accentuation of a set of criteria that have empirical referents, and that serves as a basis for comparison of empirical cases.

Now that the constructed type has been described both positively and negatively it is perhaps appropriate to reiterate its relationship to other constructs, and comment on the prevalence and indispensability of the type. The aspect of "unreality" of the type seems to be of greatest concern to those who are dubious of the typological technique. "Unreality" is a characteristic of all concepts, even of those with the closest perceptual counterparts. Take such empirically legitimate terms as the median, mean, and mode and one finds that they are all conceptual creations that "exaggerate" the empirical referent that they supposedly

---

[10] Talcott Parsons, *The Structure of Social Action* (Glencoe, Illinois: The Free Press, 1949), pp. 603-4.

represent. These average are merely "central tendencies" of a distribution and hence their "representation" of the extreme items is necessarily quite unreal. In contrast the constructed type is representative of a distribution in a different fashion in that it is formulated as *the ideal limiting case* from which degree of deviancy is potentially measurable. The task that the averages and the constructed types perform is simply a different one, and their relative research status cannot be decided on the basis of the assertion of unreality.

No concept is ever a "copy" of anything real. This is most strikingly evident in the realm of physical science. No scientific concept deals directly with perceptual experience, but only with the "ideal limits" as constructively formulated. In theory, for instance, a sphere and plane can touch each other in only one place. In the empirical world however, allowances have to be made for "roughness" of surface and the "pressure" of a real sphere on a plane. There are "irregularities" that are not a part of the limiting constructed case. Consequently they must be qualified as empirical deviations from the construct which made them comprehensible.

> In the words of Cassirer: "We investigate the impact of bodies by regarding the masses which affect each other, as perfectly elastic or inelastic; we establish the law of the propagation of pressure in fluids by grasping the concept of a condition of a perfect fluidity; we investigate the relations between the pressure, temperature and volume of gas by proceeding from a hypothetically evolved model to the directed data of sensation." Or as Wilhelm Ostwald has remarked: "We then stand before the fact that many and among them the most important laws of nature are asserted and hold of conditions, which in reality in general are never found." [11]

In the light of the foregoing, is it an unreasonable and invalid procedure on the part of the social scientist to construct units to work with? Is he flouting the scientific canons when he utilizes such concepts as "crowds," "groups," and "abstract collectivities" even when he knows that seldom, if ever will any concrete plurality pattern have the "pure" characteristics of any one of those structures? Is the social scientist anti-empirical when he looks for imperfect concrete versions of the constructed processes of "secularization," "accommodation," and "assimilation"? The answer is an unequivocal "no." It is scientifically advantageous and necessary to utilize theoretical constructs that are never existent in concrete reality. The constructed "pure" type is an indispensable tool in any of the sciences.

The failure to recognize the indispensability of the constructed type on the part of many social scientists may be partially attributed to considerable *misuse* of typology, and also to a prevalent *misunderstanding* of the typological method. The most wide-spread misuse of typology involves the unjustifiable reification of the types. When a set of character-

---

[11] W. H. Werkmeister, *A Philosophy of Science* (New York: Harper and Brothers, 1940), pp. 102-3.

istics have been abstracted out and formulated into a type, the users of that type tend to frequently forget that it is merely a tool for the ordering of concrete phenomena. The "orthodox" economists have been especially guilty of this and have thereby caused considerable unnecessary disillusionment with economic theory. Even such skilled typologists as Parsons, Sorokin, and Durkheim tend to reify their types and thereby obscure their scientific utility. The "as if" aspect of typology can never be sidetracked.

The prevalent misunderstanding of typology is related to this, and one form that it takes is the failure to recognize the conditional character of predictive generalizations based upon typological abstractions.[12] All that the constructive typologist can ever say is "if and when" certain factors recur under certain conditions there will be a probable result. The typologist merely creates the type, not the actual behavior that conforms to it in varying degrees. The continuing observation of actual behavior in terms of the type cannot be done away with, it is *the* scientific task.

Another kind of misunderstanding that frequently arises is the notion that all constructed types are of equal generality.[13] This is a gross error in view of the fact that types vary tremendously in their degree of generality. Necessarily so, in that the form of the type, if it is to function scientifically, has to be related to a problem area, hypothesis or battery of hypotheses, observational techniques, data, and predictive range.

It is the use of the constructive type that determines its scientific value. There are certain things it can and cannot do, and clear recognition of its functions and limitations is essential to the fulfillment of its potential. A manifest function of all types, statistically derived empirical types as well as those that are more impressionistically constructed, is to identify and simplify.[14] The constructed type performs the task of guiding the initial selection of data in terms of the schema of a given science. The construct may be used as a means of interpreting particular situations, in other words the type functions as the "general standard" by which a concrete occurrence is comprehended. The type can also be used as a generalizing concept by means of which one can extract its empirical versions from different cultural contexts. This is implicit in any search for "universals." The constructive type as such has "classificatory" significance and thereby differentiates phenomena and sets the stage for prediction. The constructed type serves as a point of reference for the analysis of the socially occurrent in that it serves as basis for comparison and measurement of concrete occurrences. First of all, the comparison of the actual processes, or situation, with the typical construct will indicate the degree of prevalence of the typical factors and thereby indicate the degree of probability of occurrence of the typical consequences. Secondly, the comparison will, through the indication of degree of prevalence of the typical

[12] Howard Becker, *Through Values to Social Interpretation* (Durham: Duke University Press, 1950), pp. 120-21.
[13] *Ibid.*, pp. 120-21.
[14] W. J. Goode, *op. cit.*, p. 473.

factors, indicate the possible need for further constructed types on a different level of generalization so as to include more of the apparently unique in a generalized scheme. Thirdly, the comparison of the construct with the empirical data should serve as a fruitful source for more specific hypotheses which in turn will be applicable on a less general level. And, finally, when the constructed type is used in conjunction with an appropriate hypothesis it may have predictive value. Using the conditional terms demanded by the degree of probability involved, the social scientist can say "if and when" these typical factors occur in the typical relationship pattern, these will be the typical consequences.

These varied aspects of the utility of the constructed type seemingly give ample justification for concern with the development and refinement of the typological method.

2. The Variables of Type Construction

For purposes of description and clarification it is possible to create a series of polar variables that are involved in the construction of the type. These are the "axes" around which types are constructed. They are not mutually exclusive, on the contrary, they are mutually implicated, hence they are used solely for the purpose of further clarifying the nature of the constructed type. These are the major variables of type construction:

Constructed—Extracted
General—Specific
Scientific—Historical
Timeless—Time-bound
Generalizing—Individuating

It is possible to analyze any given type in terms of its tendency to conform to the requirements of one pole or the other on each of the above continua.

(1) Constructed-Extracted: The characteristics of the constructed type have already been enumerated and need not be repeated. In contrast to it one has the extracted type, which is often called the "empirical" type.[15] These types are definitely not exclusive of one another. It has been pointed out that even though the constructed type is theoretically derived it must still have empirical referents in that it is based upon the particularities of actual occurrence. Conversely the extracted type, no matter how empirical its base, involves a certain amount of construction. Further, they both serve the purpose of identifying and simplifying the object world. Their difference lies primarily in their formulation which of course has implications for what they can "do" in research. The extracted type is based upon

---

[15] Winch refers to this type as the "empirical type." This is entirely justifiable, but this writer prefers the label "extracted type." Part of the negative attitude toward "ideal types" is based upon the mistaken notion that they are anti-empirical types. Consequently it seems inadvisable to in any way perpetuate the impression that there is a constructed-empirical dichotomy. See R. F. Winch, "Heuristic and Empirical Typologies; A Job for Factor Analysis," *American Sociological Review,* Vol. 12 (February, 1947), pp. 68-75.

the notions of "average" and "common" and "concrete" rather than upon those of "accentuation" and "abstractness." Kretschmer's description of how he arrived at his two general bio-types the "cyclothymic" and "schizothymic" is a classic example of the method:

> The types are not "ideal types" which have emerged, consciously created in accordance with any given guiding principle or collection of pre-established values. They are, on the contrary, obtained from empirical sources in the following way: when a fairly large number of morphological similarities can be followed through a correspondingly large number of individuals, then we begin measuring. When we compute averages the outstanding common characteristics come out clearly, while those peculiar marks which only occur in isolated cases, disappear in the average value. In exactly the same way we treat the remainder of the characteristics which can only be described from mere optical observation. So we proceed as if we were copying at the same time the picture of one-hundred individuals of a type on the same picture-surface, one on top of the other, in such a way that those characteristics which cover one another become sharply outlined, while those which do not fit over one another disappear. Only those characteristics which become strongly marked in the average values are described as "typical." [16]

The types arrived at by Kretschmer throw the "average" and "common" traits into bold relief, and not necessarily the "crucial" or "significant." The role of "interpretation" is much greater in the method of constructive typology. The constructed type involves comparison and measurement from the "ideal limits" of the case, whereas the extracted type involves comparison from central tendencies. It must also be noted that it is possible to "construct" in many instances where it is impossible to extract.

(2) General—Specific: Types can also be distinguished by their relative generality or specificity. Cognizance must be taken of the levels of abstraction involved in the formulation of types. The more general a type is the greater the simplification of the empirical attributes, and the more specific a type is the greater the number of general characteristics obscured by the mass of idiographic detail. Empirical generalization made through the use of the more general constructed types must necessarily remain relatively indefinite in the sense of being highly general. Generalization means omission and simplification of particularities, consequently as a type effects wider coverage, its adequacy in accounting for specific variations is lessened.[17] This is not to say that general types are not useful, it is merely to take account of the fact that more specific types must be used in conjunction with them for many explanatory purposes.

Such types as "Gemeinschaft," "Gesellschaft," "sacred," "secular,"

---

[16] E. Kretschmer, *Physique and Character* (New York: The Humanities Press Inc., 1925), pp. 19-20.
[17] Howard Becker, *op. cit.,* p. 122.

"communal," "associational," "rural," "urban," "folk," "state," "familistic," "contractual," "primitive" and "civilized," are obviously "sponge types" as they stand, nevertheless they have been extremely useful. Numerous subtypes are necessarily involved in their extensive application, but it is the "general" type that makes the subtypes possible, and furthermore gives them coherence within a schema.[18] The degree of generality-specificity involved in the construction of a type is unalterably related to the purposes at hand and the predictive task it must perform.

(3) Scientific—Historical: Construction of types may proceed in terms of the purposes of the scientist or in terms of the purposes of the historian. It must be recognized that they can and do use the same data, for all data are in a sense "historical." The scientist, however, is in search of the "general" and "recurrent" and the historian is primarily interested in the actual sequence of unique events. Both use constructed types to achieve their objectives.

Max Weber used the two different kinds of constructs in his historical and sociological work. His construct of "modern capitalism," for instance, is a unique or "historical" conception. It is an "ideal type" construct of behavior, but it is not generally applicable. Its sole referent as a type is to a particular time and place. It does not make sense to speak of "modern capitalism" as being existent prior to the seventeenth or eighteenth century. Further, it cannot be appropriately applied anywhere outside of the "western" world. Nevertheless it is a construct in that it does not contain within it all the behavioral minutiae of the epoch. The reference of "modern capitalism" is individual and historical, not analytical and general.

Max Weber's sociological usage of typology was in line with scientific purposes. His second kind of type dealt with recurrent and prevalent phenomena which typically appeared as constitutent elements in repetitive social occurrences. Among his concepts that had "general" application in a variety of historical contexts are those such as his four types of action: "purposive rationality," "valuational rationality," "affectual," and "traditional." Also, the concepts of "legitimacy," "routinization," "charisma," "sect," and numerous others.[19]

Georg Simmel, the initiator of "formal sociology" is another example of the user of "generally applicable," "non-historical" types. He detached such concepts as "leadership-obedience," and "superordination-subordination" from their historical or concrete settings, and maintained that they were applicable in even the most diverse groups, and regardless of

---

[18] For good illustrations of the use of sub-types see Howard Becker, "Sacred and Secular Societies," *Social Forces*, Vol. 28, (May, 1950), pp. 361-76; C. P. Loomis, "The Nature of Rural Social Systems: A Typological Analysis," *Rural Sociology*, Vol. 15 (June, 1950), pp. 150-74; and C. P. Loomis and J. A. Beegle, "A Typological Analysis of Social Systems," *Sociometry*, Vol. 9, (August, 1948), pp. 147-91.
[19] See Max Weber, *The Theory of Social and Economic Organization*, Talcott Parsons (tr. and ed.) (New York: Oxford University Press, 1947); and Max Weber, *From Max Weber: Essays in Sociology*, H. H. Gerth and C. W. Mills (trs. and eds.) (New York: Oxford University Press, 1946).

their social setting. The "form" of the types made them universally applicable. Hence, they were scientific rather than historical tools.[20]

Constructed types of "historical" value tend to be highly complex, dated and localized, whereas those of "scientific" value tend to be relatively undated and non-localized, relatively simple, contain a limited number of criteria, and consist in content that makes them appropriately applicable in many diverse historical situations. The "historical" construct is general in the sense that it does not depict the "full concrete reality" in all of its concrete manifestation, and the "scientific" construct is historical in the sense that the behavior it symbolizes necessarily bears a resemblance to that which has historically occurred.

(4) Timeless—Timebound: This axis is very closely related to the one just treated in that the scientific "universal" is the closest approximation to the "timeless" pole of the continuum, and the "historical" construct is the closest approximation to the "time-bound" pole. Nevertheless it is important to treat it separately to get at the *relative* timelessness of the scientific construct. Recognition must be given the fact that scientifically useful constructs *vary* in the extent to which they are timeless. They stand in different relative positions on the timeless—timebound continuum.

The concept *Gemeinschaft* as Tönnies used it is unquestionably as time-less as the sociologist can make a concept.[21] Tönnies regarded all social relationships as the creations of human will. He designated two types of will, *Wesenwille* (essential will), and *Kurwille* (arbitary will). *Wesenwille* refers to any process of willing originating in the traditional adherence to beliefs and sentiments common to the group. *Wesenwille* is responsible for the Gemeinschaft relationship and makes it as timeless as the natural behavior of man. On the other hand, *Gesellschaft,* the presumed antithesis of *Gemeinschaft* is not timeless to the same extent. Being the product of *Kurwille,* the arbitrary will, and involving the expedient adaptation of means to ends, it necessarily is restricted to a more *particularized* behavioral development, and hence in point of time must be a development out of *Gemeinschaft.* Consequently it is timeless to a lesser degree.

To use another illustration, the concept of "superordination-subordination" appears to be quite timeless in view of the fact that some type of hierarchical relationship can be found in even the most primitive of contemporary societies. It is not necessarily entirely timeless, for if there were ever such things as hordes or mechanical solidarity it would not have been applicable. As a principle however it seems to be a close approximation to the timeless pole. In contrast, take the sociologically

---

[20] Georg Simmel, *The Sociology of Georg Simmel,* K. H. Wolff (tr. and ed.) (Glencoe, Illinois: The Free Press, 1950); and N. J. Spykman, *The Social Theory of Georg Simmel* (Chicago: University of Chicago Press, 1925).

[21] Ferdinand Tönnies, *Fundamental Concepts of Sociology,* (*Gemeinschaft* and *Gesellschaft*), C. P. Loomis (tr. and ed.) (New York: American Book Company, 1940).

significant concept of "class," and it appears closer to the time-bound pole of the continuum than the concept of super-ordination-subordination does.

It is important to note as Becker does, that scientifically useful constructs are only *relatively* timeless.[22] It is the task of the scientific researcher to remove the time-markings from the phenomena under analysis in order to get at the general and recurrent, but his success is always a relative one. Time and location still leave discernible markings on many of the most useful scientific social types.

(5) Generalizing—Individuating: Constructed types may be conceived of as being primarily either "generalizing" or "individualizing." They are not unrelated, indeed, numerous generalizing constructs are usually required to support an individualizing concept, and conversely, an individualizing construct can frequently be adapted through modification to more general use.

Max Weber used the individualizing construct as a means of delineating what he called the "historical individual," the thing to be explained. The impossibility of handling "all" the data, and determining its relevance made it necessary to construct the individual unit to be examined. The construct of "modern capitalism" for instance, was woven out of the particularities of an historical epoch, but it was obviously simplified, selective, and limited. It contained what appeared to be the "crucial" characteristics of the capitalistic form that distinguished it from other economic configurations. To describe this complex historical individual, however, it was necessary for Weber to employ numerous *generalizing* constructs such as "rationality" and "bureaucracy" which have a range of applicability far beyond the particular case of "modern capitalism." It is only through the use of such explanatory generalizing constructs that the historical individual is made comparable in any respect. The construction of the historical individual has the function of preparing and organizing the mass of concrete data for analysis in terms of general constructs and ultimate predictive statements of relationships.

The way in which an individualizing concept may be adapted to more general use can be illustrated by the construct of "caste." The Indian caste system is definitely an individualizing construct representing extraordinarily heterogeneous phenomena. There is only one Indian caste system and even as an historical individual it has to be enormously simplified in order to be comprehended at all. It is possible however to extract from this heterogeneous pattern a number of essential elements whose presence justifies the attachment of the label "system." When such elements are extracted out it is possible to drop the prefix Indian and talk about "caste" as a general phenomenon. The elements of: (1) rigidly endogamous groups; (2) arrangement of hereditary groups into a superiority-inferiority hierachy; (3) group relationship to the

---

[22] Howard Becker, *Through Values to Social Interpretation* (Durham: Duke University Press, 1950), p. 106.

division of labor in the form of hereditary occupations; and (4) the maintainence of sacred ritual barriers, can be conceived of as constituting caste as a general construct. This abstracting process makes it possible to observe a caste relationship in parts of the world other than India. For instance, only a procedure of this sort justifies the use of caste with regard to the Negro-White relationship in the American South. Through adaptation from the historical individual it becomes possible to conceive of a phenomenon that otherwise might be neglected.

The generalizing construct is emergent out of the particularities of history, but is a construct that is applicable in many diverse situations. Its qualities of abstract generality and logical intensification give it the ability to serve as a basis of measurement and comparison of various empirical structures and courses of action. Its hypothetical *typicality* enables it to function as a tool of analysis in an indefinite plurality of individual cases and enhances understanding of an indefinite number of concrete situations. Such a concept as the "sect" for instance has been applied to such diverse phenomena as religious status,[23] religion and power,[24] moral rearmament,[25] acculturation and secularization,[26] and the German Youth Movement.[27] It is the generalizing constructs of this sort that are of immediate scientific relevance in the predictive context. Further, it is this type that seems susceptible to formulation in statistically verifiable form in many instances.

3. Varied and Fruitful Uses of Typology

For illustrative purposes it is perhaps advisable to cite some of the varied and fruitful uses typology has recently been put to in the social sciences. This is in no sense to be construed as a comprehensive survey; such an exposition would be out of the question in terms of space limitations. Further, it is restricted to a few of the modern, better-known, explicitly labeled and constructed typologies. No attempt can be made here to deal with the truly enormous body of "implicit" typology in existence. Let it suffice to say that if one develops the ability to clearly distinguish the characteristics of the explicitly constructed type, he will concomitantly develop the ability to recognize the "unlabeled" typologies for what they are.

The "formal" clarification of the method of constructive typology must be credited to the discipline of sociology, more specifically to a

---

[23] Max Weber, The Protestant Ethic and the Spirit of Capitalism, Talcott Parsons (tr.) (London, Allen and Unwin, Ltd., 1930): Ernest Troeltsch, *The Social Teaching of the Christian Churches,* Olive Wyon (tr.), 2 vols. (New York: Macmillan Company, 1931).

[24] J. M. Yinger, *Religion in the Struggle for Power* (Durham: Duke University Press, 1946).

[25] A. W. Eister, *Drawing-Room Conversion: A Sociological Account of the Oxford Group Movement* (Durham: Duke University Press, 1950).

[26] P. V. Young, *Pilgrims of Russian Town* (Chicago: University of Chicago Press, 1932).

[27] Howard Becker, *German Youth: Bond or Free* (New York: The Grove Press, 1946).

number of the leading German sociologists of the late nineteenth and early twentieth centuries. This despite the fact that the method itself is as old as science. Such analysts of social phenomena as Tönnies,[28] Simmel,[29] Sombart,[30] Troeltsch,[31] Wiese,[32] and Weber[33] played a leading role in making the method of typology explicit. Of that group it was Max Weber who made the greatest contribution to the delineation of the method and also to the use of it in analysis.

In the United States the method was established under the Germanic influence, primarily at the University of Chicago under the leadership of Robert E. Park. In the late twenties and early thirties several excellent typological dissertations were produced there. Hughes and Redfield have carried on the tradition at Chicago, however, the continuity has been maintained primarily at the University of Wisconsin under the influence of Howard Becker. The typological method, in its explicit formulation, is currently becoming more prevalent and a larger number of competent studies are being produced in terms of it.

Now for a look at some of the more promising *modern* typologies current in American research. The sacred-secular antithesis has been utilized by many people, but it finds its most elaborate construction in the work of Howard Becker.[34] These types are by no means new in that they come out of an old tradition antithetically typing societies. They resemble in certain respects Tönnies' *Gemeinschaft* and *Gesellschaft,* Durkheim's mechanical and organic solidarity, Cooley's primary and secondary (implicit) groups, Weber's communal and associative dis-

[28] Ferdinand Tönnies, *op. cit.* The analysis is based on the distinction between the two fundamental concepts *Gemeinschaft* and *Gesellschaft.* In developing this formulation Tönnies played a role in the firm establishment on the notion of the *continuum* as being applicable to social phenomena. The contemporary acceptance of "scaling" and "measurement" of social phenomena is largely based upon the notion of the continuum.

[29] Georg Simmel, *op. cit.* The school of "formal" sociology has left a profound mark on contemporary sociology, and Simmel is considered to be its founder. Simmel's approach consisted in a typology of "pure" forms of social interaction that represented the structure of society. The currently popular "structural-functional" approach is a close relative of Simmel's typological "formal" conceptualization.

[30] Werner Sombart, *The Jews and Modern Capitalism,* M. Epstein (tr.) (Glencoe, Illinois: The Free Press, 1951); *A New Social Philosophy,* K. F. Geiser, (tr. and ed.) (Princeton: Princeton University Press, 1937); *The Quintessence of Capitalism,* M. Epstein (tr. and ed.) (London: T. F. Unwin, Ltd., 1915). The work of Sombart is pertinent to the development of typology only in the respect that it emphasized the utility of the individuating constructed type. This usage of Sombart's must be recognized as an important contribution to the development of historical sociology.

[31] Ernest Troeltsch, *op. cit.* Although primarily an historian, Troeltsch played a major role in the development of the sociology of religion. He successfully demonstrated that the analysis of religious organizations in terms of sociological types facilitated the understanding of the reciprocal influence of religion and the social order.

[32] Leopold von Wiese, and Howard Becker, *op. cit.* The greater part of Wieses' work is concerned with the typological systematizing of the processes of sociation and their repetitive patterns.

[33] See especially the Talcott Parsons translation, *op. cit.*

[34] See especially Chapter V in *Through Values to Social Interpretation.*

tinction and others. They are not synonymous with any of them however, and seem to have a wider and more general applicability.

Sacred and secular societies, obviously enough, are constructed types, but by the very nature of the construction sacred and secular are rendered applicable to groups in general wherever the notion of "social system" is employed. The primary value of the polarity lies in its use in getting at the sacred or secular aspects of a group relationship conceived of as a *system,* and in exposing the process of secularization or sacralization that might be taking place. The establishment of the relative conformity of the relationship pattern of a given type of group to the sacred or secular poles puts it within the predictive pattern of the polarity. To say that one group is oriented more toward the sacred pole than another, gives one the ability to say many things *comparatively.* These statements will be based upon the many criteria which have been made explicit within the sacred-secular formulation.

For purposes of illustration, here are simplified descriptions of the sacred-secular structures.[35] The sacred society (as constructed type) is isolated vicinally, socially, and mentally. This isolation leads to fixation of habits and neophobia, relations of avoidance, and traditional in-group-out-group attitudes. The concrete is emphasized at the expense of abstraction; social contacts are primary; and tradition and ritual play a large part in the life of the individual. There is the dominance of sacredness even in the economic sphere which works toward the maintenance of self-sufficiency, and against any development of the pecuniary attitude. The division of labor is simple. Kinship ties are strong and are manifest in "great family" relationships. All forms of activity are under sacred sanctions, and hence violent social control is at a minimum. The forces of gossip and tradition are powerful tools of control. Non-rational behavior is predominant, with an important element of supernaturalism present. Rationalism, particularly in the form of science, is largely absent. The value system is impermeable.

The secular society lies at the opposite pole of the continuum and is vicinally, socially, and mentally accessible. Habit fixation is rendered difficult by the accessibility of the social structure. There is an absence of social barriers. Social circulation is unimpeded. Ends are evaluated in terms of "happiness" and means according to the norm of efficiency. Tradition and ritual are minimal. Rationality is dominant, and science is pervasive and powerful. The kinship group is manifest in the conjugal family form. Change is sought after and idealized as progress. Innovation is frequent. Informal sanctions are weak, and formal law prevails. Offense against the law invokes little social disapproval. Legal contracts are the rule. Individuation is prominent in society. The value system is permeable.

These two constructed types cannot be found except in empirical

---

[35] *Ibid.,* pp. 248-80. Also Wiese-Becker, *op. cit.,* pp. 222-25.

approximations to the major sub-types derived by Becker. The *folk-sacred* society is best exemplified by the old-fashioned, and primitive groups in the world. The *prescribed-sacred* finds its closest approximations in the Geneva theocracy of Calvin, the Jesuit state of Paraguay, Fascist Italy, Nazi Germany, and Soviet Russia. The *principled-secular* is an equilibrating society wherein the extreme aspects of the sacred are lost, and yet a principle derived from a sacred value system puts a check upon rampant change and reduces the potential of mental accessibility. The *normless-secular* is the anomic form of the secular society. Instances are most frequently found in centers of culture contact wherein the devices of communication generate social accessibility.

These types are not merely classificatory, they perform the function of giving understanding of empirical instances and have predictive power. Numerous observers have pointed out that Germanic folk culture provided the indispensable base for the Nazi society. Becker, through the use of these types, was able to point out that Germany had been rapidly moving in the direction of normless-secularism. Nazi Germany was a devised *prescribed-sacred* society, but in spite of the indispensability of the folk-values for its emergence, there was within those folk-values no explanation of the Nazi hatred of non-German things. This leads to the conclusion that the Nazi movement was really a perversion of the folk values that could only have been brought about by the deliberate operation of the leaders. Fixation of German-guilt in the area of leadership is demonstrable in terms of these types. The sacralization of Germany was an observable process, just as the attempted sacralization of the Soviet Union is observable. Knowledge of the extent of the process is essential to the success of dealing "practically" with these societies.

The versatility of the sacred-secular polarity is demonstrated by its use in very different spheres. For instance, one of the earliest uses of the polarity was by Hughes with regard to the division of labor.[36]

> The objects of occupational selection are persons most of whom have been reared in families in which they have inherited sets of social objects and attitudes more or less common to the community. The division of labor operates on these persons in an urbanized world, by mobilizing them from their *milieu natal* (Durkheim) and making them available at the points where competition will give them a place. The completeness of this mobilization varies in different types of occupations; the completeness of personality change of those who enter the occupation varies with it. Sometimes the mobilization of the person is of another sort, involving conversion, long professional training, and development of esoteric skill and interests. The more mobile and esoteric the occupational type, the more completely are familial and local ties and mores left behind. The person finds a "life

---

[36] E. C. Hughes, "Personality Types and the Division of Labor," *American Journal of Sociology,* Vol. 33, (March, 1928), pp. 754-68.

organization" in the occupational group, social objects and attitudes, and definitions of his wishes.

A division of labor may be sacred or secular. In a caste system one is born to a station and a set of prerogatives; his personality is a stereotype. In our world but few are born to their stations. A man's trade thus becomes more important than his family.

Each occupation tends to have its peculiar realm of sacred and secular objects. The sacred objects are its interests and prerogatives. The secular objects are within the realm of its technique.[37]

There are numerous implications in the foregoing, perhaps the most important is the suggestion that personality type and the division of labor are closely related. This suggests that the classification of personality can be fruitfully accomplished on the basis of the objective criteria of the occupational categories of the division of labor.

Another, and very different use of the sacred-secular polarity has been made by Young in the study of the Molokan sect. This is a study in acculturation within the American society. The structure of the sect was folk-sacred and when the group migrated to Los Angeles it had every intention of avoiding contact with the "sinful" secular world. The group was almost "ideal-typically" equipped to combat assimilation. It had a long tradition of social isolation in Russia, deeply rooted habits of collective action, social customs powerfully supported by religious sanctions, intelligent and purposive leadership, and an explicit determination to remain "pure." Despite all this, within a span of two generations the group exhibited striking examples of loss of cultural integrity in the form of secularization. Young's conclusion was that this was important evidence in support of the thesis that American city-life does not long permit the permanent segregation of cultures but inevitably influences even the most sacred.[38]

From this necessarily brief citation of illustration, it is possible to point out that the sacred-secular polarity is both useful and versatile. It is applicable to the processes that these structures undergo. Further, it seemingly is closely related to the imputation of "function" when the concept of "social system" is utilized.

Related polar types that have been applied to societies, and have been useful are Redfield's "folk-urban" continuum,[39] Odum's "folk-state" continuum,[40] Sorokin's "ideational-idealistic-sensate" triad,[41] Bateson's

---

[37] *Ibid.,* p. 754.

[38] P. V. Young, "The Russian Molokan Community in Los Angeles," *American Journal of Sociology,* Vol. 35 (November, 1929), pp. 393-402.

[39] Robert Redfield, *The Folk Culture of Yucatan* (Chicago: University of Chicago Press, 1941).

[40] H. W. Odum, "Folk Sociology as a Subject Field for the Historical Study of Total Human Society and the Empirical Study of Group Behavior," *Social Forces,* Vol. 31 (March, 1953), pp. 193-223.

[41] P. A. Sorokin, *Society, Culture, and Personality* (New York: Harper and Brothers Publishers, 1947).

"steady-state-unsteady state" pair.[42] and such non-personalized distinctions as "rural-urban," "primitive-civilized," "non-literate-literate," and "static-dynamic."

Some suggestive typological work has recently been done in the area of "social movements." This is an area that has been grossly neglected in American research, and seems promisingly susceptible to typological analysis. Heberle's formative work can be taken as one example.[43] Heberle starts with Weber's typology of motivation and reduces the motives of individuals in joining and supporting a social movement to four pure types. (1) *Value-rational* motivation is the case wherein the goal of the movement as such is held to be desirable and good, and success of the movement is wanted for the sake of the "cause." The conviction of "goodness" is based upon deliberation and careful inquiry into the validity of the ideas supporting the movement. (2) *Emotional-affectual* motivation is the case wherein an individual is emotionally aroused against the persons or conditions that the movement attacks, or is affectionally bound to the leaders or people in the movement. (3) *Traditional* motivation has reference to the fact that many individuals belong to a social movement because there is a traditional affiliation within the groups to which they belong. (4) *Purposive-rational* motivation refers to the attachment to a social movement in the expectation of personal advantages. It is expedient to join.[44]

The use of such subjective categories obviously involves difficulty. Nevertheless, the attainment of statistical data with regard to the motivation of the participants in a social movement, would assist tremendously in determining the solidarity, cohesiveness, and chances for persistence of a given movement.

Heberle goes on to distinguish the following types of movement. (1) The *spiritual community,* the fellowship of a value-oriented movement. (2) The *following* of a charismatic leader. It is the divine endowment of the leader that accounts for the maintenance of the movement. (3) The *utilitarian association* between individuals or groups.[45]

Heberle distinguishes further between two types of participants in any movement.[46] The *enthusiast* is primarily inspired by the ideals, ideas, and symbols of the movement. The *fanatic* is primarily concerned with action, and the goals of the movement do not mean as much to him as the group action and combat. The goals are typically conceived as dogma, and hence give justification to violent action. Knowledge of the extent to which a movement is peopled by enthusiasts (who can be disillusioned),

[42] Gregory Bateson, "Bali: The Value System of a Steady State," *Social Structure: Studies Presented to A. R. Radcliff-Brown,* Meyer Fortes (ed.) (London: Oxford University Press, 1949), pp. 35-53.
[43] Rudolf Heberle, *Social Movements* (New York: Appleton-Century-Crofts, Inc., 1951).
[44] *Ibid.,* pp. 95-98.
[45] *Ibid.,* p. 131.
[46] *Ibid.,* pp. 114-15.

or fanatics (who can shift readily from one movement to another) can assist in evaluating the force for change and persistence of a movement.

Heberle also suggests a relationship between motivation and membership in social movements and Spranger's six types of men. Spranger's types of men are drawn from types of attitudes expressing basic values. They are really expressions of value orientations. The relationship between type of value orientation, type of social movement, and type of role played in the movement is certainly worthy of investigation.

Pigor's types of followers are somewhat similar to the Heberle typology and seemingly could be useful in determining the character of a movement.[47] He distinguishes four types: (1) *Constructive* followership involves those who understand the collective aim and feel a direct responsibility for it. It covers a range from the young leader of the future to the intelligent assistant. (2) *Routine* followership refers to the case where the collective aim is unimportant or a matter of indifference. The range is from the faithful subordinate to the drudge. (3) *Impulsive* followership denotes an emotional tie to the leader or cause that need not be long-lasting. The range is from the hero-worshipper to the faddist. (4) Subversive followership covers a range from the self-interested man to the disguised traitor. The analysis of any movement must concern itself with the leader-follower relationship. The determination of relative extent of membership of any of the foregoing types in a movement would materially assist in interpreting its possible impact.

Linton's typology of nativistic movements could conceivably aid in understanding an increasingly common phenomenon.[48] He defines a nativistic movement as any conscious organized attempt on the part of members of a given society to revive or perpetuate selected aspects of its own culture. He then distinguishes four types: *revialistic-magical, revialistic-rational, perpetuative-magical,* and *perpetuative-rational.* Any nativistic movement presupposes close and continuous contact with other societies and the phenomenon of acculturation. The situations which are likely to produce the above types, and in turn, the types of situation likely to be created by them constitutes the area of hypothesis and potential research.

With a small handful of basic types Becker carried out an exceptionally penetrating study of the German youth movement.[49] The basic concepts were: sacred-secular, cult-sect-denomination-ecclesia, and charisma. The varied uses of the sacred-secular continuum have already been dealt with. The cult-sect-denomination-ecclesia pattern is an elaboration of the older Weber-Troeltsch formulation of church-sect. This work definitely establishes the applicability of these concepts outside of the strictly religious

[47] Paul Pigors, "Types of Followers," *Journal of Social Psychology,* Vol. 5 (August, 1934), pp. 378-83.

[48] Ralph Linton, "Nativistic Movements," *American Anthropologist,* Vol. 45, (April-June, 1943), pp. 230-40.

[49] Howard Becker, *German Youth, Bond or Free* (New York: Grove Press, 1946).

sphere. Charisma is a Weberian concept that already has had wide applicability.

Becker hypothesized that the German youth movement came into being because the ends and prospective life situations of its adherents had been defined by adults in patterns that were in sharp and observable contrast with the things adults actually did. There was a readily distinguishable difference between what parents said "should" be done and their actual deeds. Parents were seen to practice expediency under the guise of sanction and tradition. They visibly utilized affective outlets that they verbally condemned. Youthful idealism, fed on idealized patterns of the past, was rudely shaken by the harsh reality of adult deviousness. This demanded a redefinition of life by confused youth.

This dissent and rejection of adult values and standards gave rise to like-mindedness and resulted in the emergence of youth conventicles which later fused into sects. It became possible for rebels to join forces against a despised way of life. There was an emotional and collective youth reaction against the insincerities of rapid secularization. The emergence of hundreds of groups manifesting certain basic similarities of conduct was typed as the German youth movement.

Becker then delved into the important relationship between the youth movement, youth tutelage, Hitler youth, and ultimately the Nazi movement itself. Becker was able to show very clearly how the youth movement was perverted by the Nazis. The loose framework of fellowship (conventicles and sects) was eventually converted into a highly organized ecclesia. This was in direct contrast to the avowed aims of the early leaders and participants. Youth movement became youth tutelage, and a hugh paramilitary organization emerged that was in sharp contrast to the early romanticism and anarchism. The external manifestations of the youth movement such as the dress, the "roaming," the "nest," the "camp," the "leadership" principle and the songs, were borrowed by the Nazis, but they were utilized as means to the accomplishment of specific ends. These were the Nazi ends of converting and utilizing youth in their system of control and expansion.

All of this is of extreme significance for the current international scene. The phenomenon of "perversion" of a movement, the invidious use of tutelage for doctrinaire purposes, the buttressing of one movement by depicting it as the "ideal" realization of a powerful "folk" movement, the erection of a devised sacred society, are all of significance for the understanding of the Nazi movement, and the continued strength and appeal of its ideology. Beyond that, however, all of these phenomena are of *general* significance as typical forms of behavior under typical circumstances.

Typology has also recently been related to the problem of "nationalism." Nationalism is obviously one of the crucial aspects of the current epoch, consequently any advance in the understanding of it is important. Handman in a pioneer derivation distinguished between "oppression-nationalism," "irredentism," "precaution-nationalism," and "prestige-national-ism."[50] Wirth conceived of a typology that is somewhat similar, but which might be much more useful because it was derived from the categories of "opposition" and "conflict." In its empirical manifestation the signifi-cance of nationalism lies in conflict, hence types devised on that basis seemingly have a better chance of enhancing knowledge of the general phenomenon. Wirth's types are "hegemony," "particularistic," "marginal" and "minority" nationalism.[51]

In the area of the sociology of religion the recent work of Yinger follows in the tradition of Troeltsch. Using the sect-church and sacred-secular polarities Yinger attempted to study religion as a factor in inter-human behavior. The central problem involved the analysis of the socio-logical significance of religion in terms of its influence over other aspects of behavior, and conversely its effectiveness in reaching its own ends in conflict with other interests. The sect and church tendencies within re-ligion are clearly delineated and related to different strategies and his-torical developments. His conclusion was that religion seems to maximize its power as an agent in social change when it manages to combine the sect-church tendencies by means of an organizational principle. The broader significance of the study is that it furthers the notion that the struggle for power can be effectively studied typologically.[52]

Riemer has suggested that the systematic incorporation of constructive typology into the area of criminological research might aid in resolving some of its dilemmas. The major progress in this area in recent years has been in the field of prediction (parole success, recidivism, *et al.*) studies. Relatively little has been accomplished with regard to fundamental uni-formities. The establishment of relationships between certain types of crime, types of criminal, and types of situations would lend theoretical clarity to a field that obviously suffers from empirical diffuseness.[53]

Following the lead of Durkheim with respect to the sociology of law, Gurvitch has given an example of the relationship of "types of sociality" and "types of law." He differentiates between sociality by interpenetration in the "we," and sociality by simple interdependence between individuals. He divides the latter type into "rapprochement," "separation" and a com-binatory form, and then proceeds to consider the types of law engendered by such social relationships. Origins, character, and sanctions of law can seemingly be fruitfully studied in this way.[54]

An area wherein constructive typology seems to represent the only

---

[50] M. S. Handman, "The Sentiment of Nationalism," *Political Science Quarterly*, Vol. 36, (March, 1921), pp. 104-21.
[51] Louis Wirth, "Types of Nationalism," *American Journal of Sociology*, Vol. 41, (May, 1936), pp. 723-37.
[52] J. M. Yinger, *op. cit.*
[53] Svend Riemer, "The Ideal-Type in Criminal and Delinquent Behavior," in W. E. Reckless (ed.), *The Etiology of Criminal and Delinquent Behavior*, Bulletin 50, Social Science Research Council, New York, 1943, pp. 138-43.
[54] Georges Gurvitch, *Sociology of Law* (New York: Philosophical Library, 1942).

possible approach is in "cyclical theory." Cycles, sequence patterns, or process series have intrigued many analysts, and with some significant results. Cyclical theory suffers from the reputation given it by the "sweeping theory men" such as Toynbee, Spengler, and Sorokin, but that does not negate the fact that there has been some work done that is of empirical value. To repeat, constructive typology has to conform to the strict rules of scientific method, consequently the relation between the constructed type and empirical evidence must be held steadfastly in view. The grand-scale cyclical theories simply do not afford the opportunity for empirical examination. In a much more limited fashion, however, it is possible to build "patterns" that have significance in either retrospective or prospective prediction. The "business cycle" is a case in view when economists use it within its legitimate confines and do not yield to business or governmental pressure to "time-bind" it and thus engage in prophecy. Simmel's "conflict cycle"[55] seems to be empirically useful, as does Bogardus's "race relations cycle."[56]

The "revolutionary cycles"[57] of Brinton and Edwards, as well as the "strike cycle"[58] of Hiller are in this "pattern" tradition. Whatever value lies in the notions of "pattern," "cycle," "periodicity," or "sequence" seemingly must be extracted and exploited by the constructive typologist if it is to be salvaged at all.

The foregoing sample of typological contributions is in no sense comprehensive, it is merely illustrative of the use the method has been put to in recent years. To reiterate, the constructed type is an indispensable analytic tool in the sciences generally, and it is particularly indispensable in its explicit form to the social sciences. It is useful in the examination of a "time-sequence," that is, the same set of processes and structures in their occurrence over a period of time. It is useful in the examination of "systems" of any sort, that is, the interrelations of processes and structures and the imputation of their "function" within a conceptual whole. Further, it is useful in the extraction of regularities of order in generalizable form from the empirical chaos.

4. The Relationship of the Constructed Type to Systematic Theory

In order to clarify the role of the constructed type further it is necessary to shift the focus of attention over to related aspects of the scientific method. The essential relationship of the constructed type to systematic theory must be demonstrated if the type is to claim major scientific significance.

It is generally accepted that the ideal of science is to achieve a

---

[55] Georg Simmel, *op. cit.*

[56] E. S. Bogardus, "A Race Relations Cycle," *American Journal of Sociology,* Vol. 25 (January, 1930), pp. 612-17.

[57] Crane Brinton, *The Anatomy of Revolution* (New York: W. W. Norton Co., Inc., 1932) and, L. P. Edwards, *Natural History of Revolution* (Chicago: University of Chicago Press, 1927).

[58] E. T. Hiller *The Strike Cycle* (Chicago: University of Chicago Press, 1928).

systematic interconnection of facts. This means a systematic interconnection of observations made of some aspect of the universe. Isolated propositions do not constitute a science. Such propositions merely create the opportunity to find the connection between them and other propositions. Such an arrangement of propositions attains coherence "as a whole." It is permissible, then, to speak of a system of propositions. However, it is not merely the propositions that are responsible for the system, indeed, they presuppose the existence of a body of logically interdependent generalized concepts of empirical reference. These concepts are the *categories* within the system which give rise to empirical proposition.

A theoretical system, then is a conceptual scheme which may be taken to mean a set of concepts that stand in relation to one another and wherein each individual concept assumes meaning relative to the others. Integration of such a scheme is a matter of degree, and reflects the extent to which each concept is a function of the relationship pattern. According to Parsons such a scheme performs two functions.[59] One consists in furnishing the *frame of reference*. This is the most general framework of categories within which empirical work takes shape and "makes sense." The second function of a conceptual scheme is to provide structural categories. This implies that in empirical reality phenomena are interrelated and thus constitute systems. Structure is then the static aspect of the descriptive treatment of a system. The conceptual scheme enables one to view a system "structurally" as it is composed of units and their interrelations.

Conceptual schemes as scientific systems may vary in terms of a number of different characteristics. All such systems are abstract, therefore, they vary in terms of their *construction*. The characteristic of *generality* means the inclusion of many particulars or specifics under a common rubric. The question of "how general" refers to the relative number of particulars that have been subsumed under a given category.

Complexity as a characteristic refers to the intricacy of the system in terms of the stated relations of its parts. The use of broad "general" categories would mean simplicity, in contrast to the use of numerous specific categories which would make the interrelationship of the parts more complicated.

The characteristic of *integration* refers to the internal unity of the system. This is manifest in the degree to which relations within it are derivable from the logical presuppositions of the system. This refers to the extent to which an alteration in relationships can be foretold upon the basis of the manipulation of a part.

Coherence refers to the internal consistency of the system: the extent to which its elements sustain the system.

[59] Talcott Parsons, *Essays in Sociological Theory; Pure and Applied* (Glencoe, Illinois: The Free Press, 1949), pp. 18-19.

Closure as a characteristic of a system refers to the exclusion of all concepts not definable within the framework and through the principles of the system itself. It is based upon the act of closure which means to encompass, or shut off, and thereby establish the boundaries of the system. This is the terminal phase of the construction of the system.

Taking the above variations into consideration, a theoretical system is a body of interrelated generalized concepts based upon a coherent series of premises and assumptions that are non-contradictory in nature. The development of such theory is best exemplified by the physical sciences. Among the social sciences, classical economics is the closest approximation. In general it may be stated that the social sciences are in what Parsons calls the "categorical system" phase of development.[60] This means that the fields have only a fragmentary knowledge of the "laws" or "principles" of the behavior that they are concerned with, but they do have a rough grasp of the general patterns of that behavior. This results in a delineation of structural categories that are not merely *ad hoc,* but are bound together in a state of interdependence that roughly fits the interdependence of the subject matter. There is an articulation of the categories commonly used that reflects the state of the phenomena as it is empirically observed. These relations are not spelled out to any great degree as propositions however, and consequently they are not verified as "laws" to any significant extent.

Conceptual systems seemingly can perform two major functions. First, they aid in the codification of our accumulating concrete knowledge. Discrete hypotheses and observations can be unified under general categories. They can be tentatively "placed" in a larger context, consequently their "meaning" can be assessed or interpreted in the light of more general implications. Second, theory of this order can serve as a guide to research. It enables us to locate and define the areas of our knowledge and ignorance by pointing up problematic areas. In the light of a system one can "see" problems of interest and significance relative to presumed "interconnections" or relationships. Problems in a sense are a function of ways of looking at things, and to look at behavior from the point of view of a system of categories gives the possibility of establishing a set of hypotheses that are also interrelated. This consequently can increase the possibility of correlating empirical observation with theoretical systems possessing coherence.

The importance of the theoretical system, even in its highly imperfect versions, is a matter of scientific consensus. The development of a theoretical system is another matter, and the difficulties involved are enormous. It is here that the constructed type can make (as it unquestionably has in the more "exact" sciences) a major contribution. *The constructed type can perform the important service of functioning as a bridge be-*

---

[60] Talcott Parsons and E. A. Shils, *Toward A General Theory of Action* (Cambridge: Harvard University Press, 1951), pp. 50-51.

tween *systematic substantive theory* and *relatively unstructured empirical data.* The constructed type as a conceptual device represents an attempt to advance concept formation in the social sciences from the stage of description and "empirical generalization" to the construction of theoretical systems.

It has been noted previously that a constructed type is not an ordinary concept but is a *special* kind of concept. It is special in the sense that it deliberately emphasizes and states the "ideal limits" of the case. Moreover, it is special in the sense that it consists in a set of characteristics wherein the *relations between the characteristics* are held constant for the purposes at hand. Hence, the constructed type is a *system* in itself. It has the character of a theoretical model. As such it can function as an analytic element in a more comprehensive theory. The constructed type thus, in a highly developed theoretical system can become indistinguishable from the theory of which it is a part.

There is no contradication between systematic theory and the formulaᴸ tion of constructed types. It is true that type concepts can be readily formulated *ad hoc* for innumerable empirical purposes, but their utility in such case is sharply limited. To realize their full potential, types have to be arranged in a definite order of relationships. It is in this way that they gain in both theoretical and empirical significance. The experience of Weber indicated that this cannot take place on an *ad hoc* empirical basis, but on the contrary involves the use of more general categories.[61] Weber, implicitly at least, had a generalized scheme underlying his type constructs. Social action was conceived of in terms of structural categories of social relationships and groups. Typological variation could then be stated within the structural categories. It was this implicit Weberian system that served as the point of departure for Parsons in his development of the structure of social action. This development indicates that although systematizing on the constructive typological level is difficult, it is inevitable. The explanatory use of the type involves reference to elements external to it. Explanation necessarily entails putting a type in context, hence types are either theoretically or intuitively bound to more general categories. Their appearance within these categories forces the statement of propositions regarding their relationships. System to type and type to system is a two-way developmental relationship. Parsons states this succinctly as follows:

"Indeed, it is impossible to work out a systematic classification of ideal types without developing at the same time, at least implicitly, a more general theoretical system. For the relations between the types in the classification can only be stated by employing the categories that comprise such a generalized system. Thus, by virtue of the fact that maximiza-

---

[61] Max Weber, *The Theory of Social and Economic Organization*, Talcott Parsons, (tr. and ed.) (New York: Oxford University Press, 1947), pp. 28-29.

tion of economic rationality is common to them, traditional and free enterprise belong, for certain purposes, in the same class."[62]

The constructed type, no matter how independent it might seem, is an initial selection of data in terms of a schema of a given science. It is theoretically derived as a means of defining and structuring the empirical situation. Therefore, it is mandatory that it be an extract from a generalized scheme. Since it is a selection from a substantive theory on the basis of a given class of data, it is not interchangeable with the constructed types of other sciences. Every science has its constructed types but they are indigenous to those sciences. Further, in so far as the constructed type is derived from a generalized scheme it serves the important function of orienting empirical research to systematic theory. This is an important step in the elimination of the sterility of trial and error, or empirically random research. The constructed type aids in lending direction to research by pointing up problematic areas that are of theoretical significance.

Systematic theory is valued in terms of its explanatory utility. This explanatory utility is scientifically bound to the procedures of empirical verification.[63] Empirical procedures directly reflect the systematic frame of reference. It is here that the constructed type fits in as a legitimate scientific instrument in the theoretically directed examination of the empirically given. On the one hand it is derived from a theoretical construct and therefore, it is heuristic. On the other hand it serves as the unit for comparison and probability statement of empirical occurrence. When used in conjunction with a suitable hypothesis it serves as a device that can bridge the gap between the interrelated set of propositions emerging out of the system of categories and the empirically occurring events. The cogent comment of Hobson should suffice to terminate this phase of the discussion:

> The development of the conceptual scheme "has actual physical experience as its essential condition, but the *constructive* and generalizing work of thought is no less essential. The original function of such a scientific theory or conceptual scheme, is to provide an *ideal* representation of some more or less restricted range of physical phenomena as actually observed, that is of certain sequences and regularities in percepts. But the functions of a conceptual scheme are much wider than those of merely describing symbolically what has actually been observed. The scheme is applied hypothetically to predict what will be observed, in circumstances which differ in some degree, or in some characteristics from those in which the experiments or observations which led up to the theory were made. The value and the range of validity of the particular conceptual scheme have to

---

[62] Talcott Parsons, *The Structure of Social Action* (Glencoe, Illinois: The Free Press, 1949), pp. 618-19.

[63] See C. G. Hempel, *op. cit.,* for an important analysis of the explanatory status of the constructed type.

be estimated by its actual success in the fulfillment of this function of prediction." [64]

5. The Constructed Type and Experimental Method

Systematic theory is commonly looked upon as being constitutive of the base of the deductive aspect of science. The "experimental method" is accorded the same status with regard to the inductive aspect of science. The notion of the experimental method, however, is rather loosely used in the social science. Optimistic expressions regarding the application of the method to social data have frequently been made. The term has also been applied to empirical studies wherein it is an obvious misnomer with reference to the actual procedure. One of the brute facts that social scientists have to face is that the great bulk of human behavior is not susceptible to the sort of control that is the distinctive characteristic of the experimental method. This is not to say that the logic of the experiment is not just as important in the social as in the natural sciences, it is merely to say that the manipulatory control which accompanies that logic to a high degree in the natural sciences is largely lacking in the social sciences.

Briefly, the methodological core of the experiment is represented in the ability to isolate a set of factors or immunize them to external influence. These factors are the potential variables within the defined "boundaries" of the experiment. Then, a single determinate change is effected with reference to one variable with all the other potential variables being held simultaneously constant. Determinate differences in the end result are then noted. Scientific custom then decrees that the variation in results was produced by the change induced in the variable. *Manipulatory* control is evident throughout in this, the prototype of the experimental method.

With numerous exceptions which should not be discounted, such manipulation is impossible in the realm of human behavior.[65] The social scientist then frequently settles for the use of the logic of the experiment in his search for uniformities.[66] It is this limitation to the logic of the method that dictated the adherence here to Becker's definition of science wherein the phrase "prediction of the *hypothetical* or actual recurrence of social phenomena" was used. It was necessary to use the term hypothetical along with actual for the reason that much of the recurrence that the social scientist deals with is hypothetical rather than actual. The use of the *if* and *when* proviso means that certain types of results occur when certain factors combine under certain conditions. These conditions are *usually* not producable at will. The social scientist usually cannot actualize them, and if they do become actual they usually do so

---

[64] E. W. Hobson, *Domain of Natural Science* (New York: Cambridge University Press, 1923), p. 31.
[65] For illustration of exceptions see Stuart Rice (ed.), *Methods in Social Science* (Chicago: University of Chicago Press, 1931), pp. 683-728.
[66] Howard Becker, *Through Values to Social Interpretation* (Durham: Duke University Press, 1950), pp. 102-3.

independently of the scientist. The social scientist is primarily a controlled *observer,* not a controlled manipulator.

As Weber and Becker have suggested, the social scientist can use the constructed type as tool to engage in a "mental experiment" in the attempt to fulfill the *if* and *when* proviso. Weber remarks that in the absence of experimental control "there is available only the dangerous and uncertain procedure of the 'imaginary experiment' which consists in thinking away certain elements of a chain of motivation and working out the course of action which would then probably ensue, thus arriving at a causal judgment."[67] Weber reached his judgment of "objective possibility" by establishing what *would* have happened *if* certain factors in the situation had operated differently. The *if* and *when* proviso is only hypothetically fulfilled.

Schelting gives a convenient summary of the steps involved in this type of causal imputation. The construction of the historical individual (the individuating type—the thing to be explained) is presupposed. The procedure is then outlined as follows:

> (1) Analysis of this complex phenomenon (or process) in such a way that it is broken down into elements of such a character that each of them may be subsumed under a general law. (2) There is presupposed previous knowledge of such general laws. (3) Hypothetical elimination or alteration of one or more factors of the process, concerning which it is wished to raise the question of its (or their) causal significance for the result. (4) Hypothetical construction of what would *then* (after the elimination or alteration) be the expected course of events (application of the category of objective possibility). (5) Comparison of the hypothetical conception of a possible development (really that which would *have been* possible had certain things happened differently) with the actual course of events. (6) On the basis of this comparison, the drawing of causal conclusion. The general principle is that in so far as the two, the actual and the possible, courses of events differ, the difference may be causally imputed to the factor "thought away" or considered as changed. If, on the other hand, this hypothetical change fails to make a difference, the judgment is justified that the factors in question were not causally important.[68]

Briefly, the researcher, on the basis of evidence, constructs a type. This may be a type of process, structure, social organization, personality or the like. It is then hypothesized that under given circumstances this type would probably behave in a particular fashion. The researcher then looks for the "set-up" that approximates the ideal circumstances in order to effect a comparison between the construct and the empirical approximation. The differences are imputed to the factors thought

---

[67] Max Weber, *op. cit.,* p. 97.
[68] Alexander von Schelting as interpreted by Talcott Parson, *op. cit.,* pp. 610-11.

away in view of the fact that they were not a part of the objectively possible pattern.

There are numerous implications in the Schelting formulation and it is necessary to examine some of them. As the series of steps stand they are in the tradition of some of the best work in physical science, for of course the "mental" or "imaginary" experiment is quite common in all of the sciences. On the basis of points (1) and (2) it is possible to distinguish, between two kinds of imaginary experiment: the *experiential* and the *derivative*.[69] It is the experiential type that prevails in the social sciences and the derivative types that prevails in the physical sciences. The difference accounts for significant differences in validity of the result.

The derivative type of imaginary experiment presupposes a set of explicitly stated general laws. The outcome of the experiment is anticipated in terms of deductions made from those principles in combination with a set of conditions constituting the experimental situation. The experiment is imaginary in the sense that the situation it refers to cannot be technically produced. Ideal gases or pendulums or perfectly elastic impacts cannot be created for manipulatory purposes. The question of what would happen *if* an ideal pendulum were at work, is not answered by thinking away the physical aspects of a pendulum at variance with the ideal, and then attempting to envisage the difference in outcome. On the contrary the question is answered by rigorous deduction from available theoretical principles or laws.[70]

Obviously the type of imaginary experiment envisaged by Weber and Becker cannot employ this type of deduction because the general laws are not there. The type of imaginary experiment they are concerned with is of the experiential variety. Imaginary experiments of this kind do not have deductive access to general laws that serve as the base for systematic prediction. Prediction here is guided by experience with empirical "regularities," assumed general "principles," and often in terms of assumptions and data that are not made explicit in the predictive process at all. Even the most ingenious experiential mental experiment, such as those of Weber, cannot give results that may be considered to be conclusive evidence in the strict scientific sense. The method is fruitful, however, when it performs a recognizable heuristic function. It can serve to suggest hypotheses and can give theoretical insights. It can also serve in the construction of a type that can be examined under other circumstances. Causal imputation based upon it must admittedly be extremely tentative. It must be emphasized that the difference between the experiential and derivative imaginary experiments is the relative absence

---

[69] These two types of experiments correspond with those called "intuitive" and "theoretical" by Hempel. The author feels that this is an unfortunate terminology due to the fact that the word "intuitive" is so amorphous in meaning. See C. G. Hempel, *op. cit.*, pp. 76-77.

[70] *Ibid.*, p. 77.

or presence of theoretical laws that have independent verification. An experiential experiment may attain the status of a derivative experiment when it can be related to general theory that has some empirical verification. This again emphasizes the close relationship of the constructed type and systematic theory.

Returning to the Schelting formulation, it is necessary to examine further the explanatory significance of the constructed type. Note that the final steps listed by Schelting involve a comparison of the construct and the actual with a resultant causal imputation. Explanation is thus given on the basis of a comparison, but it must be noted that here again a significant difference exists between contemporary physical and social scientific procedure.

Typical social scientific procedure imputes cause to the factors thought away insofar as they are held accountable for the difference obtained between the hypothetical and actual. This procedure assumes that the constructed type contains within it all the relevant criteria and that the area to which the type is applicable has been clearly delineated. Although both assumptions are currently pragmatically necessary, they must be recognized as assumptions that are impressionistically arrived at.

It must be remembered that any constructed type is really an explanatory schema. The "structure" of the type consists in a postulated relationship between a set of criteria. This structure is an implicit theory. The drawing out of this theory results in the explicit statement of hypotheses about the type. What these hypotheses will be however is determined by the structure of the type. The type is really a hypothetical "model" course of action, process, structure, entity, *et al.* What one is saying when one uses a constructed type is that this is the *expected* behavior of the "sect," the "ecclesia," the "baron," the "union man," the "falling body," the "pendulum" or whatever it might be. But, something different has actually happened. What factors have interfered with the expectancy? That is the question that must be answered before empirical explanation can be said to exist.

In any science, to explain an actual occurrence amounts to showing that it had to be expected in view of the presence of certain factors prior to and/or contemporaneous with it. The set-up is there which is supposed to give a particular result. It is here that the physical and social sciences frequently part company at the present time. In the physical sciences such explanation frequently consists in the deduction of the occurrence from general principles and limiting conditions describing the relevant antecedent and contemporaneous occurrences. The "logic" of the social scientist is the same. The difference lies in the fact that he does not have general principles to draw upon as freely, but must depend upon particular empirical uniformities. Also, he is usually not in a position to accurately state the explicit limits of the applicability of the construct which he has used. The "ideal" use of the constructed type as a predictive schema involves a statement specifying its area of application. An empirical interpretation must be given the type, thus link-ing it to observable phenomena. It is not enough to say that the ideal gas exists under ideal-conditions—that is a tautology. Hypotheses about the ideal gas must be stated in terms of its characteristics which can be found to be existent to varying degrees in actual gases. Similarly, state-ments about economically rational behavior must be stated in terms of the economic variables it is specifically concerned with such as "money," "profit," "utility," etc. It is only when the theoretical parameters are made explicit that the hypotheses about the construct attain full empirical import. It is then that they become susceptible to disconfirma-tion as well as confirmation and thus satisfy the canons of scientific ex-planation.

In the light of the foregoing analysis it is evident that the *logic* of the experimental method is as important to the social scientist as it is to those scientists possessing manipulatory control over their data. The logic of the experimental method is the logic of the explanatory use of the constructed type. The use of the constructed type as a predictive schema demands that it be testable under empirical conditions. This means the making of *comparisons* in the sense of experimental logic. The fact that most of these comparisons must be made with reference to "naturally" occurring data, and often cannot be "willfully" produced, is a handicap to the social scientist, but it does not deny him explanation in the scientific sense.

When a constructed type is conceived of as an explanatory schema it embodies certain empirical propositions which function as a theoretical system. Any constructed type is thus a system in its own right. Its full potential as a system has only been partially realized in the social sciences. Hempel lists the following objectives as being essential to a full realization of that potential.

> The constructed type can serve as a theoretical system by: "(a) specifying a list of characteristics with which the theory is to deal, (b) formulating a set of hypotheses in terms of those characteristics, (c) giving those characteristics an empirical in-terpretation, which assigns to the theory a specific domain of application, and (d) as a long range objective, incorporating the theoretical system as a 'special case'," into a more com-prehensive theory."[71]

The attainment of these objectives would mean the absorption of the constructed types into a systematic theory where they would have the status of analytic elements. This would not mean the disappearance of constructed types, however, it would merely mean that more of them, with varying bases of abstraction, could be profitably deduced from the system itself.

---

[71] *Ibid,* p. 84.

6. The Constructed Type and Statistical Method

The experiment has been identified as the "prototype procedure" of the inductive aspect of science. Obviously it cannot be used under all circumstances. In the area of the social sciences the "statistical method" is frequently used as its empirical substitute. Consequently the statistical relationship to constructive typology is worthy of examination.

It may be asserted that *there is nothing anti-quantitative in the method of constructive typology*. It has been the historical case, however, that researchers skilled in the use of the constructed type have not been strongly interested in the statistical validation of their findings. Conversely, researchers possessing considerable statistical skill have not felt it worthwhile to carefully inquire into the presuppositions and working methods of constructive typology. An unfortunate limitation has been placed upon the fruitfulness of social research due to the failure to capitalize on the complementary relationship of quantitative and typological procedures. The emergence of a number of social scientists who are procedurally competent in both typology and statistical techniques would unquestionably enrich the contemporary research perspective.

One primary value of the constructed type is that it serves as a basis for *comparison* and potential *measurement* of concrete occurrences. The constructed type serves as a point of reference for the analysis of the empirically occurrent. The analysis can only proceed in terms of the *comparison* effected between the empirically occurrent and the heuristic construct. Both quantification and measurement are implicit aspects of comparison even with respect to constructs. Consequently the adaptation of quantifying and measuring techniques to typological procedure represents its *natural* line of development. It must be noted that this has reference only to the generalizing constructed type, not to the individuating type.

Scientific observation is concerned with qualitative distinctions, and the constructed type represents those distinctions. Science also aims at quantitative discernments between those distinctions. The reason for this is accuracy of statement with regard to comparison. Scientific accuracy demands that one say, not merely that A is heavier, warmer, larger, taller, more secular, more sacred, or more solidary than B, but that A is *so and so much* heavier, is *so and so much* more secular, is *so and so much* more solidary, etc., than B. Statements of this kind involve that aspect of quantification called measurement which is the procedure for the assignment of quantitative values to certain *qualities* of objects or events.

Scientific accuracy can also demand that one say, not merely that A occurs more frequently than B, but that A occurs *so and so much* more frequently than B. Statements of this sort entail counting, and objects or events can be counted. The process of counting culminates in "statistical" surveys. Counting and statistical surveys involve an *enumeration* of objects or events. Statements of relative frequency can then be made. Measurement and enumeration are companionate features of the *comparative* statements involving constructed types and their empirical approximations.

With respect to measurement it must be recalled that the abstract type deviates from "reality" in that it accentuates to a logical extreme some attribute or group of attributes that are relevant to a system of analysis. In a sense it is a distortion of the concrete in that all occurrences will be individually different in some way from the constructed types. One will get nothing but deviations when empirical courses of action are observed. But, these deviations will be relative—to each other and to the constructed type. Logically, then, the typologist is led to the problem of measurement in terms of *degree* of deviation. This is not an end in itself, for it facilitates further scientific activity. First of all, the comparison of the actual actions or structures, with the typical construct will indicate the relative degree of prevalence of the typical factors and thereby indicate a degree of probability of occurrence of the typical consequences of those actions or structures. Secondly, the comparison will, through the indication of degree of prevalance of the typical factors, indicate the possible need for further constructed types on a different level of generalization so as to include more of the apparently unique in a generalized scheme. Third, the comparison of the construct with the empirical approximations should serve as a fruitful source of more specific hypotheses which in turn will be applicable on a less generalized level.

With reference to enumeration it must be recalled that the generalizing constructed type is applicable to varied historical and cultural contexts. The *extent* of prevalence of a given type within a given universe can often be of problematic significance to the researcher. For example, the relative *frequency* of occurrences "democratic" as opposed to "autocratic" orientations within a concrete group can assist the typologist in interpreting the behavior of that group. Similarly the relative numbers of "constructive," "routine," "impulsive" and "subversive" followers within a "movement" indicates relative possibilities to the researcher with regard to the realization of the aims of the movement. Likewise, the relative frequency of manifestations of "rational" behavior as contrasted to "valuational," "traditional," or "affectual" behavior within various concrete groups gives the analyst the ability to make significant comparative statements about the value and action systems of those groups.

Whatever may be said about the constructed type it must be clearly understood that it is not anti-quantitative in nature, indeed, the realization of its scientific potential seemingly binds it to quantitative procedures. The reduction of the role of "impression" and "intuition" in the approach of the constructive typologist would seem to be related to the development of his ability to practice quantification. The constructed type is a theoretically plausible course of action or structure. It is the concept of statistical probability that enables the typologist to avoid the false reification of his construct. It is the concept of probability that puts an empirical interpretation to the constructed type and bridges the gap between the heuristic device and the empirical occurrence.[72] The generalizations based upon the constructed type are always probability statements. Weber, for example, carefully cast his statements in the form of: "typical chances for the expectation of a certain course of action under the presence of certain conditions." [73] Both enumeration and measurement are implicit in such a formulation.

Statistical control is a desirable adjunct of the constructed type for it enhances the predictive power of the theoretical device. The constructed type isolates the behavior that is theoretically significant. It does not in itself say anything about the frequency of that behavior; that is a function of enumeration. Neither does it say anything about the *degree* of deviation; that is a function of measurement. Whatever statistical controls are used, however, are put on the empirical data that the type has reference to, not on the type itself. The type is a structured *unit*. The criteria of the constructed type are structurally interrelated. The relations that obtain between the elements of the type are postulated, and hence the type is a system that need not be manipulated. The way in which it can be held accountable for empirical variations is through the extraction of sub-types that isolate lesser universes for statistical manipulation. Quantitative methods can be applied in the empirical validation of the predictions based on the type, but not to the type itself.

From the foregoing exposition it should be evident that the constructive typologist and the statistician stand on the threshold of an important research relationship. At bottom both adhere to experimental and probability logic, and hence there is nothing except time and effort that stands between them and a fruitful procedural merger. It must be frankly admitted, however, that such a merger has been slow in developing. Constructive typology is still largely in a prequantitative state. Certain contributions have been made, however, both in the area of enumeration and measurement. For illustrative purposes three such contributions will be cited here in some detail.

One of the pioneer usages of statistics was that of Durkheim in his study of suicide.[74] His enumeration in that study had reference to constructed types. He distinguishes four types of suicide which spring from the peculiarities in the relations between the individual and society. "Altruistic," "egoistic," "anomic," and "fatalistic" are constructed sociological types. The "altrustic" type of suicide refers to the case wherein

---

[72] Attention is directed to the scheme propounded by Howard Becker for empirically examining hypotheses about types. It takes the form: "If P, then Q, and if Q, then P." See *Through Values to Social Interpretation* (Durham: Duke University Press, 1950), pp. 262-75.

[73] Theodore Abel, *op. cit.*, p. 146.

[74] Emile Durkheim, *Suicide,* George Simpson (tr. and ed.) (Glencoe, Illinois: The Free Press, 1951).

the individual is so immersed in his social relationships that his own life counts for little. This is a self sacrificing type of suicide. On the other hand "egoistic" suicide springs out of the opposite situation. It is a self-asserting type of suicide emergent out of a social system stressing individuality. "Fatalistic" suicide derives from excessive regulation in the form of oppressive discipline. Aspirations and passions are so blocked and choked off by an inflexible order that life has no "holding power." [75] Standing opposite the "fatalistic" is the sociologically intriguing "anomic" type. This is a type reflecting the "normlessness" of a society. There is confusion with regard to the "standards" of behavior and the equilibrium is upset. The stability of the individual is seen as reflecting his ability to preserve his customary standards and thus his social role.

Utilizing these types it was then possible for Durkheim quantitatively to check their rate in various concrete groups. For instance he shows the suicide rate is higher among the Protestants than among Catholics and interprets this as being due to the fact that Protestantism stresses individuality more and puts more responsibility on individuals than some of them can bear. Mother Church encompasses the Catholic, whereas the Protestant faces God alone. The result is a higher incidence of "egoistic" suicide among Protestants.

Durkheim's verification of the "anomic" suicide is largely based upon the correlation between suicide and the business cycle. "Peaks" as well as "troughs" indicate an absolute increase in suicides. Loss of money is obviously disturbing and makes life intolerable for some people. Durkheim points out that the opposite can also be true. Sudden access to fortune can cause as much stress as the loss of fortune. This can only be interpreted as meaning that people are closely fitted into their social niches and the drastic alteration of a style of life is in itself intolerable for some people. "Anomic" suicide as a societal current thus reflects the relative "normlessness" or flux of standards in society.

This brief treatment of Durkheim's suicidal currents should merely serve to illustrate the possibility of enumerating concrete cases in concrete groups and relating them to heuristic types. This amounts to saying that certain suicides may be considered to be empirical approximations of a given type, and hence may be considered to be "identical for the purpose in hand." [76] When variation of type incidence in various groups can be detected, then the analyst is in a position to make certain general statements about those groups. The heuristic type has been given an empirical interpretation through enumeration of relative frequency.

With reference to measurement, certain things are now being done that show promise for the constructed type. It is the peculiar advantage of the constructed type that it lends itself to statement in the form of polar anti-

---

[75] The fatalistic type is not a part of the main scheme. See p. 276, *ibid.*, for a brief treatment.

[76] The constructed type is obviously not a "class," nevertheless it can serve a classificatory function.

theses. The constructed types constitute the limits of a conceptional continuum. The problem of measurement for the constructed type is the familiar problem of the continuum. When a continuum is assumed the task becomes one of *scaling* it. Scaling consequently offers considerable promise to the constructive typologist in the matter of enabling him to make statements of *degree* of deviation from the ideal limits of a case. Much of the work done by people interested in scaling involves the implicit usage of constructed types. Such well known distinctions as "liberal-conservative," "progressive-traditionalist," "democratic-autocratic," "introvert-extrovert" and numerous others are of this character. A continuum is comprehensible only in terms of its limits, hence the necessity for the constructed type.

For illustrative purposes two scaling adaptations of the constructed type will be cited in detail. The Allport-Vernon *Study of Values* aims to measure the relative prominence of six basic interests or motives in personality: the *theoretical, economic, aesthetic, social, political; and religious.*[77] These types are recognizable as being Spranger's types of men.[78] Spranger defends the view that the personalities of men are best known through a study of their values or evaluative attitudes. These types are then ideal value perspectives and the problem becomes one of determining degree of deviance from them on the part of individuals identified with different concrete groups.

The Allport-Vernon test consists in a number of questions based upon a variety of familiar controversial situations wherein either two or four alternative answers are provided. An equal number of questions on the test refer to each of the value perspective. The subject records his preferences numerically by the side of each alternative answer. His score is then determined. Norms are then established for different concrete groups and significant differences are demonstrated with regard to their value perspectives. Table 32 indicates the various value forms (means and standard deviations) with references to different groups of college students. A glance will indicate that students of engineering and medicine are more theoretically oriented than theological students. Students of engineering and business administration are more economically oriented than students of medicine, education, and theology. Theological students are more socially oriented than students of engineering and business administration, and so on. One can state a different value expectancy with reference to each concrete group on the basis of the scaling of the deviance from the constructed value types.

Loomis has done some pioneer work in the area of scaling types of social systems.[79] To get at the differences in the value orientation of social systems Loomis introduces the basic concepts of *familistic Gemein-*

[77] G. W. Allport, P. E. Vernon, and Gardner Lindzey, *Study of Values,* rev. ed. (New York: Houghton Mifflin Co., 1951).

[78] Edward Spranger, *Types of Men,* Paul Pigors (tr.) (New York, Stechert-Hafner, Inc., 1928).

schaft, contractual Gesellschaft and *compulsory Gesellschaft.* In oversimplified terms *familistic Gemeinschaft* embraces those relationships and associations arising from an emotionally based inclination to associate. *Contractual Gesellschaft* flows out of rational and calculated consideration of the ends to be served by the associations. *Compulsory Gesellschaft* re-

TABLE 32.

ILLUSTRATIVE OCCUPATIONAL DIFFERENCES	Theo-retical	Eco-nomic	Aes-thetic	Social	Polit-ical	Reli-gious
53 Students of	46.62*	45.79*	37.25*	34.70*	43.08*	32.59*
Engineering (male)	6.97†	7.66†	8.43†	7.37†	8.12†	10.13†
173 Students of	42.09*	49.25*	32.58*	35.16*	45.68*	35.24*
Business Administration (male)	6.36†	7.69†	7.34†	5.96†	5.96†	8.42†
93 Students of Medicine	50.68*	33.90*	44.83*	38.12*	38.86*	33.48*
(male)	7.52†	9.18†	9.85†	8.45†	6.80†	11.70†
68 Graduate Students of	44.31*	37.14*	43.76*	41.98*	39.17*	33.64*
Education (male)	8.30†	8.29†	9.34†	7.27†	6.22†	10.63†
24 Clergymen	37.07*	27.12*	35.54*	43.67*	38.57*	58.07*
	6.44†	5.93†	7.01†	4.95†	4.17†	3.84†
15 Theological Students	35.67*	27.40*	40.73*	45.20*	36.80*	54.20*
	5.82†	7.16†	7.97†	5.79†	4.74†	5.97†

Table is taken from G. W. Allport, P. E. Vernon, and Gardner Lindzey, *op. cit.,* p. 9.

* Indicate the means on the above table.

† Indicate the standard deviations on the above table.

fers to relationships wherein certain members are powerless to resist their participation on the basis of ends other than their own. Each of these are constructed types. Loomis then subsumes under these basic constructs a series of continua based upon sub-types of each variety. He then proceeds to effect comparisons between concrete social systems with references to the constructs. Table 33 is self-explanatory, and a careful perusal of it will indicate the procedures Loomis used in scaling the difference between "families" and "military organizations."

Loomis used a similar technique involving only one major variation in scaling three other social systems. The variation from the approach outlined in Table 33 was with regard to the use of "judges." An Amish family, a Latin-American ditch association, and a federal government bureau in the U. S. Department of Agriculture were compared as social systems. Professional sociologists who were intimately familiar with at least two of these systems were requested to rank them on a series of continua subsumed under the *familistic Gemeinschaft-contractual Gesellschaft* antithesis. A series of continua were set up with regard to hierarchical interaction, non-hierarchical interaction in roles, and prevailing value orienta-

[79] C. P. Loomis, "The Nature of Rural Social Systems: A Typological Analysis," *Rural Sociology,* Vol. 15 (June, 1950), pp. 156-174; C. P. Loomis and J. A. Beegle, "A Typological Analysis of Social Systems," *Sociometry,* Vol. 9 (August, 1948), pp. 147-91.

tions. Each social system was rated by the judges on a ten-point scale with reference to the series of continua. Figure 11 indicates the consensus profiles established with regard to the prevailing value orientation. The rankings which were made independently were consistently in close agreement. The distinctions between the social systems on the basis of the rankings are clearly shown in Figure 11.

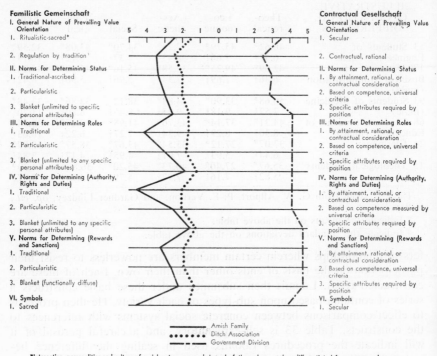

*Interaction, personalities and culture of social systems are ends in and of themselves—ends undifferentiated from norms and means.

Figure 11.

Figure 11 is taken from *ibid.*, p. 162.

The foregoing examples of enumeration and measurement are given merely to illustrate the possibility of eventually quantifying many constructed types. The utility and predictive value of the generalizing constructed type would unquestionably be enhanced if quantifying procedures were followed whenever it was feasible.

7. The Constructed Type and Historical Method

The relationship between typological and statistical methods show promise of becoming increasingly fruitful. It has been repeatedly noted, however, that quantification is always quantification of *something*. Statements as to what that something is involves description of the empirically

TABLE 33.

Average Scores Which Ninety Veterans Who Were Students of Rural Sociology During the Winter and Spring Terms of 1949 at Michigan State College Gave the Military Units They Knew Best and Their Families of Orientation When These Veterans Were 5 to 15 Years of Age, as Related to Continua Which Are Used as Components of the Types: Familistic Gemeinschaft, Contractual Gesellschaft, and Compulsory Gesellschaft.

	Average Scores*	
HIERARCHICAL RELATIONS‡	Families	Military
FAMILISTIC GEMEINSCHAFT vs COMPULSORY GESELLSCHAFT		
1. Two-Way or Two-sided vs One-Way or One-sided	7.3	3.0
2. Voluntary vs Compulsory	8.3	3.2
FAMILISTIC GEMEINSCHAFT vs CONTRACTUAL GESELLSCHAFT		
3. Solidary vs Antagonistic	9.4	5.0
4. Short, face-to-face vs Long, secondary	9.4	3.5
5. Sacred vs Secular	7.1	4.1
6. Non-rational vs Rational, *i.e.*		
a. Traditional vs Efficient	6.4	4.6
b. Emotional or spontaneous vs Planned	7.4	3.2
7. Personalized Authority vs Impersonalized Authority	8.1	2.7
8. Blanket Rights and Responsibilities vs Limited Rights and Responsibilities	7.9	3.8
NON-HIERARCHICAL RELATIONS		
*9. Highly Integrated Roles in System vs Conflicting Roles	7.9	5.8
10. Required Integration of Roles in and Out vs Irrelevance of Roles in and Out of System	7.3	4.3
11. Complete Community of Fate vs Limited Responsibility ...	9.8	3.9
†12. Interaction Confined to System vs Interaction Distributed to Many Systems	5.4	5.4
GENERAL VALUE ORIENTATION		
†13. *Norms:*		
a. Functionally Diffuse vs Functionally Specific	7.2	3.3
b. Determined by Tradition vs Rationally Determined or by Contract	6.9	6.0
c. Sacred vs Secular	7.3	3.8
†14. *Ends:*		
a. Functionally Diffuse vs Functionally Specific	6.9	2.9
b. Determined by Tradition vs Rationally Determined or by Contract	6.5	5.7
†15. Sacredness of Symbols vs Secular Nature of, or Lack of Symbols	7.5	5.3

* Items 1 through 11, with the exception of item 9, are calculated for ninety rural sociology students who were veterans in World War II. On the instruments as used by the students, the terms familistic Gemeinschaft, contractual Gesellschaft and compulsory Gesellschaft were not used. The instrument used by the ninety students and filled out in the fall and spring terms of 1949 carried definitions of the extremes on each continua. The instructions given the students are indicated below. Item 1 is reproduced below to indicate how the continua were set up on the instrument filled out by the students.‡

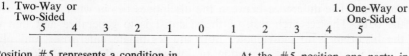

1. Two-Way or Two-Sided										1. One-Way or One-Sided
5	4	3	2	1	0	1	2	3	4	5

Position #5 represents a condition in which there is no difference in individuals of the system in response and response-provoking and/or requesting and granting of permission.

At the #5 position one party in the interaction only responds as in the case of hypnosis or a robot being manipulated.

The scores are calculated on the basis of arbitrarily assigned numbers running consecutively from 1 to 11 from right to left, so that position 5 at the right is numbered 1; 0 in the middle, or the neutral point, 6; and position 5 at the left, 11. Thus the higher the average score, the nearer the social system under consideration was placed toward the familistic Gemeinschaft, and the farther from the Gesellschaft types. As stated above these types were not used on the instrument.

Standard deviations and corresponding "F" ratios of these standard deviations were first calculated for all items. The items which showed no significant differences between family and army scores on standard deviations were then tested by a "t" score showing the difference between the means of family and army scores. Only items 6a, 12, 13b, and 14b were found to give insignificantly different scores for family and army unit at the 5 per cent level. Standard deviations for the separate items ranged from .15 to .35.

† Items 9, 12, 13, 14 and 15 were used on a different sample of veteran students attending rural sociology classes in 1948. The following number of students filled out the respective items: Item 9, 72 students; Item 12, 73 students; Item 13, 42 students; Item 14, 43 students; and Item 15, 68 students. When these latter items were used there were no definitions of position 5 as above, and there were no specific situational definitions given.

‡ Among instructions used in comparing the continua were the following:

In each case please assume the following conditions: A sudden emergency about which no member of the group had any warning required that the permanent location (residence of the family, and offices or quarters of the other group or groups) be moved within twelve hours. All possessions and equipment used by the group and its individuals must be moved by the group itself to a new location several miles away.

1. Please place an F on each of the continua which indicates approximately the correct description of the relationship between your own father and yourself which would have existed under the crisis situation if it had occurred during the 5-year period before you were 15 years old.

2. Assuming that the above described crisis occurred, please place an M on the continua which would represent the position of the relationship between yourself and your immediate superior in the unit of the armed forces with which you are most familiar. If you had no military experience, assume your immediate superior to be a second lieutenant and yourself a private and rely on your reading and general knowledge.

NOTE: Place all relationships on each continua or line before proceeding to the next.

Thus, below, place the father-child (your father and yourself) and military relationship on each line so that their relative position may be noted on each continua before going to the next continua. Do not attempt to place the parent-child relationship separately on each continua and the other relationship separately.

Table 33 is taken from C. P. Loomis, "The Nature of Rural Social Systems: A Typological Analysis," *Rural Sociology,* Vol. 15 (June, 1950), pp. 158-59.

occurrent. It is here that the data of the historian is of importance to the typologists, and hence the relationship of the typological and historical methods must be subjected to analysis.

There is a sharp distinction between social-scientific and historical procedure for their procedures answer to their respective research purposes. All data are historical, consequently the date of history and science are the same. The difference between the disciplines lies in what they do with the data. The research task of the scientist is to generalize and that of the historian is to individuate. Both are legitimate enterprises and play important roles in the accretion of knowledge and no confusion need exist between them.

It is acceptable to hold that all objects or events are unique in time and space. No scientist has any quarrel with that. Such a thesis need not involve the argument that objects or events are *merely* temporal and that they can be known only in their uniqueness, with their time and space markings clearly evident. On the contrary it is possible through the use of conceptual constructs to conceive of the "identical," "recurrent," and "typical." History is "event structured" even to the historian, and events cannot only be viewed chronologically and individually, but can be viewed as relationship-series involving necessary and sufficient antecedents of consequents. Such conditions and consequents can be categorized, and types and the relations involved can be abstractly stated as general relations. It is thus the perspectives of the historian and scientist that differ.

The field of the historian is the whole range of human activities. The social sciences in their division of labor cover the same range. But whereas the historian is concerned with processes and structures which are singular in their space-time occurrence and does not conceive of them as being repeatable, the social scientist adopts the opposite perspective. The social scientist is concerned with the repetitive and constant factors, or tendencies of regularity of human society. For example, a sociologist may try to state the recurrent aspects involved in the process of "urbanization"; the historian, on the other hand, will try to state the specific course which "urbanization" has taken in a given place at a given time. This is another way of saying that the sociologist attempts to extract whatever is "universal" from the phenomenon, whereas the historian attempts to expose the relevant "particulars" of one case of the phenomena. Relative to this point Rickert writes: " 'that the most comprehensive generalizing concept of natural science would represent its objects in the simplest possible form, whereas the most comprehensive individualizing concept of history would have to comprise the greatest possible heterogeneity of historically significant elements.' "[80]

To approach the problem from a different angle, it is possible to assert that there is no such thing as a "knife-edge present," for the "present" can be comprehended only in terms of events, and any event has a temporal spread. Any given event has its antecedent conditions and thus has a "past" that it is bound to, and is implicated in a "future" that in part is responsible for the course of action. The delineation of a "present" from the historical continuity of which it is a part is accomplished only through the conceptualization of events. What is then *called* the past is "history" and what is *called* the present is "contemporary," but there is no intrinsic difference between them. They are constituted of the same material.

From the foregoing it is evident that historical and scientific data are identical; for instance, each science has its own historical development, and each body of scientific knowledge has emerged historically. The difference in the disciplines lies not in the data, but in the *perspectives, problems,* and *methods.* Granted this, then it is entirely justifiable

---

[80] Quoted in Alexander Goldenweiser, "Relationship of Natural Science to Social Science," in H. E. Barnes, Howard Becker, and F. B. Becker, (eds.), *op. cit.,* p. 101.

and indeed necessary that the social scientist concern himself with data which are unquestionably historical. History is not merely the business of the historian, but is also of crucial concern to the social scientist, for it offers him a wealth of material that must be accounted for in his "general" formulations.

It is not appropriate for the social scientist to refuse to consult data merely because it is considered to be "historical." If his formulations are truly general they must stand the test of time. There "generality" lies not only in the removal of "spatial" markings, but also in the removal of "temporal" markings. The society of today is intimately related to the society of yesterday and the days and years preceding. To get at processes and structures that are not merely "unique," it is necessary to examine them in the light of the data of history. It must be remembered that social phenomena cannot in most cases be experimentally produced by the observer. Social phenomena usually cannot be deliberately created for purposes of further examination and manipulation. The social scientist must by and large accept his data as they naturally occur. Consequently it is essential that he utilize whatever data that fits the "if and when" set-up of his predictive schema, regardless of when it occurred.

As Becker has pointed out, prediction can be either *retrospective* or *prospective*.[81] In other words, the typical conditions, factors, and emergent phenomena may be searched for in the data of history as well as in that of the contemporary or future scene. For example, on the basis of an hypothesis a type of leadership can be constructed. One can then look for the situations in history that meet the "if and when" requirements, and check for verification or refutation of the initial hypothesis. If "charismatic" leadership is to be a genuine sociological construct, then it must have applicability to leaders outside of a given epoch. It explains the position of a Christ or a Mohammed as well as that of a Hitler or a Mussolini. The prediction involved is based upon events that have already occurred, but all events that are comprehensible have already occurred. Retrospective prediction is entirely legitimate in that it involves relatively timeless processes and structures. This type of prediction also serves to illustrate the fact that a social scientist cannot prophesy the occurrence of a given phenomenon at a given time, because the factors and conditions essential to the occurrence of the phenomenon are beyond the control of the social scientist. He can merely state conditional occurrence in terms of typical action. The constructed type makes a contribution here in that it serves warning to the social scientist to abide by the limitations of his "if and when" proviso. This demands the avoidance of the unjustifiable habit of prophesying on the empirical level and requires greater expenditure of effort toward statement of prediction in probability terms on the typical level.

---

[81] Howard Becker, *op. cit.*, pp. 106, 112, 118, 163, 166, 175-76, 178, 240, 285-90.

Merton makes the following critical remarks about the validity of retrospective prediction:

> Post factum explanations remain at the level of *plausibility* (low evidential value) rather than leading to "compelling evidence" (a high degree of confirmation). . . . The logical fallacy underlying the post factum explanation rests in the fact that there is available a variety of crude hypotheses, each with some measure of confirmation but designed to account for quite contradictory sets of affairs. The method of post factum explanation does not lend itself to nullifiability, if only because it is so completely flexible—. The analysis is fitted to the facts, and there is no indication of just which data would be taken to contravene the interpretations. As a consequence, the documentary evidence merely illustrates rather than tests the theory.[82]

The foregoing is a good statement with reference to explanation based upon the use of individuating types. It is a statement that also has reference to what can happen to the generalizing constructed type when its area of applicability is not clearly stated. With regard to the individuating type it is seemingly impossible to overcome the problem of nullifiability. That is why it would be so difficult to negate such an hypothesis as Max Weber's connection of Protestant and capitalistic ethics. Alternative hypotheses cannot be readily dispensed with, hence any hypothesis based upon individuating types has low evidential value.

With regard to the generalizing construct, however, the situation is different. When the parameters of the constructed type are clearly stated, the internal criteria of the type made explicit, and the hypothesis properly qualified, explanation based upon the generalizing construct can constitute compelling evidence. It must be remembered that one does not look for the *type* in history. On the contrary one looks for the "if and when set-up." If a set-up satisfying the requirements of a given constructed type is found and the consequent behavior is not in some degree of accordance with that which is hypothesized on the basis of the type, then the hypothesis may be considered to be inadequate if not nullified. Because the behavior cannot be in *exact* accordance with the behavior of the construct there is a necessity for statements involving relative degree of accordance. Because several empirical cases can be examined and compared, due to the general character of the construct, it is possible to demand a high degree of consistent and general accordance with the expected behavior. If it is not found, then one is forced to reformulate the hypothesis and devise a substitute type or types that will expose consistent regularities in the empirical behavior.

Neither a type nor a hypothetical course of action based upon it can be sacred to the scientist. The sole justification for the existence of a constructed type is that it can serve to expose empirical regularities;

---

[82] R. K. Merton, "Sociological Theory," *American Journal of Sociology*, Vol. 50 (May, 1945), pp. 468-69.

if it does not do so then it must be discarded. The ultimate test of the constructed type is that of the instrument. It has to pass the pragmatic test of being useful as an instrument.

Returning again to the distinction between historical and scientific objectives, it is legitimate to say that the historical approach is concerned "ideally" with a description of the particular and unique aspects of a given phenomenon. On the other hand, the scientific approach is concerned "ideally" with the *comparable, repetitive* and *typical* aspects of phenomena. The type constructs that enable the scientist to conceive of phenomena in this light are *necessarily* woven out of the particularities of the historian. The historian has much to offer the social scientist in view of the fact that the scientific constructs presuppose a knowledge of the particulars from which they are drawn.

It must be noted that a generalizing constructed type can be drawn from only two different places. It can be *derived* from theory or more general types that have already received substantial empirical verification, or it can be *constructed* directly from the particulars of an historical situation. In view of the limited character of theory available in the social sciences, the latter case is most frequent. Constructed types are at their working best when they are derived from a substantial theoretical scheme, but in the absence of such a scheme it is essential laboriously to proceed from the particularities. In such case, the construct cannot be deliberately designed with "generality" as the primary aim.[83] The construction of the "individuating type"—the "historical individual" or "thing to be examined" is the necessary first step. The logic of induction demands this.

Once the type has been constructed it is then possible and advisable to check its applicability to other epochs and cultures. The example given earlier was the ecclesia-sect formulation, which has achieved increasingly general significance through its application to diverse phenomena in various studies. Likewise, it is possible to construct devices such as "economic," "scientific," or "academic" man, but their areas of applicability cannot be determined ahead of time. Obviously there are numerous *time* and *place* restrictions on their applicability. Most of recorded history as well as many contemporary cultures are immune to analyses based upon these types. It is nonsense to talk of "economic" man (and the presumptions entailed) with reference to typical behavior prior to the emergence of capitalism. It is likewise nonsense to speak of "scientific" man with reference to primitive societies, or of "academic" man prior to the emergence of the occupational role upon which it is based. Constructs cannot ignore facts; on the contrary, they must account for facts. Clearly, then, the historian with his facts has much to offer the social scientist in the way of data. The social scientist takes up where

---

[83] Becker stresses the importance of this. See *op. cit.,* pp. 145-46.

the historian leaves off, and puts the same data in a different perspective—that of the comparable, repetitive, and general.

8. The Constructed Type and Case Method

The relationship of the constructed type to the case study is essentially the same as to the historical approach. It is doubtful that the study of cases should be called a method at all. The study of cases is an essential aspect of science and is preliminary to the formulation of types and generalizations. The case study is a way of ordering social data with the view of preserving the unitary character of whatever is being studied. It merely selects out and treats some socially defined object or act as a *whole*. This whole constitutes the case unit, and the case unit may involve any level or base of abstraction. The case may be a person, an episode in a person's life, a group, a concrete set of relationships, a specific process, a culture; any aspect of empirical reality reacted to as a unit. The function of the case study is to describe the case in terms of the particularities that are observable. This means an intensive examination of the specific factors implicated in the case.

The wholeness or unitary character ascribed to this concrete case is a *construct*. There are no concrete limits to any object or act. The limits imposed reflect the perspective and theoretical interest of the observer. The limits defining an individual may be "dissolved" when one is observing from the perspective of the group. In turn the limits defining the group may be dissolved when one is conceptualizing in terms of a social order. All units are thus constructs delimited for pragmatic purposes. Whatever unit has been abstracted out may be examined and described in its uniqueness. This is what the historian and ethnologist do, and the descriptive work that they produce is important data to the social scientist interested in generalizing.

Whatever unit has been abstracted out is temporally and spatially bound. It has a particular historical development and is a unique configuration. This unit may be described as a case by an indefinite number of facts. These facts may be obtained from many diverse sources, depending upon what the case is. They may be obtained from documents, life histories, from the individual, from members of a group, from participant-observation; from all the avenues open to the historian and ethnologist. The imputation of these facts to the case merely describe, they do not have explanatory value in the scientific sense.

It is here that the scientist with his method of constructive typology can take over. The sociologist, for instance, may be interested in the repetitive characteristics and uniform relations involved in "revolutions." He desires theoretically to predict revolutions by use of the "if and when" proviso. This involves statements of uniformity and regularity with respect to revolutions. Such statements are based upon answering questions with regard to typical "elements," and "sequences" occurrent in revolutions in general. The ability of the sociologist to make such statements and answer such questions is based upon his ability to construct types on the basis of intensive examination of specific revolutions as empirical cases.

The constructive typologist on the basis of his familiarity with empirical uniformities appearing in a thoroughly described case or several cases pragmatically classified as being similar, erects a model revolution in the form of a type. Initially this type will be dated and localized as an "historic individual," and closely resembles the empirical case or type. The collection of such dated and localized types is representative of the first step toward "generality." Types of revolution that are relatively free from time and space markings can only be developed by accumulating these dated and localized types and modifying them to make them applicable to more and more empirical cases. This means that the type becomes increasingly generalized and can consequently explain an increasingly wider range of cases of revolution.[84]

In brief, the case is an abstraction. The case-study preserves the unity of that abstraction and involves the accretion of facts describing it in its particularity. The individuating constructed type marks a first step away from the "uniqueness" of the case, in that it selectively pulls out what seem to be significant uniformities. This type is temporally and spatially bound. The attempt to free it from these bonds involves the examination of other empirical cases with the view of modifying the type or types to represent ideal manifestations of a variety of cases. The constructed type is thus inductively established as a "model" and basis for comparing and generalizing empirical cases.

9. An Illustration of Type Construction

The foregoing treatment is intended to be a statement of the general considerations with which a typologist must concern himself. The introductory section and section I were concerned with the identification of the constructed type as a scientific instrument. Section II involved the dismemberment of the type in terms of the variables of its construction. Section III dealt briefly with some of the more fruitful modern applications of typology in the social sciences.

Before attempting type construction one should certainly acquaint himself with these varied uses. Section IV should serve to establish the point that types are never really established *ad hoc*. Either implicitly or explicitly, types are embedded in a background of theory consisting in the general categories of the discipline. The remaining sections represent an attempt to relate typology to the traditional methods of science. These relationships are important, for they are working research relationships, and hence indicate the instrumental value of the type. Because this treatment has been relatively abstract it is now perhaps advisable to make the *process* of type construction more concrete. For the sake of clarity and simplicity we will put aside most of the considerations

---

[84] *Ibid.*, p. 216.

dealt with so far and focus directly upon the *procedure of type construc-tion.* The question is "What does a typologist do when he is constructing a type?" In order to answer that question we will establish an illustrative case and make explicit the *steps* involved in the procedure.[85]

(1) *There must be a problematic situation.* The typologist never works in a vacuum. On the contrary he is concerned with problems appearing in the substantive area covered by his discipline. These problems will arise relative to his interests and theories. Let us say that the general problem "is the assessment of German war guilt." Now for the extraction of a research problem from that general area. Let us say that the typologist is interested in the German intellectual. Formulate the problem then as follows: "What was the role of the German intellectual in the conduct of an agressor nation?" The typologist now can begin to search for an answer, however tentative, to this question.

(2) *The typologist must acquaint himself with the data provided by the historian with regard to the problematic situation.* The typologist must immerse himself in the particularities of the German situation. The facts provided by the historian give a descriptive account of Germanic be-havior. Some knowledge of recent German events and modern German behavior is *essential* before proceeding further.

(3) *Inductive derivation of hypotheses about relationships and se-quences.* Although the type itself may be an hypothetical process, struc-ture, or system, it is impossible to construct that type until an hypothesis or battery of hypotheses is set up. The "form" the type will take will directly reflect the purposes for which it was constructed, and these in turn will be directly related to the hypotheses one holds with regard to the problematic area.

On the basis of what the typologist knows about 20th century German behavior and the Hitlerian movement, he might hypothesize a negative relation between intellectuals and the power regime of the Hitlerian order. For the purposes at hand we define the intellectual as being the "profes-sional man of knowledge." On the basis of observation the typologist believes the Hitlerian order to be charismatic, affectual, traditionally oriented, prescribed sacred, and anti-rationalistic. Such an order would scarcely emphasize the role of knowledge, consequently the intellectual as the possessor of that knowledge would probably be relegated to a minor and passive role in the scheme of things. The hypothesis can be formulated as follows: "The intellectual was an impotent factor in the Hitlerian order." Numerous sub-hypotheses would unquestionably be built around this. Then, the next step.

(4) *Delineation of empirical uniformities and pragmatic reduction to type.* It must be recalled that the constructed type is a *compound of at-*

[85] For varied treatments of procedure see: Howard Becker, *op. cit.,* pp. 93-127; Paul Lazarsfeld, *op. cit.,* pp. 118-38; R. C. Angell, *The Family Encounters the De-pression* (New York: Charles Scribner's Sons, 1936), pp. 265-307; Paul Meadows, "The Scientific Use of Historical Data," *Philosophy of Science,* Vol. 12 (January, 1944), pp. 53-58.

tributes. The compound itself as a *system* is constructed, but the attributes included should each have empirical bases. The attributes are empirical uniformities. This is not synonomous with statistical uniformities although such would be included. All that is involved at this stage is this: The area of the intellectual has been roughly blocked out as consisting in "professional men of knowledge," the typologist then is in search of attributes of this group; he makes use of whatever knowledge of such attributes is already available, including statistical uniformities and correlations, and uniformities occurring in intensively examined individual cases; he selects the attributes that "stand out" as being the most obvious (on the basis of consensus), and those that appear to be most "crucial" (on the basis of whatever theory he is using); the typologist has *interpretively* (on the basis of the frame of reference and back-log of knowledge) selected these attributes as being *significantly representative* of the intellectuals behavior with regard to the social order; the typologist then *imputes* the character of *system* to these attributes, in other words he assumes that they belong together and hence are representative of the system of behavior called intellectual. The type then is an hypothesized compound of empirically observed attributes of the class being dealt with.

The attributes included within the construct "impotent German intellectual" include the following: "(1) strong although sometimes unavowed nationalism; (2) great respect for the traditions of the German armed forces; (3) fear of Russia so great that the Nazis appeared as the lesser evil; (4) placing of primary responsibility for the rise of Hitler on the outside world rather than on German docility; (5) failure to participate in political activity; (6) opposition to the Nazis expressed in 'bitching' or like grumbling rather than in more determined ways: (7) dislike of collaboration with working-class opposition to the Nazis; (8) pride in intellectuality as an end itself ('ivory towerism'); and (9) self-pity." [86]

This "type construct" is a product of *pragmatic reduction* of a series of attributes to a single unit.[87] Nothing has been said so far about the numerical frequency of this type within the class (intellectuals) which it presupposes, nor has anything been said about those who could not be regarded as approximating the type. These are important empirical questions which cannot be handled until further typological steps are taken.

(5) *Substruction of type to attribute sphere from which it is drawn.*[88] The act of substruction may be performed as a "check-up" prior to

---

[86] This type is "borrowed" from Howard Becker. See "Propaganda and the Impotent German Intellectual," *Social Forces*, Vol. 20 (March, 1951), pp. 273-76. The type is used *illustratively* here. The intent of this section is to clarify the procedural steps of typology and the substantive material involved is purely illustrative. No assertions of empirical validity are made; this is a purely speculative exercise. Becker should not be charged with saying any of the things about his type that we are speculatively saying here for the purposes of illustration.

[87] See Paul Lazarsfeld, *op. cit.,* pp. 126-33 for a differentiation between types of reduction.

[88] For an analysis of the process of substruction involving a plurality of types see *Ibid.,* pp. 132-38.

empirical examination of the type. The type "impotent German intellectual" necessarily implies the existence of a concrete class of intellectuals. This class of intellectuals will be characterized by a series of
attributes that will be *more* varied and inclusive than those contained
within the single type constructed thus far. In other words we cannot
assume that all German intellectuals will be impotent. Each of the attributes contained in the "impotent" construct is a *serial* attribute definable in terms of *degree*.[89] A serial is an attribute which can be predicated
of an object only in comparison with another object. It permits the
ranging of any number of objects in a certain order, in this case, intellectuals with regard to *more* or *less* manifestation of "self pity,"
"political participation," *et al.* Granted this, then at *least* one other type
must logically exist within the universe of intellectuals. This is the polar
opposite of the "impotent" type, and might be called, for want of a better
name, the "potent" type. The attributes of that type would be the obverse
of those enumerated for the "impotent" type. Moreover, the attributes
of the intellectual class might lead to reductions other than the ones engaged in so far. The typologist in placing his "impotent" type in the
attribute sphere of the more inclusive class of intellectuals might find it
advisable to include the use of the polar opposite type and other potentially reducible types in his research. Or he might decide that for the
purposes of his research it is possible to ignore the attributes of the
class of intellectuals and their potential reductions. He in effect decides
that he can examine cases within the universe of intellectuals by searching
for degree of approximation to the "impotent" type. He then can simply
give a statistical accounting of the cases that are not approximations at
all and of those that consistently manifest the opposite traits. The point
of significance is that the typologist has looked at his type in terms of the
attribute pattern of the class within which it is a special case. This can
result in the discarding of certain attributes ahead of time, the elimination
of overlapping attributes, the addition of attributes previously overlooked,
or even the establishment of a system of types other than the type or
types started with. The typologist is then ready for the next step.

(6) *Adaptation of available theories and principles to give a tentative
explanatory accounting of the type.* The type should be put within the
context of available theory. For example, it might be possible to conceive
of the "impotent German intellectual" in the light of the Parsons' theory of
the "social system" with its constituent parts, particularly the "role-
status" element.[90] Or, it might be fruitful to put the type within the
"sociation" theory of Simmel or Wiese-Becker and concentrate upon the
types of relationships that are potentially involved.[91] Whatever theory
that seemingly acounts for the uniformity of behavior of the type should
be given consideration as context. Theoretical significance beyond the

---

[89] See *Ibid.,* pp. 120-26 for a differentiation between types of attributes.
[90] Talcott Parsons, *The Social System* (Glencoe, Illinois: The Free Press, 1951).
[91] George Simmel, *op. cit.;* and Leopold von Wiese and Howard Becker, *op. cit.*

problem is thus given the type; it is deductively articulated with a system; and, the type benefits from whatever inductive verification has been given that theory. At this stage it is possible to hypothesize certain forms of behavior that the type will *probably* manifest with regard to the situation it is in. Utilizing the *if* and *when* proviso it should now be possible to say that within the German social system with its constitutent roles, statuses, values, traditions, *et al.* the "impotent" German intellectual (as a model actor) will *probably* act in a particular way. This is not a statement of statistical probability. At this stage it is merely a statement of belief based upon; (1) theory which seemingly is applicable to this constructed type, and (2) the empirical uniformities from which the type was constructed in the first place. The next step should be obvious.

(7) *Empirical verification of the type: Examination of rate of incidence and degree of approximation.* The constructed type has isolated the behavior that is theoretically significant. It is at this stage that statistical control is a desirable adjunct of the constructed type for it enhances the predictive power of the instrument. The type does not in itself say anything about the frequency of the behavior it represents; that is a function of enumeration. Neither does the type say anything about the *degree* of deviation; that is a function of measurement and serial ranking.[92]

The task now of the typologist is to examine intellectuals. Preferably this should involve the selection of a statistical sample.[93] In the examination of intellectuals the typologist now can determine degree of approximation of empirical cases to the type through ranking and scaling devices.[94] One simple way of ranking the empirical approximations to the type would be to simply categorize them by the number of attributes they demonstrated. For instance, intellectuals manifesting seven of the attributes would be closer to the type than those manifesting six.[95]

At this stage the typologist can remodel his type if necessary. If he finds that none of the intellectuals in his sample manifest a particular attribute, he can deduce that it is atypical, and a unique aspect of the case from which it was taken. He then may conclude that it is not a part of the "pattern" constituting the type.

Not only can the typologist make statements about the type approximations he has discovered, he can determine the frequency of their appearance within the universe represented by the sample. This is a matter of enumeration, and in its simplest form consists in a statement of "how many empirical approximations to the type (of a given degree) were discovered within the sample." When the typologist has enumerated his cases and distinguished *degree* of type approximation he is ready for the next step.

---

[92] See Chapter IV and VI of this work.
[93] See Chapter IV of this work.
[94] See Chapter VI of this work.
[95] Howard Becker, in using this type, interviewed approximately 600 intellectuals and never found one that manifested all nine attributes contained within the type. See his "Propaganda and the Impotent German Intellectual," *op. cit.,* p. 276.

(8) *Interpretation*. Interpretation is an important aspect of any scientific procedure, and certainly has a role here. Now that the typologist has theoretically and empirically verified the type, and examined its degree of approximation and rate of incidence, he is in a position to make an interpretation with regard to the problem.

The problem was: "What was the role of the German intellectual in the conduct of an aggressor nation?" The type formulated was: "the impotent German intellectual." Giving even a tentative answer to the problem means responding to the question: "To what extent does the 'impotent German intellectual' (as type) represent the intellectuals (as class)?" If the typologist has found that the type occurs with great frequency and has a proportionately large number of empirical approximations, he may conclude that the German intellectuals played only a minor role in the aggression, and that no other types representing the class need be constructed or examined.

On the other hand, the typologist may have found that the type incidence was not overwhelming enough (statistically) to warrant any general statements on the basis of this type alone. It appears that this is only one of several that are necessary to represent the empirical attributes of the class. Under these circumstances the typologist is compelled to construct other types and empirically examine them before he can give even a tentative answer to the research question. He has, however, constructed and demonstrated one type that should prove useful as a springboard for the construction of others.[96]

10. Summary

1. The constructed type may be identified with the general aspect of method in that it is applicable to the logical ordering of an array of discrete data. The constructed type is not confined to any particular science; it is a method that is applicable to the data of any science. The particular type-constructs as substantive entities, however, are not interchangeable among the sciences.

2. The scientific function of the constructed type is to "order" the concrete data so that they may be described in terms which make them comparable, so that the experience had in one case, despite its uniqueness, may be made to reveal with some degree of probability what may be expected in others. The constructed type is a heuristic device created for predictive purposes. The type is a means of reducing diversities and complexities of phenomena to a coherently general level. It does not describe or represent a concrete course of action or situation, but it does represent an objectively probable course of action.

3. The constructed type is a devised system of characteristics (criteria) that is *useful* as a basis of understanding empirical reality. It is a con-

---

[96] There is no intention of suggesting that the typologist "has to" follow these steps. Obviously, most typologists haven't, and yet that does not negate their contribution. It is suggested, however, that adherence to the procedure just set forth would enhance the empirical value of much typological work. See footnote 85.

struct made up of abstracted elements and formed into a unified conceptual pattern, wherein there is an intensification of one or more aspects of concrete reality.

4. It must be recognized that a constructed type is *not* (1) an hypothesis, (2) a description of concrete reality, (3) an average, (4) a class, (5) a homogeneous universe, (6) a stereotype, or (7) the most common form of a phenomenon.

5. A manifest function of all types is to *identify* and *simplify*. The constructed type performs the task of guiding the initial selection of data in terms of the schema of a given science.

6. There are seemingly five major "axes" around which types are constructed. The variables of type construction involve these polarities: constructed-extracted, general-specific, scientific-historical, timeless-time-bound, and generalizing-individuating.

7. The constructed type is a logical expedient that serves as a means by which concrete occurrences can be compared, measured, and comprehended within a system of general categories underlying the types.

8. Although examination of empirical cases never reveals anything more than "approximations" or "deviations" from the constructed type, it is essential that the type should be formulated as being "objectively probable." When formulated in this manner it throws actual structures or courses of action into a comparative light. The type focuses on *uniformity,* and it is only through the notion of uniformity that one can comprehend variations or deviations.

9. As the constructed type is, in a sense, a distortion of the concrete, all individual concrete occurrences will deviate from the type. These deviations will be relative—to each other and to the constructed type. Therefore, the type can serve as a basis for the measurement of the degree of deviation. The quantification process then may be carried further within the "if and when" predictive framework, and statements of probability may be made relative to the recurrence of the typical course of action.

10. A primary contribution of the constructed type is that it serves as a basis for *comparison* and potential measurement of concrete occurrences. The constructed type serves as a point of reference for the analysis of social reality. The analysis can only proceed in terms of the comparison effected between the empirically occurrent and the heuristic construct. Both quantification and measurement are implicit aspects of comparison even with respect to constructs. Consequently the adaptation of quantifying and measuring techniques to typological procedure represents its natural line of development.

11. Statistical control is a desirable adjunct of the constructed type for it enhances the predictive power of the theoretical device. The constructed type isolates the behavior that is theoretically significant. It does not in itself say anything about the *frequency* of that behavior; that is a function of enumeration. Neither does it say anything about the *degree* of

deviation; that is a function of measurement. Whatever statistical controls are used, however, are put on the empirical data that the type has reference to, not on the type itself. The type is a structured *unit*.

12. The logic of the experimental method is the logic of the explanatory use of the constructed type. The use of the constructed type as a predictive scheme demands that it be testable under empirical conditions. This means the making of comparisons in the sense of experimental logic. The fact that most of these comparisons must be made with reference to "naturally" occurring data, and cannot be "willfully" produced, is a handicap to the social scientist, but it does not deny him explanation in the scientific sense.

13. Prediction on the basis of the constructed type can be either *retrospective* or *prospective*. The typical conditions, factors, and emergent phenomena may be searched for in the data of history as well as in that of the contemporary or future scene.

14. The constructed type that enables the scientist to conceive of phenomena as being *comparable, repetitive,* and *typical* is necessarily based upon the particularities of history. The historian has much to offer the scientific typologist in view of the fact that scientific constructs presuppose a knowledge of the particulars from which they are drawn.

15. A generalizing constructed type can be drawn from only two different places. It can be derived from theory or more general types that have already received substantial empirical verification, or it can be *constructed* directly from the particulars of a historical situation.

16. The constructed type can perform the important service of functioning as a bridge between systematic substantive theory and relatively unstructured data. The constructed type as a conceptual devise represents an attempt to advance concept formation in the social sciences from the stage of description and empirical generalization to the construction of theoretical systems.

17. The constructed type is not an ordinary concept, but is special in the sense that it deliberately emphasizes and states the "ideal limits" of the case. Moreover, it is special in the sense that it consists in a set of characteristics wherein the relations between the characteristics are held constant for the purposes at hand. Hence, the constructed type is a *system* in itself. It has the character of a theoretical model. As such it can function as an analytic element in a more comprehensive theory.

18. In so far as the constructed type is derived from a generalized scheme it serves the important function of orienting empirical research to systematic theory.

SELECTED REFERENCES

Abel, Theodore, *Systematic Sociology in Germany* (New York: Columbia University Press, 1929).

Angell, R. C., *The Family Encounters the Depression* (New York: Charles Scribner's Sons, 1936).

Allport, G. W., Vernon, P. E., and Lindzey, Gardner, *Study of Values,* rev. ed. (New York: Houghton Mifflin Co., 1951).

Bateson, Gregory, "Bali: The Value System of a Steady State," *Studies Presented to A. R. Radcliff-Brown,* Myers Fortes (ed.) (London: Oxford University Press, 1949).

Becker, Howard, "Constructive Typology in the Social Sciences," *American Sociological Review,* V (Feb., 1940), 40-55.

————, "Constructive Typology in the Social Sciences," in H. E. Barnes, Howard Becker, and F. B. Becker (eds.), *Contemporary Social Theory* (New York: D. Appleton Century Company, 1940).

————, "Culture Case Study and Ideal-Typical Method," *Social Forces* (March, 1934), 399-405.

————, *German Youth: Bond or Free* (New York: Grove Press, 1946).

————, "Propaganda and the Impotent German Intellectual," *Social Forces,* XXIX (March, 1951), 273-76.

————, *Systematic Sociology on the Basis of the Beziehungslehre and Gebildelehre of Leopold von Wiese* (Gary: Norman Paul Press, 1950).

————, *Through Values to Social Interpretation* (Durham: Duke University Press, 1950).

————, and H. E. Barnes, *Social Thought from Lore to Science,* 2 vols, 2nd ed. (Washington, D. C.: Harren Press, 1952).

————, and Meyers, R. C., "Sacred and Secular Aspects of Human Sociation," *Sociometry,* 6 (Aug., 1942), 207-29.

Benjamin, A. C., "On Formation of Constructs," *The Monist,* XXVIII (April, 1928), 404-11.

Bogardus, E. S., "A Race Relations Cycle," *American Journal of Sociology* (25 January, 1930), 612-17.

Brinton, Crane, *The Anatomy of Revolution* (New York: W. W. Norton Co., 1932).

Durkheim, Emile, *Suicide,* George Simpson, tr. and ed. (Glencoe: The Free Press, 1950).

————, *The Division of Labor* (Glencoe: The Free Press, 1947).

Edwards, L. P., *Natural History of Revolution* (Chicago: University of Chicago Press, 1927).

Eister, A. W., *Drawing Room Conversion: A Sociological Account of the Oxford Group Movement* (Durham: Duke University Press, 1950).

————, "The Oxford Group Movement," *Sociology and Social Research,* XXXIV (Nov.-Dec., 1949), 115-24.

Foreman, P. B., "Negro Lifeways in the Rural South: A Typological Approach to Social Differentiation," *American Sociological Review,* XIII (Aug., 1948), 409-18.

Francis, E. K., "Toward a Typology of Religious Orders," *American Journal of Sociology,* LV (March, 1950), 437-49.

Goode, W. J., "A Note on the Ideal Type," *American Sociological Review,* XII (Aug., 1947), 473-74.

Gurvitch, Georges, *Sociology of Law* (New York: Philosophical Library, 1942).

Handman, M. S., "The Sentiment of Nationalism," *Political Science Quarterly,* 36 (1921), 104-21.

Heberle, Rudolf, *Social Movements* (New York: Appleton-Century-Crofts, Inc., 1951).

Hempel, C. G., "Typological Methods in the Natural and the Social Sciences," *Proceedings, American Philosophical Association: Eastern Division,* I (1952), 65-86.

Hiller, E. T., *The Strike Cycle* (Chicago: University of Chicago Press, 1928).

Hobson, E. W., *Domain of Natural Science* (New York: Cambridge Press, 1923).

Hoffer, Eric, *The True Believer* (New York: Harper and Brothers, 1951).

Hughes, E. C., "Institutional Office and the Person," *American Journal of Sociology,* XLII (1937), 404-13.

————, "Personality Types and the Division of Labor," *American Journal of Sociology,* XXXIII (March, 1928), 754-68.

Klapp, O. E., "The Fool as a Social Type," *American Journal of Sociology,* LV (Sept., 1949), 157-62.

Kluver, H., "M. Weber's Ideal-Type in Psychology," *Journal of Philosophy,* XXIII (1926), 29-35.

Kolb, W. L., "The Peasant in Revolution: A Study in Constructive Typology," Ph.D. dissertation (Madison: University of Wisconsin, 1943).

Kretschmer, E., *Physique and Character* (New York: The Humanities Press Inc., 1925).

Lazarsfeld, Paul F., "Some Remarks on the Typological Procedures in Social Research," *Zeitschrift fur Sozialforschung,* VI (1937, Alcan/Paris), 119-39.

Linton, Ralph, "Nativistic Movements," *American Anthropologist,* 45, (April-June, 1943), 230-40.

Loomis, C. P., "The Nature of Rural Social Systems: A Typological Analysis," *Rural Sociology,* 15 (June, 1950), 156-74.

————, and Beegle, J. A., "A Typological Analysis of Social Systems," *Sociometry,* LX (August, 1948), 147-91.

MacIver, R. M., *Social Causation* (Boston: Ginn and Co., 1942).

Martin, Alfred von, *The Sociology of the Renaissance* (New York: Oxford University Press, 1944).

McKinney, J. C., "The Role of Constructive Typology in Scientific Sociological Analysis," *Social Forces,* 28 (March, 1950), 235-40.

Meadows, Paul, "The Scientific Use of Historical Data," *Philosophy of Science,* XI (Jan., 1944), 53-58.

Merton, R. K., "Sociological Theory," *American Journal of Sociology,* 50 (May, 1945), 468-69.

Odum, H. W., "Folk Sociology as a Subject Field for the Historical Study of Total Human Society and the Empirical Study of Group Behavior," *Social Forces,* 31 (March, 1953), 193-223.

Parsons, Talcott, *Essays in Sociological Theory: Pure and Applied* (Glencoe: The Free Press, 1949).

————, *The Structure of Social Action,* 2nd ed. (Glencoe: The Free Press, 1949).

————, and E. A. Shils, (eds.), *Toward a General Theory of Action* (Cambridge: Harvard University Press, 1951).

Pigors, Paul, "Types of Followers," *Journal of Social Psychology,* V (1934), 378-83.

Redfield, Robert, *The Folk Culture of Yucatan* (Chicago: University of Chicago Press, 1941).

————, "The Folk Society," *American Journal of Sociology,* LII (Jan., 1947), 293-308.

Rice, Stuart, (ed.), *Methods in Social Science* (Chicago: University of Chicago Press, 1931).

Riemer, Svend, "The Ideal Type in Criminological Research," in W. C. Reckless (ed.), *The Etiology of Criminal and Delinquent Behavior:* Bulletin 50 (New York: Social Science Research Council, 1943).

Rose, A. M., "A Deductive Ideal-Type Method," *American Journal of Sociology,* LVI (July, 1950), 35-42.

Schmid, R. C., "German Youth Movements: A Typological Study," Ph. D. dissertation (Madison: University of Wisconsin, 1941).

Simmel, Georg, *The Sociology of Georg Simmel,* Kurt Wolff, tr. (Glencoe: The Free Press, 1950).

Sombart, Werner, *A New Social Philosophy,* K. F. Geiser, tr. and ed. (Princeton: Princeton University Press, 1937).

————, *The Jews and Modern Capitalism,* M. Epstein, tr. (Glencoe: The Free Press, 1951).

————, *The Quintessence of Capitalism,* M. Epstein, tr. (London: T. F. Unwin, Ltd., 1915).

Sorokin, P. A., *Society, Culture, and Personality: Their Structure and Dynamics* (New York: Harper and Brothers, 1947).

Spranger, Edward, *Types of Men,* Paul Pigors, tr. (New York: Stichert-Hafner Inc., 1928).

Spykman, N. J., *The Social Theory of Georg Simmel* (Chicago: The University of Chicago Press, 1925).

Strong, S. M., "Negro-White Relations as Reflected in Social Types," *American Journal of Sociology,* LII (July, 1946), 23-30.

————, "Social Types in a Minority Group: Formulation of a Method," *American Journal of Sociology,* XLVIII (March, 1943), 563-73.

Tönnies, Ferdinand, *Fundamental Concepts of Sociology,* C. P. Loomis, tr. (New York: American Book Co., 1940).

Troeltsch, Ernest, *The Social Teaching of the Christian Churches,* Olive Wyon, tr., 2 vols. (New York: Macmillan Co., 1931).

Weber, Max, *From Max Weber: Essays in Sociology,* H. H. Gerth and C. W. Mills, trs. (New York: Oxford University Press, 1946).

————, *The Protestant Ethic and the Spirit of Capitalism,* Talcott Parsons (tr.) (London: Allen and Unwin, Ltd., 1930).

————, *The Theory of Social and Economic Organization,* A. M. Henderson and Talcott Parsons trs. (New York: Oxford University Press, 1947).

Werkmeister, W. H., *A Philosophy of Science* (New York: Harper and Brothers, 1940).

Winch, R. F., "Heuristic and Empirical Typologies," *American Sociological Review,* XII (Feb., 1947), 68-75.

Wirth, Louis, "Types of Nationalism," *American Journal of Sociology,* XLI (May, 1936), 723-37.

Yinger, J. M., *Religion in the Struggle for Power* (Durham: Duke University Press, 1946).

Young, P. V., *Pilgrims of Russian Town* (Chicago: University of Chicago Press, 1932).

————, "The Russian Molokan Community in Los Angeles," *American Journal of Sociology,* 35 (November, 1929), 393-402.

Chapter 8

THE CROSS-SECTION FIELD SURVEY [1] *

DISCUSSIONS about the survey method are frequently heated. Some social scientists argue that data gathered by a survey is of little or no value. Others argue that the survey is just about the only way a social scientist can collect significant and reliable social data. Probably few social scientists would agree on just what the survey is and what it can do. Different conceptions of the method probably account for the vehemence with which it is either attacked or defended. The purpose of this chapter is to discuss both the conditions under which the social survey is an effective tool for the social scientist *and* the conditions that seriously impair its usefulness. We need to clarify what it can do adequately as well as what it should not be expected to do.

1. Background of the Contemporary Survey

Some of the confusion about the survey method results from its being identified with a particular type of survey where limited use was made of it for census taking or market research or public opinion polling or attitude testing.

The Early "Census-Type" Surveys: Surveys carried on during the late nineteenth and early twentieth centuries were mainly designed to collect "facts." The surveyors usually had their eye on some immediate social problem in a community and they gathered facts that dramatized its pressing nature. They frequently turned over the census-type data they collected to public officials, hoping to influence governmental policy. Surveys gathered facts about housing conditions, kinds of employment, health, income and expenditures, the incidence of crime, and so forth. Follow-up surveys sometimes tried to evaluate changes that occurred.

The broad scope of these studies led many people to believe that a survey is primarily an instrument for getting an over-view of some broad social situation. Few of these early surveyors set out to test any explicit hypotheses or to relate their findings to any body of theory. Hypotheses were sometimes suggested in the kinds of data that were gathered or

---

[1] We will be primarily concerned with the use of the questionnaire in *face-to-face interviews* with *individuals* drawn from a sample. Questionnaires can also be administered by mail, telephone, and in supervised groups. Institutions and communities can be sampled as well as individuals. Many of the considerations discussed here would also apply to these other uses of questionnaires.

We are indebted to the discussions of the Cornell Faculty Committee on Structural Research Methods for many ideas presented in this chapter. In addition to authors, the committee's members were Edward A. Suchman, Edward O. Moe, Gordon F. Streib, and John Summerskill.

* Written by John P. Dean and Robert L. Eichhorn.

in the interpretation they made of the data; *e.g.,* that poverty was a major cause of crime.

The first surveyors performed several services for present-day social science. They stressed the need for going to the field and systematically collecting data rather than depending upon impressionistic or armchair speculations. More important, and frequently forgotten by those who think of the survey as solely a means for collecting attitudes about some issue, the early surveyors concentrated on factual data about the social environment of the respondents. They asked, "What do you eat?" "Are you working?" "How do you spend your wages?" "Do you have a bath-tub or toilet in your home?"

These early surveys have had another effect. They led many social scientists to identify the method only with the collection of facts about social problems. Social theorists sometimes disdain the survey because they identify it with a "social problems" emphasis; social reformers, con-versely, often feel that a survey is just a way of avoiding constructive action by studying the problem instead of doing something about it.

2. Uses of the Survey

Use of the Survey in Market Research. Another use of the survey method has been made by market researchers. Here the manufacturer has an economic interest in understanding what the buyer's reaction is to his product. In attempting to answer this kind of question, market research people have made several contributions to the development of better survey techniques. They have perfected better instruments for getting at the "why" of respondents' reactions, feelings, and beliefs; they have developed more standardized and systematic interviewing procedures. Unlike many social scientists, the market research surveyors have a means of evaluating their findings. They can often test whether changes in the product, or in the merchandizing techniques based on the findings, actually are reflected in consumer purchases.

The market research surveyors have had little interest in theory or in the testing of broad social science hypotheses. They have been pri-marily interested in predicting the success or failure of a product in the market. Therefore, those social scientists who think of the survey in this sense understandably feel that it is adequate only for superficial problems.

The Public Opinion "Pollsters": The "pollsters" want to know how many people support the Republican candidate or favor agricultural price supports, and how many are opposed. Since they want to generalize from their sample to all of the voters in the United States or all the farmers in the "Wheat Belt," they need a representative cross section of these people. As a result, they have contributed much to field sampling procedures. They have attacked the problem of how to make a sample most representative with least cost and effort.

Since the public opinion surveyors are primarily concerned with people's opinions and attitudes, some social scientists believe that the survey is appropriate primarily for this purpose. For getting at sociological variables other then attitudes, they lean toward some other method.

Psychological Testing: Side by side with these developments, the psychologists were improving the testing instruments that they use for measuring intelligence, aptitudes, manual dexterity, and various kinds of attitudes. They gave more attention to questions of reliability and validity than the surveyors, and were concerned about the relationship between their conceptual variables and the question indexes that stood for them. The psychometrists devised new ways for defining variables (scaling, factor analysis, etc.) and stimulated interest in a mathematics for the analysis of data. All of these are problems that concern today's survey researchers.

Today's Cross-Section Field Survey as a Research Instrument. While the survey can be profitably used for each of these special types of investigation—census-type fact gathering, market research, opinion polling, and attitude testing—the social scientist who thinks the survey method must be confined to these objectives underestimates the survey as a social research tool. By incorporating and improving upon the achievements of these forerunners of the survey in sampling questionnaire construction, interviewing, reliability and validity checks, and quantitative analysis—the survey emerges today as one of the more effective instruments the social scientist has for testing and discovering meaningful relationships among the variables of social science.

Those characteristics that make the survey an important research instrument also limit it and leaves it open to criticism. Perhaps its major advantage is that it gives to social scientists *a quantitative method of establishing relationships and of generalizing about known populations.* The survey is able to do this because of its standardized or uniform data-collection procedures. What is the nature of this standardization? A systematically selected sample of individuals is exposed to a fixed set of questions; then their reactions to those questions are systematically classified so that quantitative comparisons can be made. The survey analyst can then establish whether a larger proportion of union or of non-union workers favor the Taft-Hartley Act; whether a higher proportion of respondents who said they had happy childhoods, or of those who said they had an unhappy childhood, agree that "Jews are dishonest in their business dealings."

This standardization also creates one of the survey methods' greatest weaknesses: *It exposes each respondent to identical questions and classifies his responses into a few simple types regardless of the distinctive qualities of each response.* Many things determine how a given respondent answers a given question asked by a given interviewer. Any particular respondent's answer is determined by such things as:

(1) What he interprets the purpose of the question to be;

(2) What particular meanings he attaches to the words in the questions and in the response categories;

(3) How willing he is to say what he "really" thinks to an outsider;

(4) What he thinks he *should* say;

(5) How he thinks his family and friends might feel about his answers;

(6) How much he feels the interviewer is interfering with his work or his leisure;

(7) How much he thinks the questions are an invasion of his private world;

(8) How much guilt and anxiety he has about the subjects being discussed;

(9) What kind of mood he is in;

(10) How much he fears his answers may be revealed to people he knows;

(11) How much he wants to put himself in the "best light" to the interviewer;

(12) How much he lacks or has formulated information on, attitudes about, or feelings toward the subject of the questionnaire;

(13) How willing he is to have his opinion written down;

(14) How objectionable he finds it to be "pigeon holed" by having to choose among a few limited categories.

The survey assumes that there is enough common understanding of the words in the questions, and of the problems that are being inquired about, for the response categories to apply realistically to a substantial number of respondents, *but not to all of them*. The survey analyst compensates for the limits this assumption imposes in two ways. First, he tries to construct meaningful questions and response categories and to understand the context in which they are answered. Secondly, he analyzes the data quantitatively by comparing groups or classifications so that the mis-classification of some respondents will not affect the major relationships he aims to establish. Quantitative comparisons are implicit in the logic of the survey method.

The survey method is at best an approximation of the controlled experiment. The classical experimental model calls for a control group and an experimental group. After these groups have been equated on the crucial control variables by some measurement, the experimental group is exposed to the test variable or stimulus. Then both groups are re-measured on the test variable and if all other possible causes of the effect have been controlled, the difference between the experimental and control group is assumed to be the effect of the stimulus.

For example, pairs of Republican party members matched on socio-economic status, age, education, religion, and birthplace of father are assigned at random, one to the experimental group, one to the control group. Both groups are interviewed in December on their political leanings and show no differences; then during the winter the experimental group is exposed to a barrage of Democratic propaganda. Then in May both experimental and control groups are re-interviewed on their political leanings. If no other influences can be discerned that might have influenced the experimental group more than the control group, the excess of pro-Democratic sentiment in the experimental group over the control group is assumed to be the effect of the propaganda.

CLASSICAL EXPERIMENTAL MODEL

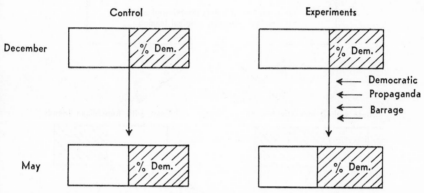

Figure 12.

Experiments of this sort are not possible for many problems where the survey can be used. Often there are multiple causes that make it impossible to isolate one variable as *the* experimental stimulus. At other times, the respondents cannot arbitrarily be assigned to experimental and control groups. For example, suppose you are interested in studying why people vote for a particular Republican or Democratic candidate. There are many factors associated with a person's vote: his economic class, his family background, his current associates, his exposure to party propaganda, and so forth. We cannot arbitrarily take one group of subjects and expose them only to Republican friends, and another group and expose them only to Democratic friends in order to test the relative effects of friendships on voting behavior. But *after* we have surveyed a sample of voters, we can divide them into those who have predominately Republican friends and those with predominantly Democratic friends. We can also divide them into those who have been exposed to Democratic propaganda and those who have not. But unfortunately *these will not be matched groups as in the experimental model.* In fact, it is highly probable that those exposed to Democratic propaganda will *also* be those who have more Democratic friends, have fathers who are democratic, and so forth. So the survey tries to study specific effects of these variables by *ex post facto* analysis.

By comparing "A" and "B" (or "C" and "D") we can see the difference exposure to Democratic propaganda makes while *holding constant* or *controlling* on the political complexion of the respondents' friendship group. Of course some of the other factors that are not held constant might account for the relationships established. Furthermore, by comparing "A" and "C" (or "B" and "D") we can see the effect of friend-

MODEL OF SURVEY ANALYSIS

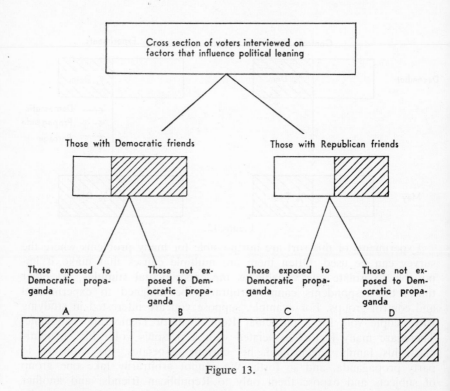

Figure 13.

ship patterns on political leanings while controlling an exposure to Democratic propaganda. And since it would be difficult to set up an experiment that systematically varied respondents' friendship grouping, this is an advantage the survey has over experiments: it can study more realistic situations that cannot be brought into the laboratory.

Thus, survey analysis falls somewhere between (1) the strict rigor of the classical experimental design that is often hard to adapt to natural settings and (2) the unstructured techniques such as participant observation and non-schedule interviewing that are adaptable to field conditions but do not generally yield quantitative comparisons among variables.

In summary, then, the survey as a research instrument aims to arrive at generalizations by making quantitative comparisons of data gathered by uniform question-answer procedures. Because of its stress on *ex post facto* quantitative comparisons, the survey method is clearly inappropriate for studying problems that such quantification can throw little light on. The survey is of little use for studying a unique historical event. Since survey data are collected from living individuals, the past must be reconstructed from the living memories of those persons most closely associated with the events. While a cross-section study throws some light on the event, the best reconstruction of "what actually happened" usually has to be made by cross checking historical documents and the testimony of the most reliable witnesses. Similarly, the survey is not generally useful for studying the on-going processes and structure of an institution such as, say, a social club or union. A cross section of the rank and file of a union may throw light on how the members perceive and feel about the leaders, but it won't yield information on how the leaders perceive and feel about the rank and file or how they make their decisions about union policies and practices. Day-by-day observation of the interaction that goes on among union leaders would be more productive. Finally, since the survey method compares group or category differences and admits a margin of error in classifying individuals, it is not usually reliable as a means of understanding a particular individual in the sample. An individual questionnaire does give a kind of overview on how a person reports verbally his attitudes, opinions, perceptions of other persons' and his own past. But it cannot substitute for the detailed life history that analyzes the developing stages of a person's life in terms of the rich experiences of his interpersonal life. The survey is just not suited to the detailed interweaving of qualitative causal variables in analyzing social process.

The survey method operates in this way: It involves a problem of theoretical importance; explicitly stated hypotheses; operational definitions of the major variables in the hypotheses; the conversion of these variables into a questionnaire for gathering data to estimate or measure the variables; the systematic exposure of a group of individuals to those questions and the systematic classification of their responses; the sorting and counting of different response patterns to establish quantitative relationships among variables and, thus, test the initial hypotheses or suggest new ones. The appropriateness of the survey for research purposes is not dependent upon the special uses made of it in the past but upon the suitability of the method in the light of its underlying assumptions or logic for answering a particular research question. The method should be adopted or rejected in these terms.

3. The Survey as a Problem in Communication

The crux of a successful survey is the communication process that takes place in the interview. In the question and answer exchange, the information the researcher is interested in leaves the field and becomes data of the social scientist. There are two components of this process: the research questions and response categories that the social scientist has incorporated in the questionnaire; and the interviewer's modes of interaction with the respondent as he solicits cooperation and handles the questionnaire during the interview.

Good communication between the respondent and the interviewer depends upon the respondent's accepting the role and behavior of the interviewer as appropriate. One of the hardest problems for interviewers is conveying an understanding of social research. Respondents unfamiliar with social research often ascribe to the interviewers some role or set of motives they are familiar with; this can cripple communication. For example, interviewers are sometimes thought to be tax collectors, salesmen, secret government investigators, public opinion pollsters, IQ testers, unwarranted university snoopers, or foreign spies.

Good communication also depends on the respondent's feeling that interviewing itself is appropriate. In some cultures, direct questioning by strangers about personal matters could not be done. Even in societies such as our own, where this is acceptable, respondents sometimes feel that "outsiders" have no right to "barge right in and take up a lot of time asking questions." Such an attitude impairs good communication.

Finally, the survey method usually throws the interviewer and the respondent into an immediate face-to-face relationship. Good data, therefore, depend upon the interviewers being able to establish and maintain some level of rapport while meeting the demands imposed by the questionnaire.

The other aspect of the communication process involves the respondent's reaction to the questionnaire. For his responses to questions to be meaningful, he must understand the symbols of communication employed in the construction of the questions; the words must convey what the researcher wants them to. Therefore, in writing questions, the surveyor must not only be familiar with the language and culture of the different types of respondents in his survey, but he must also know something of their language habits, idioms of expression and subtleties of word meaning. In the United States we can assume a rather wide universe of shared language and experiences to begin with. But if surveys are undertaken in other societies, other cultures, or even among sub-groups of our own society such as ethnic groups, children, old people or illiterates, the research worker must see the questions as these groups see them.

The survey method assumes that the respondent has information or experience that bears on the problem being studied. The respondent must also be able to communicate the information asked for or convey his reactions to experiences inquired about. In the survey this must be done verbally and thus requires a certain level of articulation about the research area. Finally, the respondent must be *willing* to communicate.

In a successful survey both components of the interview must operate smoothly. The communication *via* question-answer interaction must be as systematic and meaningful as possible. The interviewer must handle the fixed-question stimuli and response categories so as to bring about a uniform and unbiased collection of data. But at the same time, he must handle the interpersonal situation in terms of whatever peculiar social or human demands it poses. How reliable and how valid the data are depends on how skillfully the interviewers handle hundreds of these double-edged communication situations.

If the problems of communication in a given survey situation are insurmountable, then it does not make sense to try to get quantitative data by means of a survey. Many anthropologists feel that where wide differences in culture are present, surveys are meaningless. Yet recently the Cornell University sociology and anthropology staff conducted a successful survey among a group of Indians in the mountains of Peru. Many of the limitations of the survey can be offset by proper field procedures that minimize the biases of poor communication and maximize the validity and reliability of the data. The major field procedures that minimize bias are five: (1) careful construction and pre-testing of the questionnaire; (2) proper use of the questionnaire; (3) training interviewers how to contact respondents; (4) selection of appropriate interviewers; and (5) thoughtful and flexible administration of the survey in the field.

4. The Survey Procedure

(1) *Reducing bias by careful construction and pre-testing of the questionnaire.* A number of potential obstacles to communication between respondent and interviewer may arise out of the survey instrument itself. Serious bias in responses can result. There are at least five such obstacles that survey researchers need to recognize and try to minimize in advance of going into the field with a finished questionnaire. These five, along with corrective precautions survey administrators should take, are listed below. Although the list does not pretend to be complete, it does include the sources of bias that are serious and consistently encountered in survey research.

(a.) *Irrelevance of the research problem to respondents.* This obstacle to communication is not, of course, exclusively a feature of survey research. It is basic to all social research, and becomes particularly acute in the case of research that crosses cultural lines. Relevance or irrelevance of a research problem to respondents has two aspects. The first involves relevance of the *central* problem of the research to a majority of respondents; the second, relevance of a particular sub-problem to an individual respondent. Obviously the survey researcher solves the first problem by selecting his sample so that a majority of the population finds the main focus of the research relevant and meaningful. For example, if the research focuses on social and psychological problems of aging, with emphasis on retirement from employment, the sample should include only respondents over sixty years of age. Following the same example for the second problem: an interviewer would be embarrassed to find himself asking an elderly woman who has been a housewife through all her adult life, how she feels about retiring from her job. The point seems simple, but it can present real difficulties in questionnaire construction. The mechanics of the questionnaire should make it possible for an interviewer to skip irrelevent items without interrupting the smooth flow of the question and answer exchange. Very often, the questionnaire that flows most easily and naturally in the interview situation is the questionnaire most intricately constructed.

Sometimes, the inapplicability of an item or problem cannot be mechanically "built out" of the questionnaire. For example, the research may concern the effect of teen-age peer group friendships on adult friendship formation. An interviewer suddenly encounters a respondent who spent his adolescence with missionary parents in Western China. Since he had no opportunities for peer-group friendships, the items concerning this problem simply do not apply to this respondent. But since a questionnaire clearly cannot make mechanical provision in advance for such unique respondents, the interviewer can do nothing but note that the items did not apply, and explain why.

(*b.*) *Irrelevance or insufficiency of questionnaire items to the variable being investigated.* Construction of a survey instrument should begin with unstructured, "free-directive" interviewing around the major variables the questionnaire is intended to measure. Before he can frame appropriate survey questions, a researcher has to know how people like those he will eventually sample, think and talk about the problems he wants to investigate quantitatively. For example, he may be studying membership activity in a local union. He cannot assume that what represents high activity to him will also represent high activity to his potential respondents. Regularity of attendance at union meetings, for instance, might be an insufficient index of union activity for construction workers whose jobs frequently take them miles away from the town where meetings are held. In other words: if a researcher wants questionnaire items that will measure his variable realistically, he must know what constitutes this particular reality for the kinds of people ultimately surveyed.

(*c.*) *Ambiguous or inappropriate item wording.* While the researcher is interviewing free-directively to determine what kinds of items are most relevant to his variable, he will also get some idea of how the items should be worded. To insure maximum communication, a survey question should (a) mean, as nearly as possible, the same thing to the respondent as it means to the researcher; and (b) be phrased in language that is familiar and natural to both the interviewer and the respondent.

For example: One survey, in an effort to measure respondents' perceptions of their own social class, asked, "Which of the following groups do you think your family belongs in—upper class, middle class, working class, lower class?" It soon become apparent that some people were taking the phrase "belongs in" to mean "deserves to be in" or "actually *should* be in," rather than "*is* in." The question was reworded to read, "If you were asked to put yourself (your family) in one of these four groups, would you say you are in—the upper class, middle class, working class, lower class?"

As for ease and familiarity of phrasing and language: this same question could have read: "To which of the following social classes would you assign yourself (your family)?" The *meaning* here is more precise, in terms of the variable it is intended to measure, than in either of the other two wordings. But its disadvantages are glaringly apparent. It is pompous and stilted, impossible to ask conversationally. And it states a concept, "social class," by no means universally familiar.

The best way to correct for ambiguous and inappropriate wording is to try out a number of alternative wordings informally, with a few people similar to the people who will eventually be interviewed, until the item wording is as nearly perfect as possible for the people and purpose it is meant for.

(*d.*) Inadequate *categories for responses.* A good questionnaire item must not only *ask* a question well; it must also provide response categories that permit respondents to answer it in a way that is meaningful to them. If the variables can be measured in terms of "more" or "less," categories can be set up without much effort. Standard forms are "Often—Sometimes—Hardly ever," "More—Some—Less." "Very (happy)—Fairly (happy)—Not so (happy)." But there are other questions that have no clear dimensionality. For instance, "Who is living in the household with you at the present time?" For theoretical reasons, the researcher may decide that he is only interested in distinguishing those who live alone, those who live with their spouse or children, or live with other persons. If so, he can arrive at categories in advance and ask the interviewers to check the proper place. If he is not sure of the categories he wants to use, he must phrase the question so that the interviewer lists everyone the respondent is living with. Responses are then classified at the coding or analysis stage. This is cumbersome, since there are many combinations of people a respondent might be living with. It is a saving in time if the categories can be worked out in advance by asking open-ended questions in a trial run then classifying the spontaneous responses.

(*e.*) *Inappropriate item sequence; over-lengthiness; insensitivity to the emotional impact on the respondent of an item or series of items.* All of these are sources of bias that can be minimized by careful pretesting. Some people apparently believe that the pretest is just a brief trial run that follows the construction of a questionnaire assumed to be ready for the field. A good pretest is a careful examination of the communication process that is going on in the interviewing situation. In one survey with only 350 respondents in the sample, there were five successive pretests with 20 respondents in each trial. While this almost doubled the cost of the survey, the questionnaire that was finally used was a well constructed, sensitive instrument providing high order correlations in the analysis stage.

(2) *Reducing Bias by the Proper Use of the Questionnaire.* No matter how good a questionnaire instrument the survey staff constructs, its effectiveness will be impaired by improper use. The major bias dangers in the interviewing situation are: (a) that the interviewer will influence the respondent in giving his answer or (b) that he will misrepresent the respondent's answer in the way he classifies it. This is a more serious problem for "information" questions than for "stimulus" questions.

Information questions are designed to establish some fact about the respondent. For instance, the questionnaire might want to know the respondent's occupation. Probe questions may be necessary before the respondent answers this question satisfactorily. For example, a typical interview might proceed as follows:

Interviewer: "What is your occupation?"

Respondent: "I'm in business."

Interviewer: "What kind of business are you in?"

Respondent: "The machine tool business."

Interviewer: "What sort of job do you have in the machine tool business?"

Respondent: "I'm foreman at Anderson Tool and Die Works."

The interviewer may find this adequate to classify the respondent and so move to the next question. It is not necessary that information questions and probes be asked exactly the same way to every respondent. If the study director is sure that the interviewers understand the purpose of the question, they can be shown how to probe for the required information. This probing may vary a little from one situation to the next. To make sure that uniform data are collected, a careful survey will include the specifications for given questions in the body of the questionnaire at the appropriate point. For instance, the instruction beside the occupation question might read, "Get job description in sufficient detail to tell how skilled or unskilled and how much responsibility job entails."

Instructions for handling the mechanics of the questionnaire also should appear in the questionnaire where they apply. Instruction sheets handed to interviewers separate from the questionnaire are often forgotten. Even with instructions "built in," the procedure to be followed in the administration of the questionnaire can be quite complex and interviewers need practice in following these instructions. As an example, this section is reproduced from one questionnaire:

IF MARRIED AND LIVING WITH SPOUSE, CIRCLE 1 HERE
AND GO TO QUESTION 23.

22. By the way, have you ever been married?
    2———widowed
    3———divorced
    4———separated
    5———never married

IF NEVER MARRIED, SKIP QUESTION 23 and 24.

23. How many living children do you have———? (number) IF NONE
    GO TO Q. 25.
24. How many of your children do you see every week or oftener?———
    (number) less than once a week but fairly regularly?———(number)
25. How many (other) close relatives do you have who live here in
    town or just outside?———(number) IF NONE, GO TO Q. 27.
26. How many of these relatives do you see every week or oftener?———
    (number) less than once a week but fairly regularly? ———(number)
27. Now about your friends—about how many really *close* friends do
    you have here in town that you occasionally talk over confidential
    matters with?———(number)

Before undertaking their regular assignments interviewers should run
through a few practice interviews. This serves as a check on their knowledge of the mechanics of the questionnaires, gives them a chance to get
familiar with the question wording, and to practice handling the paper
and pencil work of the questionnaire at the same time they handle the
personal relationship with the respondent. Interviewers can be asked
first to try out the questionnaire with someone in their own family,
then with an acquaintance, and finally, with a complete stranger whose
doorbell they ring. Interviewers who are having difficulty with interviewing can be given further training or discouraged from continuing. If
the interviewing situation is too uncomfortable for them they will usually
decide to drop out of their own accord at this point.

"Stimulus" questions are designed to "take a reading," *i. e.* get the
respondent's reaction to a question as uninfluenced as possible by the interviewer. For instance, the questionnaire might ask "How much un-
happiness has there been in your life?—almost none,—some but not very
much, or—a good deal." Stimulus questions present a real hazard of
interviewer bias. Despite the best training, interviewers are likely to
influence the respondent's answers by the way they ask the questions or
by unconsciously revealing their approval or disapproval of the respondent's answer. If the responses to "stimulus" questions are to avoid bias, interviewers must adhere to the *exact wording* of the question, use similar
inflections and persistently re-offer the response categories until the respondent makes a choice. Improperly trained interviewers often try to
classify the respondent's freely-given answer into one of the categories
on the questionnaire rather than insist that the respondent classify him-

self. An example will help to show how an inexperienced and an experienced interviewer might differ in handling "stimulus" questions.

Interviewer: Here are some statements that people have different opinions about. I wonder if you would tell me whether you agree or disagree with them. The first one is, "This country would be better off if there weren't so many foreigners coming in." Do you agree or disagree?

Respondent: Well, there certainly are a lot of foreigners coming in. The way the Italians are flocking into this neighborhood is a disgrace. I think it is just terrible. Don't you?

The inexperienced interviewer might nod feebly and check "Agree." But the experienced interviewer would continue as follows:

Interviewer: Mrs. Jones, we would just like to know how *you* feel about some of these statements. Let me read the first one again. "This country would be better off if there weren't so many foreigners coming in." Now, do you agree or disagree to that?

Respondent: I certainly think that is true.

Interviewer: Then, would you say you agree or disagree?

Respondent: I guess I agree.

So the interviewer checks the catagory "agree" and goes on to the next question. After bringing the respondent back to the "Agree-Disagree" categories a few times, most respondents realize that they are to make a choice. The interviewer's job is to ease them into the swing of making these choices without annoying them or influencing the answers.

In order to avoid the biases that stimulus questions invite, interviewers need to be drilled in the uniform handling of them. To do this, the trainer should impress such things as the following on them:

(1) Ask all the stimulus questions exactly as worded.

(2) Don't attempt to explain stimulus questions. Repeat the exact wording of the question slowly and distinctly, emphasizing the key words. Perhaps lead in with: "Just let me repeat the question as it's worded here" (then repeat); or, "Well, generally speaking, what would you say?" (repeat question). If the respondent still can't answer, record "don't know" as his answer. One answer to a query on what a question means is, "Well, just as it seems to you," follow by "How would you answer that?"

(3) Don't elaborate the wordings. If you "ad lib" you may distort the question.

(4) Try to overcome preliminary "don't knows" and unspecified replies by reoffering the categories with some lead-in such as "Well, on the whole . . . " (repeat question); or "Well, in general . . . " (repeat question). Do not accept a "don't know" or "can't decide" unless you are convinced that the respondent is not just sparring for time while he thinks it over. If the respondent does not want to commit himself, you can reassure him again that his views are

as important as anyone else's, that there are no right or wrong answers, that what he says is confidential or that no names are taken—depending on the source of his hesitancy.

(5) Never suggest an answer to a question. Your respondent's replies are supposed to reflect his own reactions, uninfluenced, during the course of the interview, by the interviewer or any other outside source.

(6) Don't give your own opinions, even if you are asked for them.

    (a) If respondent asks for your approval ("Don't you agree?")
        Say—"Well, I can understand how you feel about that . . . "
        (Go on to next question).

    (b) If respondent is bewildered ("I don't know, what to do you think?")
        Say—"Well, that *is* a hard question—but generally speaking, what would you say?"

    (c) If respondent seriously asks your opinion ("I've told you how *I* feel about that, now you tell me your opinion.")
        Say—"As an interviewer, I'm not supposed to give my opinions —We're just the pencil pushers, you see."

(7) Try to keep the respondent on the track. Try to avoid irrelevant chatter without, at the same time, abruptly cutting him off. Neatest trick of the week.

Some respondents resent being pushed into a choice among fixed categories, instead of being allowed to express their opinions freely. Handling this problem sucessfully is the mark of a good interviewer. You ask a question; offer the categories; accept the spontaneous response in stride; reoffer the categories; the respondent makes his choice; you go to the next question. By skillfully using the little leeway he has, an interviewer can relate himself to the respondent in a genuine and friendly way and at the same time standardize the data-collecting process.

(3) *Reducing bias by training interviewers how to contact respondents.* No matter how good a questionnaire instrument the survey has, or how well trained the interviewers are in its proper use, if they are (a) unable to contact the proper respondents or (b) unable to win their cooperation, major biases will characterize the sample as it emerges from the field.

(a) Interviewers success in making initial contacts with respondents depends, of course, on how conscientiously the interviewers carry out the sampling procedures. In designing his sample, the survey researcher can range from the expensive and hard-to-carry-out area probability sample to the inexpensive but liable-to-bias quota samples. Area probability samples are usually drawn by designating a primary sampling unit such as the city block or a segment of several blocks grouped together. A certain number of these are selected randomly, and interviewers are sent to enumerate all the dwelling units in each segment. Every *nth* house is then selected and the interviewer, when he calls, enumerates all members of the household above a certain age, say 20. Then by a random procedure, one member of the household is chosen; he becomes the respondent.

In quota samples, the interviewer is given specifications that the respondents he interviews must meet. For example, part of his assignment might be to interview four males of "D" socio-economic level between 20 and 35 years of age. Where and how he locates these respondents is up to him. He may go down to the poorer sections of town and ring doorbells; he may stop persons on the street; or he may find them in the park sunning themselves. The invitations to bias here, of course, are enormous. The more leeway the survey gives the interviewers, the more carefully the interviewers must be trained to seek out a representative range of respondents and not just interview the most available.

Many surveys compromise between these two methods in drawing samples, thus hoping to keep down costs while also avoiding the main dangers of sample bias. For example, the survey could select primary sampling units randomly, assign the number of interviews to be done in each in proportion to the number of dwelling units, then leave it to the interviewer to select the actual respondents within the segment in such a way as to fill certain quota specifications he is given.

In any case, whether the sample is probability or quota, interviewers need careful instructions and recording forms for reporting the actual operations they did. Unless these instructions and forms have been thoughtfully worked out, errors of misunderstanding or sloppy adherence to instructions will be hard to catch and may create major cumulative biases.

(b) A great deal can be done to train interviewers to avoid mistakes that draw refusals or break-offs. Most people are cooperative and friendly and welcome the opportunity to express their opinions. If they are approached in the right way, they seldom refuse. Of course, there are also a small number who appear hesitant when first approached by interviewers, and an even smaller number who appear downright uncooperative, hostile, or suspicious. But since the aim of the survey is to interview the hesitant and hostile as well as the cooperative, the interviewers must be trained (1) to avoid mistakes that might lose the cooperative, and (2) to be as resourceful as possible in finding a way of interviewing the hesitant. This training is important: it allays the natural anxieties of new interviewers as to whether they can get their foot in the door; it gives them some idea of the range of field situations they will be up against and thus cuts down the likelihood of panic when actually faced with a difficult situation; it teaches the interviewers a few of the strategies experienced interviewers have worked out; and it shows the genuine appreciation of the survey directors for what they are up against.

To keep down refusals, the interviewer trainer should make special effort to impress on the interviewers certain features of the problem of winning cooperation on the doorstep. The trainers "rules of thumb" might run as follows:

(a) The interviewers should explain who he is, in a way that is understandable and non-threatening. He might say, for example:

> "Good morning, Mrs. Jones. I'm Mrs. Robinson. I'm with the Cornell University Research Group that's making a study of this community. I wonder if I could talk to you for a few minutes."

(b) The interviewer should make any explanation of the research as brief as possible. He can't really explain the purpose of the research in the few minutes he has on the respondent's doorstep. The more thorough or elaborate the explanation becomes, the more confusing it will be to the respondent and the less likely he will be to cooperate. People don't like to get involved in things they don't understand; they're apt to feel they might be "taken in." In response to a query on what the study is all about, the interviewer might say simply:

> "You have been selected as one of our cross-section of people here in town. We'd just like to have your opinions about some things that concern the whole community."

(c) If the respondent doesn't offer to cooperate immediately, he may be just stalling for time to learn more about what he's getting into before making up his mind. In this case the interviewer must decide *why* he is hesitant. The respondent may fear the interviewer is selling something; that the interview will take too much time; or that it will be too complicated for him to handle. The interviewers should handle the situation in accordance with his diagnosis of the difficulty. He might say:

> "I'm not selling anything; we'd just like your opinions on a few things."

> "I'll just take a few minutes of your time. I'm sure you'll find it interesting."

> "There aren't any right or wrong answers; we just want your opinions."

> "I really need your help; I'm supposed to get the opinions of all the people they assigned me. I need your answers to complete my assignment."

> "All your answers will be confidential; they won't be shown to anyone—just punched on a card like this." (Displays IBM card)

(d) If the respondent is busy at the moment, the interviewer can suggest that he ask the questions while the respondent continues what he was doing. Many respondents like to have company while they're washing the dishes or darning socks. Successful interviews have been conducted while respondents prepared lunch, ironed the wash, bathed the baby, washed the car, picked strawberries, and hoed the garden. Sometimes the respondent is genuinely busy at something awkward to interrupt; *e. g.,* playing bridges with friends, or leaving for a dental appointment. If the interviewer has caught the respondent at an awkward time, or at a time when he seems irritated at being interrupted and may refuse, then the interviewer should try to arrange a convenient time to call back. He can offer a tentative time for the return call, such as:

"I'd like to come back when you're not busy. How about 3:30 this afternoon? Or would tomorrow morning be better?"

The tentative call back should be posed in terms of *when* is the best time to call back, not *whether* the interviewer should return.

(e) Interviewers should be trained not to argue with respondents, but to agree with them—even about objections to surveys or the hundreds of interruptions they put up with. Even if respondents break appointments, the interviewer should not appear critical or take the respondent to task. Interviewers should learn that these are "happenstances" of interviewing that they must learn to take in stride. If they have been "stood up" they should just try for another appointment at the "most convenient time."

If the interviewers are carefully trained on these points, given practice at role-playing with each other and the staff the various door-step obstacles, and then given actual practice in the field, they should be able to keep refusals down to a small percentage.

(4) *Reducing bias by the selection of appropriate interviewers.* Of high importance in minimizing survey bias is the selection of appropriate interviewers. An example will help to make this clear. The Cornell studies in intergroup relations decided to undertake a race-relations survey in Savannah, Georgia. Knowing the explosiveness of the racial issue in the deep South, the staff had some doubts about whether they could carry on the survey at all. If they could, they were naturally concerned about the biases created by Northerners' undertaking a survey in a city that represented a section of the country and sub-culture they were only remotely familiar with. If the survey director had brought with him a staff of trained interviewers from the University, the survey would undoubtedly have sustained many biases. The interviewer would have been perceived as an outsider as soon as he opened his mouth on the doorstep. If he convinced the respondent that even a "Yankee had some legitimate reason for poking his nose into a Savannah family's business," he would probably get a "break-off" as soon as it became clear that most of the questions were on race-relations. Even if he succeeded in getting the respondent to complete the interview, the respondent would probably not give his spontaneous reactions to the questions, but in many instances would modify his responses to allow for what he would assume to be the interviewer's position on race-relations. And if the interviewer undertook to interview Negroes, the biases would be further aggravated. White Northern interviewers are just not appropriate interviewers for a white and Negro cross-section in the South when the subject is race-relations. No amount of training or experience would have made them so. Inappropriate interviewers are likely to get an excessive number of refusals and break-offs. The impairment of communication will bias the answers of respondents interviewed. And because the interviewer is likely to experience a growing discomfort at his inadequacy in the situation, the

survey may have an excessive number of drop-outs among the interviewers, making the full completition of the sample a further headache.

What are the characteristics of interviewers that keep interviewer bias to a minimum? (a) They should have an appropriate role and status to be interviewing people in different walks of life in the area where they are assigned. And it is desirable to assign the more fashionably-dressed interviewers to the better residential areas; interviewers with working class background to the factory sections; and so on. For this reason, an interviewing staff should have different types of persons. In the Savannah survey mentioned above, local Savannah interviewers from several different social classes were recruited and trained. White interviewers were assigned to white respondents, Negro interviewers to Negro respondents. (b) Interviewers should be naturally personable and friendly people, free of peculiarities of mannerism, appearance and personality that would alienate respondents. The survey can scarcely expect to train interviewers in the basic social graces or to modify their personalities during training. Since these are highly important in winning the cooperation of the respondent and in establishing a friendly feeling during the interview, a survey that goes into the field with a peculiar set of interviewers is heading for bias. There is no real substitute for the genuine friendliness of a good interviewer. (c) Interviewers should be reasonably intelligent, at *least* intelligent enough to follow the rather detailed mechanics of the questionnaire, the complexities of the sampling procedure and the administrative details of time sheets, reports, etc. One index of ability to handle this kind of paper work is educational achievement. A high-school education is just about the lowest limit for interviewers on a survey that is going to minimize paper work errors. (d) Interviewers should have conscientious work habits and the perseverance to carry out a job under their own steam. Interviewers may at first perceive the chance to participate in a scientific survey, to interview many types of interesting people, and to earn some money in the process as an exciting experience they are eager to take on. But the novelty wears off fast; after a dozen interviews or so, many interviewers begin to see interviewing as the gruelling job it really is. If they are going to complete the survey accurately and without bias, the late interviews will need to be done as conscientiously as the first. To do this, interviewers need a stiff endowment of what we used to call "stick-to-it-iveness."

How can a surveyor recruit interviewers who meet these rather stiff requirements? Largely by recruiting friendly, interested laymen who would like the experience of working on the study; who are not dependent on the income for their livelihood, but would like some spare money. Where can such people be found in the community? Our experience has been that it is difficult to choose good interviewers by personally interviewing them for the job; the characteristics of a good interviewer, such as conscientious work habits, ability to handle paper work, even qualities of friendliness and curiosity, are extremely hard to judge in a brief face-to-face interview. It is wiser to depend on persons who have known the interviewer candidate over a long period of time. If the study director can locate a few strategic persons in communities where they are likely to know people who would make good interviewers, and convey to them in some detail the kind of interviewers the survey is looking for, there is a good chance that the persons recommended will fill the bill. The superintendent of schools may know some substitute or retired teachers who are suitable. The president of the League of Women Voters, or the American Association of University Women may have some leads. An official of the local junior college may know some faculty wives who would be interested. Occasionally clergymen have contacts with persons in their parish who would make good interviewers. By letting persons of judgment and standing in the community pick the survey staff, the director probably will come up with a group more varied in background, yet reliable, then if he tries to hand-pick his own staff. Only this kind of staff can keep bias at a minimum.

(5) *Reducing bias by the thoughtful and flexible administration of the survey in the field.* A number of biases can still arise *after* a finished questionnaire, in the hands of a trained interviewer, is actually functioning in the field. Such bias results most commonly from:

(*a*) *Cumulative interviewer errors.* Regardless of the training sessions, some interviewers will ask respondents the wrong questions or record the answers improperly. Sometimes these are the result of the interviewer not understanding the instructions; sometimes they reflect a shortcoming in the questionnaire that was not noticed in the pretest. Unless these errors are caught by the supervisor, the errors become cumulative and render some questions useless for the analysis of the data.

(*b*) *Careless work by interviewers because of low motivation.* It is difficult to sustain the morale of interviewers and to convince them of the necessity of paying attention to the details of questionnaire administration without giving them an over-view of the total project so that they can see where they fit in. A training program might well begin with a description of the history of the research project, its scientific importance and some of the findings that have come out of a previous phase of the study. It is important for the interviewer to feel that the survey directors know what they are doing and that the interviewing they are asked to do can be handled by them. It helps to answer questions about different aspects of the research. In explaining the over-all project, the director might stress at first the theoretical importance of the research problem then discuss the methods being used to study it. This finally brings the discussion to the point where the interviewers fit in. It is certainly no overstatement if the director winds up by telling the interviewers that everything depends upon how well they do their job; that through them the research data leaves the respondent and is transmitted to the social scientist, and that if the study is to be of any value they must learn to handle successfully the delicate communication process which is the crux of good interviewing.

While the survey is in the field, the director should give continuous attention to the morale of his staff. Extended interviewing can be a gruelling job. By listening to the interviewers' experiences, swapping yarns with them and keeping them informed about the project, the director can do much to keep motivation high. It is good procedure to have the interviewers report into the office every two or three days, and to set aside one period every week when all of the interviewers meet together. This helps dispel the interviewer's feeling that he is the only person in the world who has met so many cranky respondents.

(c) Incomplete interviewer assignments and the "clean up" problem. A field director usually expects a certain amount of incompleted work. He knows that some interviewers will not want to finish their assignments. This can be a blessing in disguise. Good interviewers like to interview. But some people who initially think they will like the job discover that they can't ask personal questions or meet people easily. Allowing them to drop out can preclude the collection of poor data. The good interviewers usually finish their work more quickly and are ready to take on the interviewing left by the less motivated interviewers.

The clean-up job may take nearly as much time as the main body of the survey because in this phase, interviewers must contact the "not-at-home," first refusals, and difficult-to-reach respondents. Respondents who are listed as "not-at home" are best reached by sending the interviewers out at different times of the day and different days of the week. Also, inquiries can be made of neighbors of the family about the best time to contact the respondent. Notes on this kind of information should be recorded to assist in the clean-up.

(d) Avoidable refusals by respondents. Preparation for maximum co-operation is an administrative task that begins long before the interviewer knocks on the respondent's door. How much care is given to community relations and publicity, of course, depends in part on the magnitude of the survey and how controversial it is. But because of the danger that mistaken impressions, rumors, or adverse publicity may mobilize opposition or resistance to the survey in one or more strata of the community, it is generally wise to "clear" the survey with appropriate centers of authority and information. These will generally include the mayor (unless it is a great metropolis), the police, the Chamber of Commerce, and one or more of the newspapers. An occasional respondent (perhaps mishandled by an interviewer) may object loudly to the survey or to some of the questions he was asked; it helps if he can be told that the police and the Chamber of Commerce know about the survey, have cleared it, and that he is free to call and check for himself. Newspaper publicity is often helpful in spreading the work that interviewers are making the rounds. Besides, copies of a favorable newspaper story can be clipped

from the paper and given to each of the interviewers; showing hesitant respondents the story from their own newspaper may help win their co-operation.

Refusals can also be kept down by carefully diagnosing the reasons why each respondent failed to cooperate and reassigning a more appropriate interviewer. A dapperly dressed young man may agree to be interviewed by a pretty girl, but not by the middle-aged man who first contacted him. A certain housewife may be interviewed by a "club woman" but not by a retired school teacher. Such reassignments are important in breaking down respondents who initially refused.

Competent survey administration requires thoughtful planning, unflagging patience, and skillful handling of interpersonal relations. All in all, it is not an exaggeration to say that the value of a study can be seriously impaired by inadequate attention to the administrative problems.

5. The Analysis and Interpretation of Survey Data

There are many misunderstandings about the nature of survey analysis and interpretation. Many of these revolve around the contention that a table "doesn't prove anything," that you can't attribute causation to a correlation shown in a table; that you still have to give an interpretation that goes beyond the data and is not quantitatively established. The survey analyst doesn't expect his tables to "prove anything." He hopes merely to establish as firmly as possible the kinds of relationships that hold among variables that he has hypothesized and the conditions under which they hold. He is especially fortunate if the relationships he establishes run counter to prevailing scientific or common sense explorations. Out of disproof, come new hypotheses and new theories.

For the most part the survey analyst doesn't expect the relationships he establishes to be high order correlations. He accepts multiple causation as a basis tenet: every effect was numerous "causes" modified by numerous intervening variables. He is more surprised when his correlations are *high* than when they are moderate or low. The most he hopes for is a "more plausible demonstration" of the way his key variables hold together.

For one thing, he knows the fallibility of the questionnaire as a measuring instrument and the biases of field survey procedures. Few analysts are interested in the percentage of people who agree or who disagree with any one item in the questionnaire. These marginal distributions fluctuate with minor changes in question wording or question sequence. Instead the analyst is interested in the relationship among the variables his questions index. Let us suppose, for instance, that people report that they go to church more frequently than we know to be the case. Some people who never go to church respond that they go "occasionally;" some who attend occasionally say that they are in church "most Sundays;" and some who go to church most Sundays answer that they go to church "every Sunday." As long as the people who say they go to church every Sunday or most Sundays do, in fact, attend church more often than those answering that they attended occasionally or not at all, correlations based on sorting respondents on this question and relating them to other variables correlated with church attendance will hold up. Most survey questions probably misclassify a few respondents, some misclassify many. Most surveys come up with a "male housewife" or a prize fighter who belongs to the Ladies Aid. Because the survey analyst compares groups, categories or classifications on some variable, misclassification of a few individual cases can be overlooked.

But even so, the survey analyst tries not to rest his case upon the use of a single item index of variables. In indexing a variable such as marital happiness the survey analyst may have several kinds of questions designed to tap the variable: the respondent may be asked to classify himself; the respondent may have been asked about symptoms assumed to index marital happiness (*e. g.*, "How often do you have misunderstandings over the spending of money?" "How often do you disagree about disciplining the children?" and "How many of your good friends are also your husband's friends?"); or the interviewer may have been asked to give his judgment of the respondent's marital happiness. Inclusion of all of these kinds of questions in the interview provides the analyst with several different ways of estimating the major variables of the research.

Because of the unreliability of individual items, the survey analyst often tries to combine items into scales or scores (see chapter six on scaling and scores). The selection of items used to index the variables involves the whole problem of establishing the reliability and validity of the indices, and the usual tests for establishing reliability and validity apply here: (1) Items can be selected on the basis of their manifest content. "Objective," informational items especially can be evaluated on this basis. Items designed to tap some less objective conceptual variable, however, generally require evaluation by other methods. (2) Items can be selected by testing to see if they fit a scale model such as a Guttman scale or a latent attribute scale. (3) Items can be evaluated in part by the kinds of meaningful relationships they reveal when run against other variables. As our table running increases we learn how different items "work." (4) Some items we may be able to validate by an outside check, etc., whether the respondent voted or not, or whether he was actually observed attending the union meetings he said he attended. The use of judges, expert informants, and one's own knowledge are also proposed as methods of validating the items but while these are important for *choosing* the items there is some question as to whether they are methods for validating the choices.

There are numerous procedures for the analysis of survey data. The peculiarities of the problems being studied, the personality of the analyst, or the ultimate use of the findings all influence the analysis procedure. Some analysts operate more empirically by running most of the items or indexes against other items that might conceivably be related and then attempt to think of *ad hoc* explanations for the relationship they discover. At the other extreme we have analysts that more rigorously state the hypotheses they will test, specify the items that will index the variables and test primarily *those* relationships hypothesized. A position between these would try to be at the same time both exploratory and reasonably rigorous by looking for recurring patterns of relationship among variables that are measured and indexed in several different ways. This anaylsis procedure need not be complex. When the hypotheses have been well formulated, the concepts clearly defined, and the study design thought out in advance, the analysis of the data should flow naturally from the over-all design and be relatively straightforward. More complicated procedures, involved statistical manipulation, and abstruse indices are in some ways an admission of failure at earlier stages of research planning. Analysis should become involved only when things "go wrong" (poor indices are discovered, etc.), or when special problems not previously anticipated demand corrective or secondary analysis.

The survey researcher cannot, of course, provide for all of the eventualities of analysis, but neither should he avoid careful planning in the earlier stages of the survey, feeling that he can compensate for his negligence by complex analysis. Complicated analyses often show weaknesses greater than a simple analysis of a survey that was undertaken with well-thought-out design. If the study has been well constructed a fairly straight forward analysis procedure such as the following should suffice:

(a) The analyst should probably review the major hypotheses underlying the study and decide upon the major "effect" variables he wants to "explain."

(b) The analyst can then choose the indices he will use to estimate the major variables. This usually begins with an analysis of the content of the questionnaire with the major hypotheses in mind and the construction of scales and scores from them.

(c) Having selected the indices of the major variables, the analyst might first sort on the effect variable and count on the background characteristics to see how the "effect" distributes in the population.

(d) Then the analyst might sort on the effect variable and count on possible causal variables to establish the "basic" relationships. (Sorting first on the effect variable and then counting on the causal variables is a mechanical convenience permitting one to retain the original sorts while counting on a number of causal variables.)

The major relationships the analyst establishes here (the "basic" relationships) become the central focus of the study. The tasks from here on are mainly designed to break down these relationships by showing that they are spurious, or modifying them to provide more insight into the conditions under which they hold.

(e) The analyst might next inspect the "basic" relationships to see if perhaps some of the background characteristics or other variables might be causing a spurious relationship (one that will be wiped out if a test variable is held constant). If this might occur, he introduces the test variables by sorting on both "cause" and "effect" and counting on the test variables.

(f) Then the analyst will probably design further runs to clarify, interpret or modify the basic relationships he has established among the variables. This involves the introduction of interpretive, modifying and conditional variables. This also requires sorting jointly on both cause and effect variables and then counting on the interpretive variables.

(g) Finally, the analyst sets up for running any special tables he can design that might have further testing relevance for the interpretations that are emerging from the "test variable analysis." These tables, if the findings are predicted by the interpretations, are important evidence.

In interpreting survey data, the analyst seeks to tie together theoretically the numerous relationships he has found in the data. He hopes in doing this to relate the findings of his study to the findings of other studies and to the general body of theory in the field. No one has yet provided a model of procedural steps for arriving at reliable and valid interpretation. The survey analyst left to his own resources at this point often suggests interpretations that, in going far beyond his data, contradict the limited scientific assumptions of the survey method. At this point the social scientist has risen above the techniques of the survey method into the more abstruse methodologies of the armchair.

6. Summary

The essence of the cross-section field survey is (a) the uniform collection of data by means of a questionnaire; and (b) the use of these data for establishing quantitative relationships that enable the social scientist to generalize. Because of the systematic way that the survey collects its data, it runs into many problems of communication because the standard form of the questionnaire is not always suitable for the wide variety of field situations the research worker is trying to gather information about. The question may mean different things to different respondents; the context in which the question is answered may not be understood; the categories for classifying the respondent's answer are rather gross and overlook the subtleties of meaning the respondent may wish to convey; and so on. Much of the effort of a successful survey researcher goes into maximizing the validity and reliability of the communication between questionnaire and respondent by careful construction of the instrument and careful use of it during the questioning. Many surveys sustain serious biases because the survey researcher fails to recruit his interviewers with great care, to train them effectively, and to diligently supervise their operation in the field. But even though the data-gathering process has been skillfully carried out, the survey analyst knows that individual questions occasionally fail to "work" and individual respondents are occasionally misclassified. But survey analysis can sustain these errors because its findings are quantitative results that compare classes, groups, or categories of individuals. A modest amount of error at each stage of the investigation will not generally alter the generalizable findings.

SELECTED REFERENCES

Deming, W. E., "On Errors in Surveys," *American Sociological Review* (August, 1944), pp. 359-369.

Goode, W. J., and P. K. Hatt, *Methods in Social Research* (New York: McGraw-Hill Book Co., 1952), Chaps. 11, 12, and 13.

Hyman, H., "Interviewing as a Scientific Procedure," in D. Lerner and H. D. Lasswell, *The Policy Sciences* (Palo Alto, Calif.: Stanford University Press, 1951), pp. 203-216.

Jahoda, Marie, M. Deutsch, and S. W. Cook, *Research Methods in Social Relations* (New York: The Dryden Press, 1951), Chaps. 6, 12, and 18.

Lazarsfeld, P. F., "The Controversy Over Detailed Interviews—an Offer for Negotiation," *Public Opinion Quarterly,* Vol. 8 (1944), pp. 38-60.

Maccoby, E., and R. Holt, "How Surveys are Made," *The Journal of Social Issues,* Vol. 2 (1946), pp. 45-57.

McNemar, Quinn, "Opinion-Attitude Methodology," *Psychological Bulletin,* Vol. 43, No. 4, pp. 289-374.

Parten, Mildred, *Surveys, Polls and Samples* (New York: Harper and Brothers, 1949).

Rosenberg, M., and W. Thielens with P. F. Lazarsfeld, "The Panel Study," in M. Jahoda, *et al, Research Methods in Social Relations* (New York: The Dryden Press, 1951).

Sheatsley, P. B., "The Art of Interviewing and a Guide to Interviewer Selection and Training," in M. Jahoda, *et al, Research Methods in Social Relations* (New York: The Dryden Press, 1951).

Stouffer, S. A., "Some Observations on Study Design," *American Journal of Sociology,* Vol. 55, No. 4, pp. 355-361.

Ziesel, H., *Say It With Figures* (New York: Harper and Brothers, 1950).

Chapter 9

PARTICIPANT OBSERVATION AND INTERVIEWING*

1. Introduction

MANY people feel that a newspaper reporter is a far cry from a social scientist. Yet many of the data of social science today are gathered by interviewing and observation techniques that resemble those of a skilled newspaper man at work on the study of, say, a union strike or a political convention. It makes little sense for us to belittle these less rigorous methods as "unscientific." We will do better to study them and the techniques they involve so that we can make better use of them in producing valid scientific information.

As scientists, we naturally want to be as rigorous as possible. Whenever a crucial experiment or the quantitative data of a survey will provide data of testing relevance for our theories, we will want to use them. But there are many areas of social science where at our present stage of development, this is not the case. Sometimes quantitative data are difficult, almost impossible, to obtain; sometimes the relationships we want to examine are not explicit; often the problem is in the exploratory stages of research; or perhaps we want to obtain elaborate qualitative data on an individual case history. For these or other reasons a quantitative study is often not in order. Among the most frequent uses of field participation and interviewing are the following: (a) the reconstruction of an event or series of events; (b) the case history study of an individual, an organization, or even a community; and (c) pilot inquiries into new problem areas where the purpose is the production of hypotheses rather than the verification of them.

One hesitates to characterize unstructured field inquiry as a *single* method. Research workers make use of participation and interviewing, as we have seen, in different ways depending on the specific purposes at hand. The hallmark of the survey method is standardized data gathering. *A major characteristic of participant observation and interviewing is its non-standardization.* In fact, it aims to make a virtue of non-standardization by frequently redirecting the inquiry on the basis of data coming in from the field work to ever more fruitful areas of investigation. Changes in the research direction are made in order to chase down data more critical for the emerging hypotheses. Respondents are not treated uniformly but are interviewed about the things they can illuminate most. Each field situation is exploited to yield the most helpful *qualitative data*.

---

* Written by John P. Dean.

The aim is usually a flexible and skillful guiding of unpatterned field work to make the most of the individual peculiarities of the field situation.

A second central characteristic of unpatterned field inquiry is that it makes as effective use as possible of the relationships the researcher establishes with informants in the field situation for eliciting data. He aims to establish himself as a friend who can be trusted. He often wants to ask questions that touch confidential and personal subjects; he often wants to participate in informal situations where informants are relaxed and spontaneous; he may want to be admitted to conferences or meetings that are "off the record." To do these things he must have the confidence of persons in the field. For some kinds of inquiries this "trusted relationship" is more important than for other kinds of investigation. Studying an underworld gang would be almost impossible without a confidential relationship; it would be less necessary for studying the processes of a community chest campaign.

2. Limitations and Advantages of Unstructured Methods

The major limitations of participant observation and interviewing are directly related to the major characteristics noted above. *Because of the non-standardized way the data are collected, they are not generally useful for statistical treatment.* This means that quantitative relationships cannot generally be established and the researcher has to depend on a more impressionistic interpretation of the data to establish generalizations. In the long run, social science will have to rest on rigorously established generalizations, and experimental and other quantitative methods are probably the most reliable for establishing them. The more loosely and flexibly guided field inquiries will often suggest generalizations to be tested, but seldom provide the data for that testing.

Because of the manifest difficulties of generalizing from qualitative data, participant observation and interviewing frequently result in masses of undigested data, the meaning of which is not clear. Because of the elaborate detail that can be apprehended by a good field worker, each situation, even, or person is likely to be perceived as unique (as indeed they actually are.) This uniqueness inhibits attempts at generalization and may inhibit the formulation of categories, types, and operational procedures for specifying variables the researcher is interested in. For example, if a researcher becomes genuinely familiar with a local political party committeeman, he can judge to his own satisfaction from the various activities of the committeeman how motivated, active, and energetic the party worker is in promoting the interests of the party. He can see the ways that one committeeman differs from another in his activities. He may never actually force himself to formulate what he means by "very active," "fairly active," and "not active." He may find himself reluctant to classify committeemen into "types" in accordance with certain common patterns that apply to their activities. This lack of formulation is not an inherent shortcoming of the method, but it is a frequent concomitant. The more structured methods usually require an operational formulation of variables. Free-directive field inquiry does not.

A second major limitation flows from the researcher's use of the relationships he establishes in the field: the likelihood of bias. Since the research direction changes frequently on the basis of the emerging data, there is a major danger that the research worker will guide the inquiry on the basis of the mis-impressions he has gotten from the first informants he contacted. Or it may be that his own personal characteristics or personality needs attract him into stronger relationships with certain kinds of informants than with others, and thus prepare the way for his receiving an undue amount of confidential information from persons who are biased in one direction. Perhaps, too, the first hunches or hypotheses that emerge attract the research worker to instances that confirm these notions and blind him to data that point the other way. It is difficult for the participant observer to tell how representative a picture he is getting of the field situation. Certain biases are almost certain to be present when the field situations the researcher can participate in or the relationships he can establish are limited by his role and status. A man may be able to participate in the tavern drinking of the union leaders he wants to know, but not interview the wives of leaders at home during the day. A woman researcher would find the situation reversed. The great flexibility of free-direction field inquiry, besides being a major advantage, is also a clear invitation to bias that must be guarded against.

In compensation participant observation and interviewing have a number of advantages over the survey: (1) It is not as bound by prejudgment; it can re-formulate the problem as it goes along. The Erie County Voting Study, a panel survey undertaken in 1940, based much of its data gathering on the hypothesis that the main media of communication were major determinants of how people made up their minds to vote. It paid only scant attention to interpersonal influences. When the analysis began to suggest that personal contacts were extremely important, the data for establishing this fact were quite scanty. (2) Because of his closer contact with the field situation, the participant observer is better able to avoid misleading or meaningless questions. Respondents in one cross-section sample of a middle-sized city were asked if they belonged to a union, and if the union was AFL or CIO. The largest union in town was an independent union formerly affiliated with the AFL. Thus a disproportionate number of responses fell into the "other" category, and a substantial number of members of the union said "AFL." (3) The impressions of a participant field worker are often more reliable in classifying respondents than a rigid index based on one or two questions in a questionnaire. The participant observer can classify party workers as "more active" or "less active" on the basis of considerable information about them. A survey, using number of hours spent working for the party on election day, might lump together the tireless worker who hauled voters all day long in his car, and the worker who just hung around party headquarters all day. (4) The unstructured field inquiry usually uses the highest paid talent in direct contact with the data in the field. The survey director is usually several steps removed from the data-gathering process. This remoteness frequently impairs the researcher's understanding of the difficulties of communication that his questions invoke when asked by a semi-skilled interviewer in the field situation. (5) The participant observer can ease himself into the field situation at the appropriate pace and thus avoid rebuff by blundering into delicate situations or subject matter. The survey researcher may find to his surprise that some aspects of his questionnaire are explosive in the local situation. (6) The participant field worker can constantly re-modify his categories to provide more meaningful analysis of problems he is studying; the survey researcher is usually stuck with the categories or variables he originally used in conceiving the problem. (7) Imputing motives is always hazardous in social science, even though often essential. The field participant can generally impute motives more validly on the basis of the interlocking of aspersions and actual behavior, supplemented by occasional "feed-back" reactions; (*i.e.,* the researcher's stating the motivational picture of a respondent for corroboration or modification *by* the respondent). (8) The participant field worker can select later informants in such a way as to throw additional light on emerging hypotheses. Suppose several young party workers say that the older committeemen are afraid the younger workers will take away their party posts. The field worker can then approach some of the older party workers who are in close contact with energetic younger workers to find what their reactions are. The survey researcher is likely to find redirection limited by his sample and the questionnaire.[1] (9) The field participant can generally get at depth material more satisfactorily than the survey researcher. He can postpone immediate data-gathering to cultivate the relationship, and draw out depth material only when the informant is ready for it. In one instance preparatory to designing a questionnaire on the problems of elderly persons, a field worker using unstructured interviewing, found half of his respondents moved to tears at some time in the interview. When the questionnaire was used by trained interviewers, weeping was rare. (10) The field participant absorbs a lot of information that at the time seems irrelevant. Later, when his perspective on the situation has changed, this information may turn out to be extremely valuable. The survey researcher limits himself to what he *considers* important at the time even though he has some serious misconceptions about the problem. (11) It is much easier for the field participant to make use of selected informants' skills and insights by giving these informants free rein to report the problem situation as they see it. The field worker frequently wants his informants to talk about

---

[1] This problem of redirection may be solved by *repeated* surveys; if it is possible to make them within the limits of research time and budget.

what *they* want to talk about. The survey researcher has to get them to talk about what he wants. (12) The field participant can usually move more easily back and forth between data-gathering in the field and desk analysis. He has less of an investment to junk if he started out on the wrong track than the survey researcher. (13) Difficult-to-quantify situations or aspects of a problem are probably less distorted by the free data-gathering of the field participant than by an abortive effort to operationalize them for quantification by a survey. (14) The field participant has a big advantage over the survey researcher in delicate research areas where *covert* research is essential; *i.e.,* where he wants to make observations while ostensibly just participating. For example, if one wanted to make certain estimates of politico-underworld assignments by participating in the on-going processes of a horse-room, he might participate by placing bets on the horses; he would have trouble in the direct questioning. (15) Finally, there is the ever-present dollar sign: because the survey involves expenses such as recruiting and training interviewers, administering and supervising the field work, coding and punching the questionnaires, and running the hundreds of tables for analysis, surveys are generally more expensive than field participation. They also are more scientific in providing a more rigorous basis for scientific generalization.

3. Interviewing and Observation Compared on Their Relative Advantages

The relative weight the researcher gives to participant observation as against direct interviewing depends on the problem. Interviewing and participant observation have their respective advantages and limitations. By and large, interviewing serves best to get at information, impressions, and feelings that can be verbally reported. Of course, we must always beware of *distortion in reporting,* but frequently distortions or selective perceptions are precisely what we want to get at. When distortion occurs, it is usually for one of the following reasons:

(1) The respondent consciously modifies his attitudes or feelings in reporting them in order to make them more socially acceptable.

(2) The respondent unconsciously modifies his report of a situation because of some emotional need to shape the situation to fit his conceptions. Awareness of the true facts might activate anxiety the respondent unconsciously protects himself against.

(3) The respondent reports as accurately as he can, but because his mental set has selectively perceived the situation, the data reported give a biased impression of what occurred.

(4) The respondent just forgets the content or details of what he is reporting or reports what he *supposed* happened. Data below the respondent's observation or memory thresholds cannot be reported.

A skillful interviewer can often tell when distortion is occurring: perhaps the facts reported support another interpretation equally well; perhaps the biases of the respondent are so clear that the interviewer can spot ways they are modifying the report; perhaps the interviewer has data from other sources that reveal to him the nature of the distortion.

The fact that a respondent's report is distorted does not invalidate it as data. It is still useful in revealing (1) how the situation *looks* to the respondent; and (2) facts that may have escaped other observers who perceived the situation differently.

As researchers we must remember that a respondent with experience in the research area may be in a much more advantageous position to analyze and interpret on-going events than the researcher. He is likely to know the local jargon or technical terms that are necessary to understand the events; he may understand the people involved well enough to know the meaning of their reactions; he *may* even be a better observer than the researcher.

Even when participant observation might be superior, interviewing will have to be substituted where the data are unavailable for observation; *e. g.,* past events, privacy situations where an observer would not be tolerated, exclusion situations where either outsiders are not permitted in *or* outsiders would so alter the situation as to give a misleading impression to the observer.

Interviewing has one major advantage over participant observation. The researcher can by direct questioning dig into content areas that might not naturally come up in a participation situation. Of course, often the participant observer is free to do some interviewing along with his participation, but if several other participants are involved, this may be difficult. And if the researcher wants to reconstruct past events or explore participants' relationships with each other, it may be much more satisfactory to pick off participants one at a time in privacy where he can get the respondents' own impressions and reactions about a situation unconfounded by the pressure of others.

But there are some situations where interviewing is seriously limited. Under certain conditions behavior is more depth-revealing than verbally expressed feelings. For example, behavior is often more revealing when the problem area concerns personal influence, personal aggression, and interpersonal manipulative behavior. How these tie in with and modify role and status relationships frequently comes out in overt interaction. The crucial distinction *between spontaneous behavior* and *conventional behavior* often requires on-the-spot observation. Situations where conventional patterns are the apparatus for conveying hostile-aggressive unconventional motives are hard to distinguish by interviewing. A mother may use the culturally appropriate motive of keeping her child clean as a thinly veiled punitive device. Watch the way a rejecting mother scrubs her youngster's face and imposes physical restraints and taboos upon him.

Feelings, on the other hand, are more depth-revealing in content areas where the informant is relatively uninhibited or not inclined to slant the reporting too much to protect himself, his family, or his loyalties. Where the inquiry-area involves tensions that are present and unresolved or still in the process of adjustment, the key data are likely to be near the front of consciousness and within reach of the informant and therefore relatively available through interviewing. But even though the crucial motivations are repressed or distorted to the informant, they may be revealed to an observer by being "acted out" in interacting with others. An observer often seems to have the advantage over an interviewer in getting at:

(1) *The expressed affect invoked by interpersonal situations:* the observer can make use of tones, gestures, facial expressions, body tensions, nervous mannerisms and the like, that the interviewer cannot reconstruct.

(2) *The unexpressed affect:* situations where unresponsiveness, avoidance, ignoring, etc., are important. Observation is often necessary when what *doesn't happen* is important.

(3) *Sociometric relationships that involve gestalt, proximity, physical arrangements, changes of place or speed, objects manipulated, etc.*

(4) *Social interaction that involves several people.* Interpersonal influence, inappropriate over- or under-reactions, manipulative behavior, ingratiating or defensive behavior—these are often more efficiently apprehended by a good observer at the scene of action.

On the negative side, observation is often hampered by the time commitments it requires. Sometimes an inordinate amount of observation time may be necessary in order to be present when the crucial events occur. Sometimes, too, the situations to be observed are scheduled for times when or places where the researcher cannot be present. Also on the negative side: unless the researcher interviews the participants, he must infer what the participants' perceptions and interpretations of the situation are. Most of what transpires in an interpersonal situation depends heavily on role taking, empathizing, perceptions of other participants' perceptions, and unrevealed motives—these may be difficult to infer without interviewing participants.

Clearly, in many field situations some combination of participant observation *and* interviewing is called for.

4. Establishing Field Relationships

Because the relationship between the research worker and the persons in the field situation is the key to effective participant observation and interviewing, much depends on the initial field contacts. They often determine whether the door to research in that setting will be open or shut. Although each field setting has its own peculiar circumstances, a few rough principles are worth noting:

(1) *Generally field contacts should move from the persons in highest status and authority down to the actual participants in the field situation one wants to study.* Where there are two lines of authority, (*e. g.,* a plant situation where both union and management are involved; or

a study of a local political campaign) the initial contacts with leaders of both groups may be essential to prevent either group from identifying the researcher as partisan to the other group. Top leaders are often the persons best in a position to have the vision and perspective to understand what the research is trying to get at. Once they have offered cooperation, persons farther down the status hierarchy will generally go along with the research if properly approached.

(2) The research worker needs to have a plausible explanation of the research that makes sense to the people whose cooperation he is seeking. This sounds obvious, but is *not* usually an easy thing to do. If respondents get the impression that they or their organization are going to be carefully scrutinized in all they do and perhaps evaluated in comparison with others, resistance is likely to set in. Compare the following:

Bad	*Good*
"We want to study what makes for good and bad union leadership."	"We want to learn how a union carries on its day-to-day work."
"We want to learn what the roots of effective political organizations are—how much patronage, paid-for party work, volunteer help, figure in local party campaigns."	"We want to understand how a local political party goes about a local political campaign."
"We are interested in racial tension, discrimination, and prejudice and how they interlock in a community setting."	"We are interested in the different groups that make up a city like this—the Jewish community, the Negro community, the foreign-extraction groups—how they are organized and participate in the total life of the community."

The principle underlying the good examples above is this: *The researcher should indicate interest in understanding the legitimate activities of a person or group rather than understanding or evaluating the persons themselves or their behavior.* Researchers who do not give careful advance thought to how they will explain their research—even to the selection of specific phrases they will use—often find themselves turned down.

(3) The research worker should try to represent himself, his sponsors, and his study, as realistically as possible. Bluffing, pretending naiveté, representing oneself or one's sponsors as something misleading, or trying to make out one's study to be *more* important or *less* important than it actually is, are *all* dangerous tactics. Subsequent events or other lines of communication may reveal the real situation to the field contacts and seriously damage the research worker's field relations. Further research may become impossible.

(4) The research worker should try to have in mind some rather routine fact-gathering that makes sense as the first research step in the field setting. This will provide him with a legitimate reason for

contacting persons involved in the actual field setting where he wants to be a participant observer. Gathering these facts will give other participants a chance to get used to his being on the grounds and may provide contacts for further inquiry. The important principle in this: *A person becomes accepted as a participant observer more because of the kind of person he turns out to be in the eyes of the field contacts than because of what the research represents to them.* Field contacts want to be reassured that the research worker is a "good guy" and can be trusted not to "do them dirt" with what he finds out. They do not usually want to understand the full rationale behind a study. The research worker should not, of course, give an appearance of reticence in talking about his study: being willing to tell people more about the study than they want to know is reassuring in allaying fears or suspicions about the research.

The participant observer's aim is to participate *naturally* in interpersonal situations in the social environment he is studying. He hopes this will give him deeper insight into the participants and their social environment. If he is successful as a participant observer, he will become accepted into social situations to the point where the other participants are quite spontaneous. At first the presence of a participant observer may seriously inhibit other participants' reactions. Acceptance depends in part on the participant observer's having role and status attributes appropriate to the social environment of the respondent. But even with role and status attributes that might be considered unusual in the field situation, a pleasant, sincere, unthreatening researcher can become accepted. *The major determinants of acceptance appear to be time, a sense of social appropriateness on the researcher's part, and his sincerity and genuine interest in the people he is working with.*

Since this is true, we have the following cardinal principle: *The research worker should sacrifice initial data in order to speed acceptance.* This means that he should not be an eager beaver after crucial data; he should relax and let the situation carry him along. He should participate as naturally as he can and as "socially" as he can. He should try not to give the impression that the only reason he is there is because he wants research data. He should give the impression (and, hopefully, it will not be just an impression, but genuine) that he is there because he really enjoys himself and is interested in the activities of the participants. He should avoid constantly probing with questions; better just to feed participants with his interest and comments when they are talking about things that are relevant to the research. Once accepted, there will be plenty of time to ask questions and in the meantime he can establish confidence, identify the most insightful participants, and judge what questions may be threatening to the informants.

In general, successful participant observation moves from passive participation to active participation, to participant interviewing, to experimental intervention. Trying to move down this line too fast is a quick way to short circuit the data gathering.

5. Fruitful Situations for Field Participation

How does the research worker find fruitful situations to participate in and observe? Some situations, of course, can be arranged by negotiation with key leaders in the research area. If the researcher wanted to study a union by participant observation, he might be able to arrange with the officers of the union to be present at union meetings. He could then start out as a non-participant just watching what went on at meetings. But to make the most of such a situation, he would try to develop informal contacts outside the formal conduct of the meetings. It would be a good idea for him to get to meetings ahead of time and hang around afterwards chatting with members still in the union hall.

Participant observation is likely to be especially fruitful at informal contact centers. These may be places the research worker can just drop in on; *e. g.,* a tavern or a restaurant "where the boys hang out." But sometimes he will need an invitation in order to be there; *e. g.,* a private club house of some sort. In either case it is better for the field worker to get himself taken along than to barge in on his own hook. If he knows a person or two who usually drop in at the informal contact centers, he may be able to chat with them at a time when they are likely to be on their way to the contact center. For instance, if the union members generally went somewhere after the meeting for a glass of beer, the field worker might even suggest to one of the men that they have a glass of beer together. Just how these things can be worked naturally varies from one research situation to another. But in most cases a little careful thought will suggest the most appropriate way for the informal participation to be initiated.

After the field worker is accepted as a participant, various research opportunities will open up: the researcher may be able to bring up certain subjects himself so he can get the reactions of different participants and perhaps even get a discussion going about them. Even touchy subjects can be brought up if properly introduced. One way is this: "I've heard it said that . . . (such and such) . . . I've been wondering if there's any truth in it."

Sometimes in field situations the researcher can do some on-the-spot group interviewing. He might say to the participants something like this: "One thing that I am especially puzzled about that maybe you fellows can clear up for me is this . . . ." and then ask about an important subject.

Occasionally the field participant has opportunities to bring together people that are important to the research in order to study their reactions to each other and to the situation he confronts them with. One possibility along these lines is forming an advisory committee to the research that will bring in people strategically situated as to the research problem.

In many field situations a research worker can establish personal relationships that he can develop socially outside the informal contact center. If he gets to know participants well enough to invite them out to lunch or to his home, he will have unusual opportunities to ask about the things he wants to know. And he may find himself invited to the respondent's home for social occasions. It is especially helpful to see a respondent in his own social context. Intense affective reactions are usually related to charged interpersonal relationships (perhaps long since past). Often, therefore, motives can be imputed more fruitfully through insight and analysis of the respondent's affectively-charged interpersonal ties (such as you would find when he is among his family and close friends). A person in the social context of his family and close friends is in a good diagnostic setting. You might almost say it is a projective test to see how the respondent reacts in such a setting.

6. Fruitful Informants for Intensive Interviewing

The experienced research worker in the field is well aware of the unevenness of interviews in providing new insights, hypotheses, and interpretations. One informant will provide rich and suggestive data; another will yield almost nothing. If the field researcher can guide his inquiry to the more fruitful informants, he can save himself much time. Naturally, no rigid rules can be laid down; chance and luck will always play a part. But there are a few leads that may help guide the field worker to the more fruitful informants. Selection of the most fruitful informants means selection of unrepresentative cases and naturally carries a bias-risk. The field worker should take appropriate cautions in interpretation. But any systematic checking of the findings of free-directive field inquiry will require quantitative verification at a later time.

There are several kinds of informants who are generally more helpful than the average person: (1) *Respondents who are especially sensitized to have insights in the problem area.*

—The *outsider,* who sees things from the light of another culture, social class, community, etc.

—The *"rookie"* who is surprised by what goes on and notes the taken-for-granted things that the acclimated miss. And as yet, he may have no *stake* in the system to protect.

—*The nouveau status,* the person in transition from one role or status to another where the tensions of new experience are raw and sensitive.

—The *"natural,"* i.e., the rare reflective objective person in the field. He can sometimes be pointed out by other intelligent and reflective persons.

(2) *The more-willing-to-reveal respondents:* because of their back-

ground or status, some respondents are just more willing to talk than others.

—The *naive informant,* who knows not whereof he speaks: either (a) naive to what the field worker represents, or (b) naive about his own group.

—The *frustrated person* (rebel or malcontent), especially the one who is consciously aware of blocking of his drives and impulses.

—The *"outs,"* those out of power, but "in-the-know," and critical of the "ins"—eager to reveal negative facts about the "ins."

—The *habitué* or *"old hand,"* "fixture around here," who no longer has a stake or is so accepted that he is not threatened by exposing what others say or do.

—The *"needy" person* who fastens onto the interviewer because he needs the attention and support. As long as the interviewer feels this need, he will talk.

—The *subordinate,* who must adapt to superiors. He generally develops insights to cushion the impact of authority, and he may be hostile and willing to "blow his top."

(3) *Critical cases.* A case is critical when the causal factors one is not studying are held constant so that the causal influence of those factors one is studying may be more easily discerned. Since critical case situations depend on holding factors constant, critical cases can often be found by selecting them so that one or more of the important variables are held constant. For example, if one were interested in the relation between housing and family tensions, then families of the same composition and age living in identical dwelling units would be critical cases, since both housing and family composition would be held constant. But if some of these families were about to move into the identical units and could be observed and interviewed both in their previous quarters *and* in the new identical quarters after they moved in, these families would be even *more* critical: you could now compare the *same* families in *different* housing situations and *different* families in the *same* housing.

Here is another example in intergroup relations among youth. Youth recently moved from states that have segregated schools to a state that has integrated schools would provide critical cases. But cities that are experiencing a change-over from segregated white and Negro schools to integrated schools would offer still more critical cases because the home and community environment would be held constant. The most fruitful critical cases for sociological studies are often those that enable us to compare people of similar psychological and social characteristics in *different* sociological environments. Obviously the best cases, then, are the people who move from one sociological environment to another.

Where large field canvasses or sample studies have already been made, it may be possible using data already collected on the cases, to isolate cases that will be especially critical from the point of view of the current problem area. Follow-up interviews with these selected critical cases will generally (a) insure fairly fruitful case selection, and (b) give certain "through-time" or "before-and-after" comparisons that may be especially helpful.

(4) *Trained persons in the field situation.* In many field situations there will be persons who may have had some special training in social work, social science, or psychiatry, but who also by virtue of their current job, are closely in touch with the field situation the research worker is examining. The research worker can sometimes profit immensely from their experience and greater familiarity with the field situation.

7. What Characterizes "Good" Interviewing and Observation?

Actually, little is known about the specific techniques of good research interviewing and observation in the field. Each research worker adopts whatever devices seem natural to him, perhaps modifies them under supervision or through experience when gross mistakes have been made and finally comes up with a set of custom-made "techniques" that are his own. In every sense, good interviewing and observation are still an art.

But if the methodologies of social science are to be sharpened, they will need formulation and modification by thorough cross-checking of the experiences of one research worker with those of another. With the thought that almost any formulation is better than none at all in promoting the cross-checking of experience, this chapter will set down in "cook-book fashion" the custom-made techniques developed by the author during his own years in the field. Needless to say, they have all the shortcomings that the formulation of one individual's experience is bound to have.

The free-directive interviewer faces a dilemma. The research value of the interview depends on the amount and specific quality of the data that emerge about the research problem. The more specific and valuable data usually require intensive and detailed questioning. Intensive and detailed questioning is more feasible after a firm and friendly relationship is established. In establishing relationships one is generally friendly and responsive to the spontaneous and meandering direction in which an informant leads the conversation. So the dilemma is, how much to try to guide the interview and probe for specific data, versus how much to give the informant free rein and cultivate the relationship. A skillful interviewer walks this tightrope by being an *insightful, sympathetic curious listener.* He tries to be natural, friendly and sympathetic throughout the interview. He frequently indicates by nodding or saying, "of course," or "I understand," that he *accepts* the *informant's feelings.* A good interview resembles a friendly conversation more than a cross-examination. An expert interviewer frequently seems to be just an interested listener encouraging the respondent to talk. But it is not enough just to be a good listener who nods incessantly. The interviewer must indicate by his responsiveness that he follows the feeling tone of the respondent and understands why he feels that way. Comments or questions that indicate that he understands the significant features of the situation *as they appear to the respondent,* usually encourage the respondent to amplify and reveal the deeper nooks and crannies that he might at first hesitate to tell a relative stranger.

Furthermore, *insightful listening* enables one to analyze and interpret what is being said—to piece together the little clues that reveal what is *meant* or *implied* by the respondent. Inexperienced interviewers are often taken in by glib and articulate explanations offered by respondents: these often represent justifications or rationalizations that the respondent customarily uses to convince others and himself that he is measuring up to expected standards of performance or ethics or motivation. This does not mean that the interviewer should step in and cut off or cut through these professed principles and practices, even though they may be rank generalities. In areas where the respondent's ego is invested and where cutting through would threaten or antagonize the respondent, it is usually best to wait out the exposition—let the respondent establish his integrity and accomplishments; *then* he will feel secure enough or gratified enough to reveal more of the sore spots, pet peeves, and countless irritations that he wants to get off his chest to a sympathetic listener.

The skillful interviewer is careful not to push the informant, but to take *his* pace. He tries never to give the respondent the feeling that he is pressuring him or pumping him. The word "probe" is perhaps an unfortunate word—It may give the impression that a good interviewer is always cutting in deeper with his sharp interviewing techniques. Actually, good interviewing is not laying out the respondent on the operating table and probing his insides. Good interviewing is much more like feeding a squirrel. First you throw a few nuts near the squirrel to see if he won't move a little closer—gradually you establish confidence until hesitantly and tentatively the squirrel sidles up and takes from your hand. Any false move or slip on your part and the squirrel retreats and you have to begin again. Although a respondent stays put while he is interviewed, his feeling tone in relation to the interviewer is like the squirrel. A sensitive interviewer can feel it hesitantly and tentatively come forward and recede. Only genuine warmth and reassurance can establish a fruitful relationship.

Even though the interviewer succeeds in establishing a good relationship with the informant, the interview will have little value unless he gets data that throw light on the research problem. An interviewer should learn to make a distinction between *generalities* and *data:*

Generalities are loose summary statements that convey a judgment inferred by the respondent on the basis of his selective perception of some situation or events.

Data (facts) are verifiable statements that require little generalization or inference.

Here are a few examples:

Generalities	*Data*
"The organization does not admit Negroes."	"Mr. Choate, a Negro, applied and was refused."
"Committeemen are not interested in the party as they used to be."	"Only fifteen or twenty of the committeemen showed up at the political rally we held last fall."
"Older workers are easily demoralized in trying to get jobs."	"Of a hundred older workers that come to the employment service, I would guess that twenty-five have jobs within a week. Most of the other seventy-five won't get placed for maybe three or four months or even longer. After a month most of them stop coming in."

Generalities may be important *leads* to good data. If a respondent is insightful and well-informed, they may represent excellent inferences *from the data,* but they are not the *data* themselves. Generalities are usually built up by *piecing together the circumstantial evidence surrounding discrete events selectively perceived.* It is the job of the interviewer to cut through the respondent's perceptions to whatever circumstantial evidence this respondent has apprehended that can provide the social scientist with data for (1) making his own inferences, and (2) verifying the validity of the respondent's generalities. A strategic informant may provide better inferences than the social scientist can arrive at from any available data. *But* without data that check in with the inferences, the generalities of neither social scientist nor informant are useful.

To avoid this most recurrent of interviewing errors, the interviewer should scrupulously try to differentiate *generalities* from *data* by constantly asking himself: "Are these *data* or *not?*"

A brief analysis of a generality may make this clear: "The organization does not admit Negroes." Who or what is meant by "the organization?" Sociologically, "organization" may mean a reification of the roles and operating practices of the people joined in this enterprise. Seen in this light, what we want to know about the organization that is relevant to our generality is: what steps must be taken by an individual to be admitted; who passes on whom under what conditions? What is meant by "does not admit?" Possibly, if a Negro were to try to take those steps to being admitted, he would be refused. But this is really a prediction of future action on an unknown applicant. What is meant by

"Negoes"? Negroes of all economic statuses, educational levels, backgrounds, and experiences? Experience has shown that often one Negro will be accepted in a situation, another Negro rejected. If a respondent replies to a question about discrimination with a generality that the "organization does not admit Negroes," the interviewer tries to cut through to the data. He might say:

"Have any Negroes ever applied for admission to the organization?"

If "yes," he goes on to get details, especially (1) those details that reveal who passed on the application and under what conditions; and (2) those details that would reveal whether white men of the same social, educational and personality characteristics have been admitted.

To enrich the data that bear on his research problem, the interviewer quickly appraises what is involved in cutting through a generality and phrases conversational questions to cut through. When he can do this spontaneously and effortlessly and at the same time maintain and improve his relationship with the informant, he can be called a "skilled interviewer."

8. Guiding the Course of An Interview

The interviewer's success in steering between a too direct probing for specific data and a too permissive passiveness while the informant rambles, depends on how skillfully the interviewer can guide the direction of the conversation. Although rules of thumb are always hazardous, here are a few that some skillful interviewers find it worthwhile to follow:

(1) An interviewer generally should open an interview by asking factual non-threatening questions. Suppose, for example, an interviewer is interested in whether an organization discriminates against Negroes, and is starting to interview an officer of the organization. His questions might follow some order like this:

"I really know very little about your organization, so perhaps we'd better start from scratch. When did your organization first get going?"

(Etc. etc.—maybe feed respondent as he traces rough history to date.)

"I see; about how many members do you have today?"

"What does one have to do to become a member?"

"Are people ever turned down?"

(If yes, "why is that?")

If "no" or "not unless they're not qualified": "Then I suppose you have all types of people in your group?"

"Do you get people of different foreign extractions—like the Polish or Hungarian?"

"What about Jews?"

"Any Negroes?"

If no Jews or Negroes:

"Has anyone ever proposed a Jewish (Negro) member?"

"What happened?"

"Was there any discussion about the fact that he was Jewish (Negro)?"
"How did you feel about it?"
   Etc. etc.
   There are usually facts that an interviewer needs to get clearly in mind before he moves into the area of special interest. He is wise to spend the first five or ten minutes on these questions: they offer a chance (a) to show genuine interest in things the respondent likes to talk about, (b) to get him chatting easily, and (c) to relieve the respondent's initial expectancy (if he has it) that the interviewer is going to interrogate or cross-examine him.

   (2) The interviewer should locate the major data by unstructured "lead" questions. The initial factual questions may lead the interviewer to key data he wants to ask about in more detail; but often special areas of interest are not touched on. In trying to locate the *significant* data in these areas, it is usually wise to let the respondent specify them in response to unstructured open-ended "lead" questions such as:

   "What impressed you about your experiences as a nurse?"
   "How did you feel about the meeting?"
   "What stands out in your mind about the various contacts you have had with Negroes?"
   After leads of this sort, follow-up questions on concrete examples that come to the respondent's mind will provide specific data about experiences that are especially meaningful to the respondent.
   Of course, if the respondent's perception is too oblique to the researcher's interest, the lead questions may have to be sharpened. Compare the following with the leads suggested above.
   "Did you feel the meeting came out satisfactorily?"
   "What would you say is the first *really significant* contact you ever had with a Negro?"
   Since the interviewer can always increasingly sharpen the focus of his questions to bring into perspective what he wants, the general principle is: *ask unstructured questions first.*

   (3) The interviewer should make use of occasional guide questions: A "guide" question is a pre-formulated and pre-worded question that the interviewer has prepared. In unstructured interviewing it is often helpful to have a few "guide" questions in mind before each interview. Well-prepared "guide" questions serve the following functions:
   (a) They provide the interviewer with something important to ask when sudden pauses occur, such as when a sub-topic being discussed is exhausted.
   (b) They avoid awkward or misleading wording such as might occur if the interviewer suddenly finds himself grasping for appropriate words.
   (c) They provide a carefully planned way of introducing a delicate or touchy subject.
   (d) If used in several interviews, they provide a sort of standardized

stimulus: the different ways different respondents react to the same question is likely to be revealing.

(e) If scattered over the different areas of research interest, they help to guarantee that an interview will get coverage.

(4) The interviewer should make an effort to pick up leads: Often, in spontaneously rambling on, a respondent will drop a few hints or clues that are suggestive, but not really illuminating without further probing. Naturally, a good interviewer is reluctant to keep interrupting once he has the respondent talking freely, but if a clue or a hint seems important, the interviewer should take mental note of it and at the first opportunity pick up the lead and amplify the data around it. The manner in which this is done is important: he must try not to seem to be prying, but to be merely interested in clearing up some little point he did not quite grasp. Compare the following:

Bad	*Good*
"Why did you say that Mr. Kress was 'obstructing' the meeting?" (R may feel you are accusing him of saying something unkind.)	"You say that Mr. Kress was 'obstructing' the meeting in what way?"
"Do you think the Jewish Community should fight anti-semitism?" (R will give his personal opinion rather than data about the community.)	"How do you think the Jewish community feels about fighting anti-semitism?"

If the respondent starts wandering from a subject you want to pursue further, pick up at the point where he started to wander.

Bad	*Good*
"You said good committeemen are hard to find—why is that?" (R will give his opinion, not data on process.)	"You were saying that good committeemen are hard to find—how do you go about finding someone when there is a vacancy?"

(5) The interviewer should cut through generalities with well formulated probes. Many interviewers use a few standard probes that have been shown to be especially helpful in cutting through generalities:

Respondent: "His behavior was ridiculous."
Probe A. Interviewer: *"How do you mean—'ridiculous'?"*
Respondent: "Of course, there are pressure groups on the inside."
Probe B. Interviewer: *"What sort of 'pressure groups'?"*
Respondents: "They seem to object to having Negroes around."
Probe C. Interviewer: *"How does that come to your attention?"*

Respondent: "Politics come up once in awhile."
Probe D. Interviewer: *"In what connection?"*

If these standard probes are thoroughly ingrained in the interviewer's reactions they will spontaneously, almost involuntarily, leap into the breach when appropriate.

It is often helpful to have the respondent concentrate on an example or illustration (not a hypothetical example—but a real instance that the respondent knows about). Even better is the respondent's account of the most recent instance or most significant instance in his experience. The interviewer can usually get the respondent onto concrete events by some probe such as:

Interviewer: "I wonder if you could give me an illustration of something like that that you know the details of."

Interviewer: "How recently has something like that occurred?" Then, "Could you tell me about that?"

When a respondent has set forth a generality, the interviewer should try to find out what caught his attention that made him form his judgment. He should be careful not to naively accept his judgment, but instead should try to look at the situation through his eyes. He should ask the questions that illuminate what the informant selected to see, hear, and notice.

(6) The interviewer should stick with the fruitful areas once they open up. If good data are coming forth in an interview situation around one particular topic, the interviewer should *stick with it.* It is usually better to sacrifice covering other subjects in order to enrich the data in the area under discussion. He can usually return another day to ask about other things, but if he cuts off data in an area that is opening up to ask about something else, he may never again have as good a chance at that data.

Perhaps the commonest fault of inexperienced interviewers is not staying with an area until the good data are teased out. The green interviewer sometimes seems to assume that once he asks a question about something and an answer is given he should move on to the next subject. But the lead question in an area is just the first spade of dirt. If the interviewer is going to get at hidden treasures he sometimes has to unearth heaps of useless dirt before he strikes gold. When he has struck it rich, he should try to amplify the data around the topic so that he gets it in full perspective. It is usually good to inquire about the actions or feelings or perceptions of other persons that were involved in the situation. Naturally, there is no mechanical set of precepts that can be offered for guiding the interviewer to the crucial data. But it helps considerably to watch for (or know in advance) the respondent's special areas of interest, experience, and competence. The chances are that the data he gives in this area will be more insightful and more reliable. The interviewer may want to direct the interview to those areas.

(7) The interviewer should reflect on the meaning of emerging data and ask questions that clarify or amplify their meaning for the research problem. Just what data *are* significant depend on the subject under consideration, and only an interviewer who understands his subject thoroughly can appraise the significance of the data that are emerging and frame intelligent questions to illuminate their meaning. Too often interviewers think their job is to get the data coming out, then just sit there and absorb it like a sponge. Intelligent interviewing requires intelligent analysis of the data emerging *as it is being discussed.* As the situation being discussed unfolds, the interviewer should speculate on the implications of the data and should be ready to explore the unexplained sidelines that are taken for granted. New crucial data are often implied by what a respondent has already said. For example, a woman who has been ill explains that the doctor has forbidden her to do any housework until she regains her full strength. This implies that the housework either goes undone *or* is done by children and husband *or* is done by a paid housekeeper. Any of these can have serious repercussions in family adjustment and should be inquired about.

In interviewing about subjects that involve specialized knowledge, the interviewer usually needs some sophistication about the area or he will find himself in the dilemma of either (1) interrupting the respondent to clear up technicalities that are important for understanding what the respondent is talking about; or (2) stringing along without understanding in hope that it will clear up as more data come out. Both are unsatisfactory, of course. Perhaps the lesser evil is to plead ignorance at the first sign of getting lost and try to clear up right then the details that are confusing. Then it may be possible to follow the rest with only minor difficulty.

(8) The interviewer should be especially alert to follow up only areas where the respondent shows emotional involvement. Significant research data are likely to emerge around subjects the respondent feels strongly about. In those areas the research problem has most meaning to the respondent, and his affect-laden experiences are of great help in enabling the research worker to see the problem through the respondent's eyes. Because of this the researcher should frequently *inquire after feelings* and then *follow the feeling tone* when there are signs of affect. He may initiate these "feeling-leads" by queries such as these:

"How do you feel about what happened?"

"What made you feel that way?"

"How did you react to that—did you feel strongly about it?" He should try to re-create the feeling tone of situations long since past:

"Now that you think back, how did it feel to be refused just because you were a Negro."

With insight and interpretation the interviewer can often bring forth depth material by some feeler such as:

"You seem to feel that . . . ."

He should listen not only to *what* the respondent says, but even more important, to *how he says it*. And he should watch especially for *unexpected affect:* There is often something significant going on whenever the emotions revealed by the respondent appear to be out of line with what seem appropriate (either because he shows too *little* or too *much* emotion). Unexpected affect is often revealed by such things as: self-correcting (was the "corrected" word or phrase really what the respondent felt?); flushing; stammering; tremulous voice; ambivalent reactions; embarrassed silences; or the over-protesting or over-concentration on certain emphases. The skilled interviewer watches for any emotional blocking (noticeable withholding of spontaneous responses) on the part of the respondent. It is revealing not only of how the interviewer-respondent relationship is developing, but may provide valuable leads to the key areas of emotional involvement. He may be able to detect *subtly revealed meanings* in spontaneous associations, inconsistencies in response, questions to the interviewer, obvious gaps or oversights in reporting sudden transitions, or the *taken-for-granted assumptions and practices* that are shared by the in-group the respondent belongs to. The interviewer should have the perspicacity to *wait out the pregnant silences*. When in doubt as to what to say or what to ask, many interviewers just *pause*. If not sure what to say he may say the wrong thing—or, more likely and even worse, he may cut off some crucial data the respondent was hesitating to reveal. "Dead air" presents a powerful invitation to jump in, and will often precipitate data a respondent had not intended to reveal.

The field worker has to break through the traditional taboo system that operates in all society and that is especially misleading to strangers. Social interaction often takes place on two levels (a) the socially accepted patterns of interaction, the "as if" fictions, and (b) what "really goes on." A guest leaving a party says he had a lovely time even though he was bored stiff; a person steps on your toe and says, "I'm sorry, did it hurt?" and you say, "No, not at all," as you limp away. A host and hostess bring out the "guest specials" and try to act as if this was the way they lived everyday. One of the highest skills in interviewing is calling the bluff of your respondent, thus letting him know that *you* know what the score is. But this must be done in such a way that it does not antagonize the respondent and give him the feeling that you doubt his word. When done successfully, it seems to relieve the respondent by making it unnecessary for him to maintain pretenses and be on guard. Thus relieved, he can talk more freely.

(9) The interviewer should try to re-direct the interview to more fruitful areas when useful data are not emerging. Sometimes an interviewer will have exhausted an area and want to move along to a new area of exploration, but the respondent keeps rambling on. He should,

of course, *try not to interrupt*. If he waits watchfully until he sees a chance, he can usually jump in with something that will enable him to guide the interview to new areas. For example:

"That's very interesting. It puts me in mind of one thing I want to be sure to ask you about ...."

"Yes, I understand how (difficult) it must have been, but what puzzles me is ...."

If it does become necessary to re-direct the interview, the interviewer should try to take the respondent's feelings into account:

"I can see that you feel quite strongly on that and I want to ask you more about it, but while I think of it I want to get your impressions on one thing we haven't touched on yet ...."

Sometimes the interviewer can create an easy handle for transition by relating some aspect of the area being discussed with the subject he wants to move along to:

"You just mentioned . . . (how difficult it was to get committeemen interested in politics); what about . . . (the actual work the party does in getting out the vote)?"

Note that in this last instance there is little relation between the two areas. It is not necessary that they be logically or even psychologically related as long as the transition gives the impression that it is a natural sequence.

If the interviewer *must* interrupt the respondent, he should take the respondent along by using something like the shortage of time to explain the interrupting:

"Your thoughts (experience) on that are most interesting, but since I don't want to take too much of your time, would you mind if we turned the discussion to another aspect you can help clear up for me."

If there are certain specified minimum areas that must be covered in the interview, the interviewer should have a check list of those areas committed thoroughly to memory. Then he can watch for easy transitions from one area to another. It is helpful to have guide questions prepared as leads in each of these areas in case there is no easy and natural transitions, and the interviewer has to use one of the above devices for re-directing the interview.

(10) The interviewer should be alert to "touchy" subject matters and not just blunder in. If an area or subject that comes up in the interview seems to be a little touchy and the respondent appears reluctant to talk about it, then the interviewer shouldn't move in on the area too fast. Maybe he can talk with the respondent around the edges of the area until the respondent leaves an opening. He can certainly watch for opportunities to put a mild question that will permit the respondent to reveal what he is holding back. For example:

"How do you get out such a large vote in the 4th Ward? Do you make any special efforts—use any special inducements or anything?"

Things held back often seem to act as a pressure on the respondent. Talking close to the taboo area, especially if the interviewer indicates that he is familiar with the sort of thing that the respondent is ducking, often melts the resistance of the respondent and calls forth a frank revelation of this sort:

"Well, it's really like this—and this is off the record—both parties spend a good deal deal of money on the Negro vote in the 4th Ward." Often an "I suppose" statement that is a little off the beam, will call forth a correction from the respondent that will begin to open up the touchy area.

Interviewer: "I suppose you have to use a lot of cars to get out the Negro vote."

Respondent: "Not any more than in the other Wards . . . (pause) (Interviewer *pause too!*) Of course, we usually have to give the committeemen up there a good bit of money to spend on 'helpers.' "

(11) The interviewer should try to turn back respondents' direct questions: One common experience of green interviewers that is apt to create an awkward situation is this: the respondent sometimes asks the interviewer a direct question. For the most part, an interviewer should not express any interfering biases, yet he cannot be in the position of refusing to answer or seeming to withhold information. Frequently, the best thing to do is to *seem* to answer, but really to evade giving his own opinions.

Suppose a respondent says:

"Well, I don't know—what do you think?"

One way to answer is:

"Well, it *is* hard to form an opinion on that, isn't it? Do you ever get the feeling that . . ."

This is much better than saying:

"We interviewers are not supposed to express our opinions, so I really can't tell you."

Suppose an interviewer who favors proportional representation is interviewing a respondent who says:

"I'm strongly opposed to proportional representation—it gives the left wing groups *too much* representation. I'll fight every move to get it in. Don't you feel that way about it?"

If the interviewer says, "yes," he may be embarrassed later on when his stand is made known: it is very poor interviewing policy to misrepresent one's own beliefs. This is especially dangerous if one is talking to people on both sides of a question: they may compare notes and find that an interviewer was two-facedly giving each the impression that he agreed with him. Perhaps the best response to such a question is something like this:

"I think you make some very telling points. What about . . ."— Then he can move right on to the next question. Turning back direct questions is an important interviewing skill.

(12) The interviewer should wind up the interview before the respondent becomes tired. If the interviewer is going to maintain the relationship so that he can return again, he should stop well short of the "exasperation point." When to stop is a matter for the judgment and sensitivity of the interviewer. Partly it depends on objective circumstances —how busy the respondent seems to be, arrival of new appointments, or other business to be attended to. Partly it depends on how much the respondent is enjoying the interview. In most instances it is risky to try to stretch a regular interview over about forty-five minutes. If still not finished in forty-five minutes, and there is a chance to return, the interviewer can wind off the interview and come back in a few days, "for a few other details I wanted to ask about?"

Of course, if the respondent is enjoying the interview immensely and seems eager to go on or if it is a social situation being enjoyed by all, interviews can last longer. But the interviewer should remember that even though the respondent seems eager at the time, (a) he may resent the time spent later (and blame the interviewer for it), (b) he may be really more exhausted than he realizes, or (c) he may be just too polite to indicate that he can't spare any more time. We all know the feeling of saying to our long-staying guests, "It's not very late— do you have to go?" Only to have them reply, "Well, I guess we could stay a little longer," and settle back for another forty-five minutes.

(13) Whether an interviewer should take notes depends on the situation. There are some situations where taking notes might impair the relationship with the respondent. In a participant situation where the field worker is really more an observer than an interviewer it might be inappropriate for him to whip out pad and pencil and start jotting down notes. But it is often quite possible to structure an interview situation so that note taking does not seem amiss. If the situation is clearly understood as an interview or if the field worker's role is clearly perceived as researcher, then the respondent may actually *expect* the interviewer to take notes. And if the interview starts off with factual nonthreatening questions, most respondents will have little cause for objection. If the atmosphere of the interview develops in a friendly and informal way, the respondent will hardly notice that the interviewer is continuing to take notes even though the discussion has moved along to more delicate subjects. If the research worker is an observer at a meeting and it is understood by the leaders that he is a research worker, it is usually perfectly appropriate to take notes. Perhaps the most difficult situations for note taking are spontaneous face-to-face interaction, where the researcher wants to be a real participant. But even here, if the researcher waits until some relevant factual and noncontroversial information comes out (the name of a person he might want to talk with, a date or place he needs to make note of) then he might find he could pull out his pad and say "Say, I'd better make a note of that or I'll forget it."

Then he may be able to keep the pad handy and gradually ease his way into jotting down notes.

Actually, note-taking frequently interferes with the interviewer more than the informant. He needs all his wits about him to guide the interview, ask penetrating questions that will draw out significant data, and maintain a friendly and warm relationship with the respondent. Note-taking distracts attention from all three of these and frequently results in a much less fruitful interview. In most field research, note taking should probably be limited to those situations where it is most important to ● get accurate factual information about something. General feelings and perceptions can be put down after the interview—and since they represent an analysis of the interview data as well as just note-taking they will probably bring together data from different parts of the interview along with appropriate interpretation.

9. Recording the Data of Field Interviewing and Observation

While in the field, the research worker has to face the knotty problem of how to process the multitudinous field data that comes under his scrutiny during field observation or interviewing. Somehow while guiding the field inquiry so as to elicit good data, he must sift and sort the raw data to separate wheat from chaff; note the key facts before they slip his memory; record the suggestive data for further consideration; reflect upon the data and come up with fruitful hypotheses to guide further inquiry; and seek further evidence in the field on the emerging hypotheses.

Recording is a key screening point in processing field data. Data elicited in the field situation can perhaps best be recorded according to the way the data will be used.

The major uses of field recording are these: (1) Field Training, (2) Refreshing the researcher's memory, and (3) Orienting other research workers on the field situations.

(1) Recording is a good medium for informing an experienced supervisor of what took place in the field situation. The supervisor can then constructively evaluate the interviewing or participation, point out places where different tactics might have been fruitful, recommend one technique in favor of another, etc. This purpose is usually served best by detailed transcription of the interview. Where possible, key words or phrases can be jotted down during the interview and amplified *immediately after the interview* before the significant details have faded from memory. Editing penciled interview notes *in ink* helps to preserve the notes and to distinguish what was taken down at the time from what was added afterwards. When these amplified notes are typed up it is appropriate to add opening and parting statements as nearly as they can be recalled. Parenthetical descriptive phrases that give the tone or affect of the situation can also be inserted. Articles and other non-meaningful words omitted in the field notes can be inserted only in the final report. This type of recording is called "process recording." The

main objection to it is the enormous time investment it entails. Thorough process recording probably consumes two or three times as much time as was actually spent in the field. This means that time in the field must be considerably reduced to allow for full process recording. Naturally, any researcher would rather have a full record than a scanty or partial one. The realistic choice is not between a *full* record and a *partial* one. The real choice is between (1) two or three times as many interviews per 40 hour week with only the most pertinent data and interpretation recorded and (2) only a half or third as many interviews, recorded in full. The understanding of many research problems will benefit more from (1) than (2).

(2) A second purpose of field recording is refresher notes. Relevant factual information gathered from field situations can often be noted in brief form. (Of course, if the context is revealing, fuller recording is called for.) It is important to put down pertinent identification data to indicate the source of your information: the when and where, and who and what of the occasion. Then the simple factual information can be listed succinctly under a heading "Special facts noted." Data can often be summarized thus:

I gathered from Mr. Green that:
—The liquor dealers contribute to the campaign funds of both parties;
—The supervisor in the 13th district feels he has to have at least three cars on hand Election Day to haul voters to the polls.
—Some of the older Italian voters are the only ones that still expect to get paid for voting (couldn't tell how prevalent this is).

(3) A third purpose of recording is to orient one's fellow field workers, one's supervisor, or even one's self at some later time as to what the field situation was. These are the field reports that provide the data that suggest hunches and hypotheses and indicate new lines of fruitful inquiry. These are the data that give the informant's perception of field circumstances or events. From the perceptions of many informants the researcher tries to piece together the significant variables in the field situation.

Recording of this sort is generally most useful if it includes not only the opinions and perceptions of the informant but also the impressions of the field worker, his analysis of the informant's interpretation, and any hunches or hypotheses the data suggest. It is wise even to include impressions that rest on details too fleetingly remembered or too fuzzy to report. The field worker's impressions may reveal a diagnosis of the situation. Detailed reporting of the facts should enable the reader to diagnose for himself. But since the facts selected for reporting depend on the observer's understanding of what is going on, his impression is often more trustworthy than that of a reader with only partial data before him. If the field worker follows the feeling-tone of the situation, if he listens hard for what is *not* said, if he picks up the gestures and how things are said or done—then he may absorb from the data an impression that can be distilled into a revealing word-picture. This task combines the best skills of psychiatric insight, scientific selectivity, and poetic succinctness. *Field workers seriously under-value this process.* Recording impressions also encourages the field worker to reflect or speculate on what occurred and may lead to new insights or a new formulation of the situation.

A field worker should reflect on the field situation not only *before, during,* and *after* the interview or observation; he should reflect on the data *at the time he records it.* Reflection should sensitize the worker as to the details worth recording. Going into the field situation, the worker should be sensitized to details that are important. In field work, a *few relevant details are worth carloads of run-of-the-mill data.* Free-directive field inquiry in some ways resembles detective work. Several clues that don't fit in will frequently (1) pique the researcher's curiosity and stimulate further reflection upon the meaning of the data, perhaps suggesting an hypothesis that ties together the field data; *or* (2) stimulate further probing for data that will eventually yield a new interpretation. Sensitively recorded field reports are frequently the most valuable product of field interviewing and observation.

From the above discussion, it is probably clear that the range of sound knowledge on the techniques of free-directive interviewing and observation is quite limited. Yet many disciplines other than sociology depend heavily on these methods for gathering information: the social case worker, the doctor, the lawyer, the administrator, the criminal investigator, the journalist, just to mention a few. Serious methodological research over the coming years can help to put these methods of inquiry on a sounder basis. But until it does, the findings of such social "science" will continue to rest on methods that are still an art.

10. Summary

The essence of participant observation and interviewing is the free-directive nature of the inquiry: the research worker constantly aims to direct the data-gathering to more fruitful lines of investigation. He does this largely by establishing a sound relationship with his field contacts and encouraging them to lead him by their greater involvement and familiarity with the field situation to the most significant data. He is especially interested in the perspective of his informants and often uses this perspective to reconstruct his own version of past events, organizational structures, informal leadership processes and other field situations that free-directive inquiry is especially adapted to. To do this he aims to cut through generalities and lead the informants to reveal the data that led them to the particular perspectives they hold. Guiding the interviewing (or discussion, if it is a group setting) to the significant data is the key to the skills of free-directives inquiry. But unfortunately little is known about these skills and they undoubtedly vary from field situation to situation depending on the kind of people the informants are and the nature of the problem the researcher is investigating. One thing is crucial: the researcher should be a thoughtful and analytic listener who appraises the meaning of emerging data for his problem at hand and uses this understanding to phrase questions that will develop the implication of those data. This is a real art.

SELECTED REFERENCES

Goode, W. J., and P. K. Hatt, *Methods in Social Research* (New York; McGraw-Hill Book Co., 1952), Chaps. 10 and 13.

Jahoda, Marie, M. Deutsch, and S. W. Cook, *Research Methods in Social Relations* (New York: The Dryden Press, 1951), Chaps. 5 and 6.

Kluckhohn, Florence, "The Participant Observer Technique in Small Communities," *American Journal of Sociology,* Vol. 46 (1940), pp. 331-343.

Leighton, A. H., *The Governing of Men* (Princeton, New Jersey: Princeton University Press, 1946), appendix, pp. 373-394.

Merton, R. K., and P. L. Kendall, "The Focused Interview," *American Journal of Sociology,* Vol. 51, pp. 541-557.

Whyte, W. F., "Observational Field-Work Methods," in M. Jahoda, *et al., Research Methods in Social Relations* (New York: The Dryden Press, 1951).

Chapter 10

THE PRINCIPLES OF RESEARCH DESIGN*

THE design of an actual study is basically a problem in the *practical application* of the fundamental rules of scientific method to some specific research objective. However, the design of research involves far more, in actual practice, than an adherence to the general rules of scientific method. While it is essential to understand fundamental principles, the actual conduct of a research study raises specific problems which require specific answers. This chapter presents some of these problems, together with examples of how they were met in an actual research operation.

Before presenting concrete materials, it might help to illustrate the problem by an analogy to a game or sport. The rules of a game, for example baseball or chess, are well-known and clearly stated. It is accepted that one will obey these rules. But it is not the obedience of the rules alone but how the game is played, *within the rules,* that determines whether one is a skilled professional or an unskilled amateur. To play a *good* game one must have not only basic knowledge of the rules of the game, but also skill based on practice and aptitude, resourcefulness in capitalizing on opportunities, and ingenuity in inventing better ways of performing.

1. The Definition of Research Design

The problem of research design is one of translating a general scientific model into a practical research operation. As used in this chapter, *research design will refer to the entire process of conducting a research study.* This is a crucial point: problems of design are not limited to any specific type of method or to any single stage of a study. To be sure, different methods lend themselves more readily to different kinds of problems. It will not be possible in a chapter of this general nature, however, to cover systematically each of the major methods. Rather an attempt will be made to deal with these different methods and techniques by drawing on examples from a broad research project on intergroup relations using many different methods and techniques.[1]

---

* Written by Edward A. Suchman.

[1] It might be worthwhile to look for a moment at this animal—the Research Project. There is little mention of research projects in textbooks of methodology. Forced into necessary categorization of methods, most textbooks treat techniques as if they existed by themselves and apply them to single studies also conceived of as separate entities. However, a great deal of research in the social sciences today is conducted in terms of broad projects encompassing many hypotheses and using many varied methods. A research project, characterized by long time execution and a relatively high financial budget, does create some of the most serious

253

Problems of design will be shown to arise at each of the following stages in the execution of a research project: (1) the design of hypotheses; (2) the design of sample; (3) the design of instruments; (4) the design of administration, and (5) the design of analysis.

The plan of this chapter is to take each of these steps in a research project and to examine them in terms of the problems of design that they create. Part I will deal with design problems in the *planning* of research, while Part II will deal with problems in the *operation* of research. These problems will be illustrated, for the most part, by examples drawn from the Cornell Study of Intergroup Relations. An attempt will be made in presenting these examples to give a realistic, clear picture of the many daily decisions and revisions made in the course of an actual research operation.

2. Some General Considerations:

Before looking at specific design problems, let us state briefly some general considerations. First, it seems to us futile to argue whether or not a certain design is "scientific." The design is *the plan of study* and, as such, is present in all studies, uncontrolled as well as controlled and subjective as well as objective. It is not a case of scientific or not scientific, but rather one of good or less good design. The degree of accuracy desired, the level of "proof" aimed at, the state of existing knowledge, etc., all combine to determine the amount of concern one can have with the degree of "science" in one's design.

Second, the proof of hypotheses is never definitive. The best one can hope to do is to make more or less plausible a series of alternative hypotheses. In most cases multiple explanations will be operative. Demonstrating one's own hypotheses does not rule out alternative hypotheses and vice versa.

Third, there is no such thing as a single, "correct" design. Different workers will come up with different designs favoring their own methodological and theoretical predispositions. Hypotheses can be studied by different methods using different designs.

Fourth, all research design represents a compromise dictated by the many practical considerations that go into social research. None of us operate except on limited time, money and personnel budgets. Further limitations concern the availability of data and the extent to which one can impose upon one's subjects. A research design must be *practical*.

Fifth, a research dsign is not a highly specific plan to be followed without deviation, but rather a series of guide posts to keep one headed in the right direction. One must be prepared to discard (although not

---

problems in research design today. It requires the combination and integration of many hypotheses and many separate study designs into a meaningful overall project structure. Too many projects end up as a series of only loosely related studies. They are undertaken as projects in the first place because of the complex interwoven nature of the phenomenon studied. If successful, they should end up as a synthesis of the separate analyses carried out in the different units of the project.

too quickly) hypotheses that do not work out and to develop new hypotheses on the basis of increased knowledge. Furthermore, any research design developed in the office will inevitably have to be changed in the face of field considerations.[1a]

PART A. DESIGN PROBLEMS IN THE PLANNING OF RESEARCH

Design problems begin with the formulation of one's hypotheses. To a large extent hypotheses are tentative statements of expected relationships between variables. Their demonstration will consist of a more exact statement of the kind and size of relationship based upon more systematic observation. It is this intimate connection betwen hypotheses and data that makes the initial "design of ideas" such an important one in the research process.[2]

This problem may be divided into two stages. First, there is the problem of the overall design of the study. Second, there is the translation of specific hypotheses into observable phenomena. In the first stage we are concerned with whether the method used will produce the kind of data needed to test the hypotheses. This stage involves such decisions as whether a statistical sampling survey or qualitative unstructured observation or controlled experimentation is needed. At this point one must decide on the nature of "proof" desired, taking into consideration the level of one's hypotheses, the size of one's budget, the amount of personnel and their skills, etc. For example, the study of intergroup relations was faced with two conflicting types of hypotheses concerning prejudice. One set of hypotheses viewed prejudice as the result of an individual's "psychological needs," while the other set saw prejudice as the result of "acceptance of customary beliefs and practices." To investigate the psychological explantion it would appear obvious that one's research design should involve depth level, possibly projective techniques aimed at individual cases. The alternative set of hypotheses could probably be demonstrated more adequately by a design aimed at the study of processes of group membership and communication. To a

---

[1a] For example, a study of high school students involved a careful design which required identification of the students so that: (1) sociometric diagrams could be made between different ethnic groups; (2) the answers of the students could be compared to those of their parents; and (3) follow-up interviews could be made. However, in the course of field administration, a controversy between the local newspaper and the high-school superintendent in . which the newspaper attempted to use the survey against the superintendent, forced the deletion of all identification from the questionnaires.

[2] All too often a research study will be divided into two tenuously connected parts. The first will deal with the hypotheses while the second will deal with the data. The connection between the two is often hard to discern. This is also true for many research plans wherein the statement of the problem lists the hypotheses to be studied, while a separate section on method of study lists the techniques to be used. It is rare that the research proposal indicates how the proposed methodology will afford answers to the stated hypotheses. A most serious problem in hypothesis design, therefore, springs from the need for close integration between the statement of hypothesis and the method of study.

large extent the controversy itself is a false one, stemming from the different methodological designs used by two opposing groups of researchers. On the one hand, there are the "depth" psychologists who, using a "clinical" design on a sample of "bigots," find prejudice resulting from personality defect, while on the other hand there are the "institutional" sociologists who, using field observation of discriminatory situations, find prejudice rooted in the thoughtless acceptance of current operating practices.[3] Both approaches are valid, but require integration.

In many cases the overall design of the study will spring directly from the nature of the hypotheses. For example, in studying the effect of participation in a common enterprise upon the reduction of prejudice, the overall design will determine whether one demonstrates the effectiveness of a total program or the effectiveness of a single variable. In planning a study of mixed Negro and white Boy Scout troops, it becomes important to decide whether one wishes to test the general effectiveness of an optimum combination of circumstances conducive toward successful intergroup relations, or whether one is interested in some such single aspect as whether the first Negro to be introduced should be a person of outstanding abilities or of average abilities. Similarly, in the overall design one must decide whether the experiment is to be conducted in a natural or artificial situation. The inferences for action to be drawn

---

[3] Another example illustrating the problem of overall design is provided by A. H. Leighton's current study of social stress and mental disorder. Initially, the project was conceived as a study of the relative prevalence of mental disorder occurring within groups which differed according to the amount of social stress as observed by a team of anthropological and sociological observers. The analysis design was one of rank correlation between mental disorder and social stress for different groups. It became obvious, however, in viewing the hypotheses for which data were desired, that such correlations could not serve to bring data to bear on many of these hypotheses. (Many studies which make use of ecological research designs contain a basic weakness in inferring individual correlations on the basis of ecological correlations.) The design was subsequently changed to permit the determination of individual correlations. The design now consists of the following four parts.

Social Stress	Mental Disorder
A. Anthropological observation of stress areas	C. Psychiatric clinical observation of mental disorder
B. Sociological survey of individual stress	D. Psychological screening test of mental disorder

This design permits the comparison of data obtained by four different methods. A comparison of A and B will show to what extent a climate of social stress is experienced as individual stress. A comparison of C and D will indicate to what extent standardized instruments of screening can diagnose cases of mental disorder in the same way as a trained psychiatric team. A comparison between A and C will offer the correlations desired initially. A comparison between B and D will afford the individual correlations necessary for studying individual mental disorder and individual social stress. Perhaps even more important in this design are the partial correlations which become available. For example, one can study the relationship between B and D for different social climates determined through A.

from the experiment will be highly conditioned by the degree of "natural-ness" retained in the experiment. If a scoutmaster tends to be prejudiced, does one proceed with this handicap or does one attempt to introduce a cooperative scoutmaster?[4]

The way in which the kind of question asked will indicate the kind of data needed, and therefore, the best method to be used is illustrated by the study of a court case on discrimination in Elmira. First, an at-tempt to answer the question, "Did the court case affect the attitudes of the Negro community?" dictated the use of a cross-sectional survey which both directly asked about the effect of the court case and indi-rectly measured the respondent's attitudes to be compared with his atti-tudes before the court case. Second, the question, "What motivation leads a Negro to institute a court case?" resulted in a detailed case study of the Negro individuals concerned with bringing the case to trial. Third, an answer to the question, "Do Negroes behave differently as a result of the court case?" was sought through participant observer reports on the change in behavior of the Negro community. Fourth, a documentary content analysis approach was used in relation to the question, "What kind of treatment did the media of communication give the court case?" Finally, a fifth approach, not used in the present study, would have been to set up experimental and control groups, the experimental group taking part in some form of group discussion concerning the court case, in order to study the effectiveness of such discussion. Depending upon

---

[4] In deciding upon the basic overall design of a study, one should keep in mind the essential logic of each of the main methods of social research. Each method represents some modification or approximation of the controlled experimental de-sign. In the experimental design we have four cells representing before and after observations for an experimental and a controlled group. A good experiment will concentrate upon designing matched experimental and control groups, the isolation of a stimulus to be applied to the experimental group only, and the definition of some criterion of effect to be observed in both groups after the stimulus has been applied. The survey design attempts to reproduce this pattern by statistical con-trols which match pseudo-experimental and control groups and by correlation analysis which attempts to isolate stimulus and effect. A good survey design there-fore will include information on necessary matching characteristics and a carefully thought out classification of "stimulus" and "effect" variables together with their most important preceding, intervening, and conditional variables. The panel de-sign comes closer to the experimental design in that before and after observations are made of what may be thought of as the experimental group. From such a design it is possible to increase the plausibility of one's inference of which vari-able in a correlation analysis should be viewed as "cause" and which as "effect." A trend study design uses a comparison between an "experimental" group before and a "control" group after. The problem in this design comes from the fact that there is no way of observing internal changes or of only a limited check on the matching of the experimental and control groups. Finally, there is the one cell design involving only the experimental group, after exposure to the stimulus. This design is most common in the case study method or in uncontrolled observation. Here we observe the behavior of an individual or group and infer what this in-dividual or group was like before the stimulus and how he differs from control groups not subjected to the stimulus. (See S. A. Stouffer, "Some Observations on Study Design," *AJS*, Jan., 1950, p. 355).

which method is used, a different kind of data is collected and a different sort of question answered.[5]

(a) The Definition of Concepts

In the previous discussion, the problem of research design has been limited to the determination of the overall framework. A more frequently discussed design problem concerns the translation of hypotheses into operational terms. For the most part, such discussions have been of a general nature, either attacking or defending the process of "operationalism." Little has been said about the actual problems of designing operational hypotheses.

Our position will be that hypotheses to be studied empirically must be stated in operational terms. This means on the one hand a definition of concepts in terms of observable phenomena and on the other hand, an analysis of the "causal" or "interpretive" sequences relating these phenomena. Problems of design involving concept formation are basically problems in *scale analysis, index construction* or *typological classification*. One must decide to begin with whether the concept is to be viewed as uni-dimensional or multi-dimensional. If uni-dimensional, the design should incorporate some empirical test of common meaning such as scale analysis. If the concept is multi-dimensional, it becomes important to determine the different dimensions involved and to provide for the study of their inter-relationship. A great deal of so-called "secondary analysis" results from an inadequate preliminary definition of one's concepts. Such secondary analysis is characterized by "post facto" rather than *a priori* operational definition.

The definition of prejudice provides an illustration of concept formation in the study of intergroup relations. It is essential in the study of prejudice to determine what dimension or dimensions one is concerned with. In the present study we were concerned with three concepts of prejudice— cognitive expression, affective feeling, and discriminatory behavior. We

---

[5] An important design problem which needs more methodological attention concerns the integration of different methods into a meaningful whole. One useful approach might be as follows: Observation supplies the overall impressionistic, organized total picture necessary for the development of hypotheses and the interpretation of structured data. Surveys supply objective data concerning the range of variation (marginal distribution), comparisons between groups (individual differences), and the study of relationships (interpretative and conditional). The case study offers a connected sequence of variables to illustrate and explain how and why relationships exist and finally, the experiment provides a control test of the effectiveness of specific variables.

The study could be designed to permit an interweaving between the various methods. For example, unstructured pilot inquiry would yield hunches and hypotheses. These hypotheses could be welded into a questionnaire instrument to be administered to a cross-section sample. Out of the cross-sectional, statistical analysis will come correlation tables which will enable the selection of crucial follow-up case studies. These case studies would be studied by detailed interview and personal observation. These follow-up cases would also be "followed-out" into the community at large in a study of significant institutional environments. Finally, to come full circle, these institutional environments would be related to the initial pilot inquiry.

hypothesized three types of prejudice to fit these concepts; (a) stereotyping, (b) tension and (c) social distance, each of which we postulated as being uni-dimensional. Questions were formulated to provide for a scale analysis of each of these dimensions. Subsequent analysis showed that the only clear-cut single dimension was social distance, with a coefficient of reproducibility of .94. The stereotype scale was greatly affected by educational level, while the tension items broke down into two dimensions of "liking" and "competition." [6]

Concept formation for research purposes might usefully proceed by two steps. First, one would perform a logical analysis aimed at (a) discovering the various dimensions involved within the concept, (b) correlating these different dimensions so that all possible types can be discerned and (c) reducing the number of types to be studied. After this logical exercise one may proceed to the second step of translating those types selected for study into operational categories and empirical indices. An example of this process is seen in the attempt to define the concept of the "exemption mechanism" in intergroup relations. One of the major hypotheses concerned the ability of individuals to keep their prejudices intact even after favorable contact with a member of the minority group, by exempting this individual from the total group. In an attempt to define and study this concept, a logical analysis indicated that exemption involved a relationship between the number of in-group and out-group members. Four types were derived in this way: (1) where all or most of the in-group accept all or most of the out-group, (2) where certain members of the in-group accept most members of the out-group, (3) where certain members of the in-group accept certain members of the out-group, (4) where most members of the in-group accept most members of the out-group. Type 3 seemed to come closest to the hypothesis of exemption. This limits the concept to those instances where only some out-group members are exempted by some in-group members. In Type 1 where all in-group accept all out-group persons, the notion of individual exemption does not seem to apply; these are the situations commonly described as non-discriminatory, such as riding in buses, etc. Type 2 where some in-

---

[6] The problem of concept formation is basic to the process of research design. The main difficulties are first, to find adequate categories to cover the general concepts and second, to translate these categories into meaningful, observable indices. Perhaps one of the most important causes of difficulty comes from the attempt to include in the definition of the concept, correlated variables which are not themselves a part of the definition. For example, if one is asked to define a cow, one ordinarily would not attempt to squeeze into this definition the economics of the dairy industry. Similarly, many individuals might question the completeness of William Whyte's definition of group structure as the reciprocal relations between members occupying hierarchial positions in the group. Certainly this type of definition is a perfect one for research purposes. It contains within it a picture of the actual observations to be made. However, one feels that there is more to group structure than this definition implies—as there certainly is, but it is extremely important to recognize that these other things become correlates to be studied in relation to the definition rather than something to attempt to incorporate into the definition itself.

group members accept most out-group persons seems to be a form of *situational exemption* in which certain areas are defined as non-discriminatory. Type 4 where most in-group accept some out-group members is a form of exemption but seems to be limited to a kind of "honorific" acceptance rather than real exemption.

From this logical analysis it was decided to concentrate the operational definition around the partial acceptance of only certain members of an out-group by certain members of an in-group. This operational definition was translated into categories of "feeling different" toward specific contacts, arrived at from the specific index question "Would you say he (she) is typical of the (ethnic group) or different in some respects?" asked concerning individual contacts with ethnic group members by majority group members.

The usefulness of a logical analysis preceding the operational definition lies in the awareness it creates of the underlying dimensions. If the concept is found to be uni-dimensional by such an analysis, one knows that the problem of research design must center around some form of scale analysis which would permit one to differentiate the *degree* to which this concept is present in individuals or groups. If the concept is found to be multi-dimensional, the procedure of typological classification permits one to decide what relationships one must observe and correlate before the individuals or groups can be classified. Such a correlation between dimensions also serves to check on the completeness of one's concept— all cells in the table must be accounted for. Furthermore one can proceed on the basis of a complete table to reduce the total number of possible types in which one is interested.

(b) The Translation of Relationships

Most hypotheses involve the statement of relationships between concepts. The design problem becomes one of determining how one can study such statements as "the more A, the less B" or "if A, then B," followed by other statements introducing a third concept C such as "if A, then B, under condition C," or "if A, then B, due to C" or "if A, then B by way of C." The problem of design seems to be one of first stating the basic relationship between two main variables and then, second, elaborating this statement in terms of a third variable C. It is variable C which becomes the crucial, analytical problem. This variable can be either interpretive (causal or total) or conditional (modifying or partial). It is extremely important in the design of one's research to trace carefully through the kind of relationship involved in one's hypothesis.

An example of this kind of design of hypotheses can be shown from the study of the relationship between intergroup contact and prejudice. The major hypotheses concern the relationship between personal contact of minority and majority group members and prejudice toward each other. First, the two concepts of contact and prejudice were defined in observable terms. The design of hypotheses then proceeded by taking this basic relationship and logically determining the interpretive variables and the conditional variables to be studied. First there were the intervening variables—those variables which would help explain *how* it was that contact led to less prejudice. A listing of such variables included understanding (empathy and sympathy), familiarity or feeling at ease, cooperation based on common goals, etc. Similarly, a negative list of intervening variables was determined to explain how non-contact might lead to prejudice. Such variables were suspicion, ethnocentrism, isolation, etc. To complete the picture, intervening variables were hypothesized for deviate cases in which contact would result in prejudice or no-contact in tolerance. Such variables were competition, exploitation, insecurity, etc.

The design of the above hypotheses is that of A (the contact) leading to C (intervening variable) which in turn leads to B (prejudice). Observations would be required of all three variables, the cross-tabulation of which would show the disappearance of the correlation between A and B when C was held constant.

The second type of interpretive variable included in the design would be where C preceded A. Such variables in a case of contact leading to tolerance would be initial level of prejudice, previous experiences, personality, self-selection of contacts, etc. Finally, in deviate cases where contact might lead to prejudice such preceding variables as competition, forced association, etc., were to be studied.

The above type of design would again find the correlation between A and B disappearing when C is held constant, but in this case C is interpreted as preceding A rather than intervening between A and B.

Finally, there are the conditional or modifying variables which have to be included in the design of hypotheses. These are the variables which do not destroy the correlation between A and B but rather alter it depending upon the nature of C. Such variables would be the type of contact (relative status, closeness, situational pattern, etc.), type of prejudice (cognitive, discriminatory, tension), expectations, existing definitions, personality, and status and role or background characteristics. These conditional variables rather than explain or interpret the relationship between contact and prejudice, show the conditions under which this relationship becomes stronger or weaker.

A summary statement of what has happened to the initial contact-prejudice hypothesis might take the following form: "Certain preceding variables will tend to promote or limit contacts, which contacts in turn tend to produce certain intervening variables, which variables in turn tend to promote prejudice or tolerance. These relationships become modified (strengthened or weakened) by certain conditions of contact, types of prejudice and kinds of individuals involved." A hypothetical statement involving the basic conceptual variables of contact and prejudice, but combining many variables of different kinds might read as follows: "Especially among women (modifying variable), social isolation (preceding variable), affords the opportunity for very limited contact with ethnic groups (conceptual variable), usually of an impersonal, inferior-superior relative status nature (modifying variable) which tends to produce a stereotypic labeling of ethnic groups (intervening variable), especially if the individual has an authoritarian personality (modifying variable) which finds expression in prejudice toward the ethnic group (conceptual variable) especially of the social distance, discriminatory type (modifying variable)." To be sure one cannot hope to include all of the above variables in a single demonstrative table, but some such statement must be built up based upon the integration of disparate hypotheses.[7]

PART B. DESIGN PROBLEMS IN THE OPERATION OF RESEARCH

The problems of design discussed in the previous section occur during the planning stage of a research study. It is customary to conceive of research design as limited to this stage of work. However, design problems continue to arise at each stage of the actual execution of a research project. The remainder of this chapter, therefore, will attempt to single out the more general type of design problems that are common to most studies. These will be treated in separate sections on (1) the sample design, (2) the instrument design, (3) the administrative design, and (4) the analysis design. A general characterization of the problems involved in each of these stages will be given together with brief illustrations.

(a) The Sample Design

Of all design problems, probably sampling design has been the one that has received the greatest amount of attention. This is also an area in which the concept of "efficiency" of design based upon practical considerations is used as a basis of evaluation rather than an "all-or-none," good or bad criterion. As discussed previously, "efficiency" is a much more apt basis for evaluation than "scientific."

---

[7] One of the main problems in the above type of hypothesis design concerns the need to place the variables A, B and C in some sort of time sequence. Whether A leads to B or B to A, and whether C is to be considered preceding or intervening, all depend largely upon one's ability to arrange these in order of occurrence. This is of course the basis purpose of the controlled experimental design wherein one administers the stimulus in a known time sequence. The best research design for doing this outside of the experimental set up involves the "panel" design. If one can determine whether or not A, B, and C are present and how they are related at one period of time, and then study the same variables for the same group at a later period of time, then it is possible by means of a 16-fold table design to overcome many of the disturbing weaknesses of the usual "static" analysis. For example, the panel study design used in the Elmira intergroup study permits one to determine for each individual his contact and prejudice at two periods of time. By composing separate questions and analyses for each of the 16 possible types of contact and prejudice at two periods of time, it is possible to discern the manner in which the interpretive and conditional variables are to be analyzed. For example, an individual who had no contact and no prejudice when first interviewed, but who on the second interview has gained contact and continues to be unprejudiced, could be questioned in detail on whether or not the lack of prejudice was an important causal factor in the acquisition of the new contact. It is only by means of some such dynamic design that the interpretation of intervening variables can be removed from the plausible and argumentative realm.

Design problems in sampling may be divided into those which affect (1) the definition of the population, (2) the size of the sample, and (3) the representativeness of the sample. In regard to the definition of the population, one faces the important problem of deciding what group it is about which one wishes to generalize one's findings. For example, what does a cross-section of the population of Elmira stand for? A series of cross-community studies would help to determine more exactly the degree to which generalizations can be viewed as applying to "human behavior" rather than Elmiran behavior.

The definition of sampling variables forces a consideration of one's initial hypotheses. All too often a cross-section is selected when it would be much more efficient to select some subgroup of the population. For example, in the study of contacts between minority and majority groups, it was found unnecessarily costly to include "old ladies on the shelf" who shed very little light on the problem of intergroup contact.[8]

In regard to the size of the sample there is the inevitable problem caused by the disappearance of one's cases in a breakdown analysis. It is difficult to see how this problem can be answered except through increasing the size of one's sample. One interesting type of sampling design that often has been overlooked in this respect is "double sampling." In double sampling one proceeds to study the variable which is expensive to observe by substituting a related but cheaply observable variable. For example, one can increase the size of one's sample by asking one family member about the behavior of other family members and friends. A check on the accuracy of these reports by a sub-sample of family members and friends affords some basis for adjustment of biased reporting. A new development which holds great promise is sequential analysis wherein current analyses of incoming material permits one to estimate sampling error without the full completion of the entire sample.

The third and perhaps most intricate sampling design problem arises in connection with the method used to secure a representative sample. The current controversy of area vs. quota sampling has limited its arguments too often to national public opinion sampling. It is quite often most efficient to use a combination of area and quota samples, especially when, as is most often the case, one is not so much concerned with distribution estimates as with the description of relationships. This problem of marginal *vs.* breakdown analysis has been neglected in most discussions of sampling error. A particularly common problem occurs in relation to the representativeness of subgroups used in breakdown analysis. For example, how representative is a group of 30 young, uneducated women

---

[8] Sampling problems which do not deal with a population of individuals also call for difficult decisions. For example, the study of contact situations required the setting up of some form of inventory of the kinds and number of situations that existed in Elmira. We attempted to establish such a population base by having Negro group members keep diaries indicating all situations occurring during the day in which white people were present. Time sampling in the observation of individual or group conduct is also a problem which needs careful formulation.

being compared with a group of 50 old, educated men? A related type of sample design problem which is often overlooked has to do with type I or type II errors. For example, how many conclusions are made that a relationship is not significant when what one means to say is that the population difference is not large enough for a sample of this small size to determine, although of course a larger sample might very well show a significant relationship.

In summary, it would seem that many sampling design problems must be viewed more from the point of view of the hypotheses being studied and the level of demonstration desired, than from the current emphasis upon theoretical sample error although, of course, this is still important. To a large extent it is "like using a scalpel in a butcher shop."

(b) The Instrument Design

Regardless of the method used in the study, some form of reporting device is necessary. This may be highly structured, as in the case of a check-list questionnaire, less structured as in the case of the funnel-type design of the open-ended interview, or simply a topical outline as in the case of a participant observer's report. Such reporting instruments are basically tools and, like the design of any tool, must be evaluated in terms of how well it does the job for which it has been constructed. Too many discussions on principles of question wording fail to realize that the validity of a question cannot be determined in the abstract.

The basic problem of instrument design therefore is to tailor it to the job—which requires once again a clear statement of initial hypotheses. The purpose of an instrument is to secure the data required by the hypotheses. These data may be evaluated in terms of reliability and validity. The concepts, reliability and validity, are greatly in need of more careful definition for social research. The design of a reliable instrument has traditionally centered around the construction of an instrument which produces the same measurement upon repeated use. Since repetition is an almost impossible criterion in social research (for even if one could repeat studies, one would never know whether the instruments were unreliable or whether the individuals had changed), it would seem that the problem could be stated better as one of internal consistency of concept definition. To check the reliability of a question or observation one would have to repeat the question or observation from another point of view which does not destroy the conceptual meaning of the datum. It is seen, therefore, that the reliability of an instrument relates directly to the problem of concept definition discussed previously and concerns the interrelationship of different indices of this same concept. For example, the reliability of a question designed to measure prejudice can best be determined by asking other questions also hypothesized as measuring prejudice and then studying the pattern of interrelationship between these questions.

Similarly, the problem of *valid* instrument design requires a unique solution in social research. *No estimate of validity can be given until a statement of purpose exists.* Any piece of data may be valid for one purpose and invalid for another, at one and the same time. To provide for a check on the validity of one's instrument in the design of the study, one must know the purpose for which the data are being collected. If, for example, one is attempting to *define* a concept such as prejudice, then the check on the validity of the observations made is the same as a check on the reliability of the items used in the definition. The use of the traditional criterion of comparing what a person says with what he does makes sense only when one's hypothesis involves the prediction of overt behavior from verbal responses. In many cases, even a low correlation between verbal and overt observations may be a "valid" measure of the existing inconsistency between attitude and behavior. For example, we found many white storekeepers who said they would refuse to sell to Negroes. However, when we sent Negroes to these same stores, in general, they were waited upon. If our initial question was intended to predict actual behavior, it was indeed invalid. If, however, the initial question was asked to compare behavior in hypothetical situations with behavior in actual situations (its real purpose), then the question was certainly valid.

Apart from the above general statements, a great many problems exist in the design of recording schedules. The type of item or question to be used, the check list, multiple choice or free answer, the wording of the question, direct or indirect, the ordering of the items or questions, etc., all of these contain peculiar problems of design which cannot be treated in this brief chapter. Every study will create specific problems of question design. Many of these are answered on the basis of criteria of understandability, *i. e.*, simple, clear-cut wording. Other problems are more difficult, such as the translation of questions into different wording for different subgroups. For example, in studying intergroup relations among majority group adults, Jewish and Negro adults, majority group youth, Jewish and Negro youth, it became extremely difficult to keep the same wording for all groups. There can be no doubt that direct comparisons of marginal distributions are impossible without identically worded questions. The decision was to leave questions identical where the hypothesis called for a direct comparison of marginal distributions and to change wording where we were more interested in the relation between different concepts. In summary, an instrument is basically a tool which must be evaluated in terms of its success in securing the information needed to demonstrate some hypothesis.

(c) The Administrative Design

The administrative design of a research study concerns the execution of one's original study design. The principle goal is to stay as close as possible to the previously prepared model. Field or administrative conditions will invariably create the need to change the original design. The problem is how to compromise and improvise without destroying the ideal model.

Perhaps the first problem in field administration occurs in fulfilling the sampling requirements. The design of the administration will do much to determine how large a mortality one will have. The use of call backs, telephone interviews, mail questionnaires, abbreviated question-naire forms containing only the key questions, special inducements or rewards, etc., will often determine whether or not an interview is com-pleted. Participant observation is particularly susceptible to sampling problems. For example, the observer in the Negro community in Elmira thought that he knew almost all the Negro families. However, a check on those he knew against a cross-section obtained in a survey showed the almost inevitable under-representation of uneducated respondents.

In regard to the administration of the schedule or instrument, the major design problems center around the interpersonal situation be-tween investigator and subject. How is the field worker to define his role? How are the subject's behavior and responses affected by the presence of the investigator? This problem of definition of role is most apparent for a participant observer. (It has been claimed by more than one anthropologist that there can be no such thing as a nonparticipant observer.) In the case of one Negro observer, we found that after three years his role had almost completely shifted from that of a participant observer to one of an observer participant—a new role which proved very useful to us in subsequent action experiments.

An important principle to keep in mind in administrative design is the close, continued relationship between the field worker and the study designer. The need to change design in the face of developing data is inevitable, and not always undesirable. Too many research designs are carried to completion once in the field despite an apparent need for redesign. One should benefit by the additional evidence accumulated in the course of field administration. Field conditions do not always act in a negative way. For example, in the study of intergroup relations among high school youth, a field administration problem arose regarding the singling out of Jewish, Negro, Catholic and Protestant children. This addition, not contemplated in the original design, proved extremely valu-able in subsequent analyses.

An interesting possibility in administrative design would involve the completion of a study in two or more stages. For example, if one wishes a total sample of 500 cases, one could select two random samples of 250 cases each. Upon completion of the first sample of 250, a preliminary tabulation and analysis could be made. This analysis would result in a new schedule to be administered to the second sample of 250 containing the following kinds of changes: (a) Questions to be re-peated without change in order to secure more cases; (b) Questions to be repeated with change in wording because the analysis has cast some doubt upon the meaning of the first wording or because the distribution of responses is such as to prevent a breakdown analysis; (c) New questions to be asked in order to provide additional data; (d) New, follow-up questions to be asked of specific subgroups or individuals showing specific relationships between variables in an attempt to get at more detailed information. If necessary, the above procedure could then be repeated in three or four stages. This technique would help to eliminate the current overload of "pilot" inquiries, whose main asset lies in pointing out the problems that should have been studied.

(d) The Analysis Design

Ideally, the design of analysis should be worked out in advance of the collection of data. If the design of hypotheses is any good, then the design of the analysis will follow from it almost automatically. In fact an hypothesis may be called operational only if the analysis to be made is explicit in the statement of the hypothesis.

For example, the analysis design for the study of the relationship between intergroup contact and prejudice would follow through the basic hypothesis design presented previously. First would come the test of one's operational definitions of the concepts involved. We hypothesized three separate dimensions of prejudice—social distance, stereotype, and tension. The analysis design therefore requires some form of scale analysis to test the dimensionality of each of these definitions of prejudice. The same would apply to the construction of an index of intergroup contact. What definition of contact would be most productive—availability of contact, actual contacts, or actual close friendships—or should the contact index consist of some ratio between available contacts and actual contacts?[9]

In a similar way the basic interrelationships to be studied should have been specified in the design of hypotheses. For example, following the analysis of the relationship between the dependent variable (prejudice) and the independent variable (contact), one would proceed to study the interpretive variables, both preceding and intervening (understanding, familiarity, ethnocentrism, etc.), and the conditional variables (status

---

[9] An example of a scale analysis which helped to clarify the meaning of an index is seen from the study of intergroup situations by means of hypothetical examples. In an attempt to find out how individuals react within specific situations, we formulated a series of questions which asked about their behavior in actual situations they had experienced, or if they had not experienced these situations, about their hypothetical behavior. Subsequent sale analysis showed quite decisively that the individuals were answering these hypothetical questions from an "attitudinal" rather than a "situational" point of view. Briefly, all of the hypothetical situations scaled together and were closely related to general scales of prejudice, whereas feelings expressed about actual situations did not scale together. This raises a very interesting design problem involving such techniques as socio-dramas, projective tests, etc. It would seem that wherever the subject is asked to construct an artificial situation, he will do so in general, stereotyped terms rather than with any real awareness of the specific situational components.

and role attributes, personality, type of contact and prejudice). This much of the analysis design at least should be provided for in advance.[10]

However, it would be a great mistake to think of the analysis design as cut and dried, following the original design of hypotheses without deviation. The hypotheses serve as a point of departure, but ingenuity

---

[10] The basic objective of a "breakdown" analysis is to study the effect of a series of "test" variables upon the main "cause" and "effect" relationship between the dependent and independent variables. One begins with some relationship between two variables a and b, to be "explained" or "modified" by a third variable c. What happens to the difference between a+ and a— in the amount of b+ present, when observed separately for c+ and c—? Or to use the example of contact and prejudice, what happens to the difference between those people who have intergroup contacts and those who don't in the amount of prejudice present, when observed separately for individuals with "authoritarian" or "non-authoritarian" personalities? Does personality "explain" or "modify" this relationship? The following scheme will list the 9 different possibilities and their interpretation:

(Where a = contact, b = prejudice and c = "test" variable;
+ = presence, — = absence)

		Difference in b+ present	Possible Interpretation
		a+ — a— = +	The basic relationship-contact decreases prejudices.
(1)	c+	a+ — a— = 0	Interpretative variable.
	c—	a+ — a— = 0	Total explanation. C destroys relationship between a and b.
(2)	c+	a+ — a— = +	Independent variable.
	c—	a+ — a— = +	Cumulative effect. c and a both remain related to b.
(3)	c+	a+ — a— = —	Impossible result, given initial positive relationship.
	c—	a+ — a— = —	
(4)	c+	a+ — a— = —	Conditional variable.
	c—	a+ — a— = +	Cancellatory effect. a has opposite effect depending upon c+ or c—.
(5)	c+	a+ — a— = +	Same as above.
	c—	a+ — a— = —	Types 4 and 5 would have to show + effect outweighing —.
(6)	c+	a+ — a— = 0	Conditional variable.
	c—	a+ — a— = +	Partial explanation. a is effective only if c— present.
(7)	c+	a+ — a— = +	Same as above, but for c+.
	c—	a+ — a— = 0	
(8)	c+	a+ — a— = 0	Impossible.
	c—	a+ — a— = —	
(9)	c+	a+ — a— = —	Impossible.
	c—	a+ — a— = 0	

From the above listing of possibilities, we see that an interpretive variable wipes out the initial relationship. If this variable precedes a, or intervenes between a and b in a meaningful way, we say we have a "true" causal explanation. If no logical sequence can be discerned between a, b, and c, but rather c appears independently related to a and b, we say we have a "spurious" causal explanation.

If the initial relationship persists when controlled on variable c, then we have a conditional effect. In this case both c and a may contribute to b independently, and therefore cumulatively, or dependently, either in a cancellatory way, or in a partial way.

and imagination come into play as strong as ever. The ideas one gets at this stage of research are no longer "free floating," as in the hypothesis state, but are closely limited to the data at hand. In the design of hypotheses one takes the total picture and cuts it up into a jigsaw pattern. In the design of analysis one attempts to fit the jigsaw pieces together but inevitably finds some pieces missing and other pieces added. The final picture established after the analysis should certainly resemble the hypothesized picture but undoubtedly will be changed in many respects.

The analysis stage, therefore, is a combination of the demonstration of previously formulated hypotheses and continued conceptualization leading to the development of new hypotheses. For many researchers who work better with tangible evidence, the analysis stage represents the highest moment of reflective thinking. The analysis design therefore should provide for the study of new hypotheses which become evident only in the face of the contradiction of one's original hypotheses. There is an obvious danger in the too-loose reformulation of one's hypotheses—but that is a problem of personality rather than one of method.

3. Summary

What we have tried to show in this chapter is that problems in research design are practical problems that occur continuously from the beginning to the end of a research study. The research process is one of constant decision and revision—and each decision must be made with an eye toward its effect upon a balanced study design. While the basis for many decisions will rest upon fundamental rules of scientific method, the translation of these decisions into specific operational procedures requires skill and ingenuity.

The criteria of good research design are similar to the criteria of any good structural design. The architect of a research study, like the architect of a building, strives to satisfy the following general conditions:

(1) Basic soundness of construction (the rules of scientific method);
(2) Practicality of construction (availability of techniques, and new data);
(3) Suitability to purpose (validity of findings for the problem);
(4) Originality and inventiveness (the development of new techniques and new designs);
(5) Aesthetically pleasing (the "beauty" of a balanced design) and finally, but by no means least important;
(6) Fitted to the construction budget (research without deficits or "free time" writing).

In short, research design is *science* plus *art*.

SELECTED REFERENCES

Stouffer, S. A., "Some Observations on Study Design," *American Journal of Sociology* (January, 1950).

Stouffer, A. S., et al., *Measurement and Prediction* (Princeton, New Jersey: Princeton University Press, 1950).

Wilson, E. Bright, Jr., *An Introduction to Scientific Research* (New York: McGraw-Hill Book Company, 1952).

Name Index

Subject Index